OCCASIONS to SAVOR

Our Meals, Menus, & Remembrances

DELTA SIGMA THETA SORORITY, INC.
TEXT BY EDNA LEE LONG-GREEN

AN ELLEN ROLFES BOOK

G. P. Putnam's Sons
New York

Most Putnam books are available at special quantity discounts for bulk purchase for sales
promotions, premiums, fund-raising, and educational needs. Special books or book
excerpts also can be created to fit specific needs. For details, write Penguin Group
(USA) Inc. Special Markets, 375 Hudson Street, New York, NY 10014.

G. P. Putnam's Sons
Publishers Since 1838
a member of
Penguin Group (USA) Inc.
375 Hudson Street
New York, NY 10014

Copyright © 2004 by Ellen Rolfes Books, Inc.,
and Delta Sigma Theta Sorority, Inc.
Food photography by Langdon Clay
Food styling by Roy Finamore
Food preparation by Carla Hall
The photographs on pages 94 and 112 are
by Brian Hagiwara and Jonelle Weaver,
© 2001, Brand X Pictures.
Other photographs courtesy of Delta Sigma Theta Sorority, Inc.

Library of Congress Cataloging-in-Publication Data

Occasions to savor : our meals, menus, and remembrances / Delta Sigma Theta
Sorority, Inc.; text by Edna Lee Long-Green.
p. cm.
Includes index.
ISBN 0-399-15203-2
1. Cookery. I. Long-Green, Edna Lee. II. Delta Sigma Theta Sorority.
TX715.0312 2004   2004044649
641.5—dc22

Printed in the United States of America
1   3   5   7   9   10   8   6   4   2

This book is printed on acid-free paper. ∞

BOOK DESIGN BY JUDITH STAGNITTO ABBATE/ABBATE DESIGN

ACKNOWLEDGMENTS

elta Sigma Theta Sorority, Inc., wishes to extend a heartfelt thank you to all the members who generously submitted their extraordinary recipes and meal memories. Our special appreciation goes to those members who shared their intimate life stories to serve as chapter openers and provide a glimpse into the lives of Deltas through the decades.

For their tireless efforts and unwavering commitment, huge thanks to our wonderful agent, Liv Blumer, and our favorite publisher, John Duff. Many thanks, too, to Carol Boker for her superb recipe editing and transcription, to Roy Finamore for his incredibly gifted food styling and innovative presentations of Delta traditions, and to Carla Hall for acting as our cultural food consultant. Most of all, our sincere appreciation and gratitude to Judy Kern, our text editor, now known as "Dr. Judy," for her ability to birth a book in the truest sense of the word.

Special recognition and appreciation also go to members Gwendolyn E. Boyd, Vivian Moore Lawyer, Esq., Dr. Carolyn Showell, and Edna Lee Long-Green, who helped us to provide a true visual presentation of Delta food ways by graciously allowing their exquisite homes to be turned topsy-turvy for photo shoots.

And finally, we would like to acknowledge all the members of Delta Sigma Theta Sorority, Inc., who have done so much to make this book possible.

The Founding Sisters of Delta Sigma Theta. (Left to right) Bottom row: Winona Cargile Alexander, Madree Penn White, Wertie Blackwell Weaver, Vashti Turley Murphy, Ethel Cuff Black, Fredericka Chase Dodd; Middle row: Pauline Oberdorfer Minor, Edna Brown Coleman, Edith Motte Young, Marguerite Young Alexander, Naomi Sewell Richardson; Top row: Myra Davis Hemmings, Mamie Reddy Rose, Bertha Pitts Campbell, Florence Letcher Toms, Olive C. Jones, Jessie McGuire Dent, Jimmie Bugg Middleton, Ethel Carr Watson. Not pictured: Osceola McCarthy Adams, Zephyr J. Chisom Carter, Eliza P. Shippen

To the Founding Sisters
of Delta Sigma Theta Sorority, Inc.

Osceola McCarthy Adams

Winona Cargile Alexander

Marguerite Young Alexander

Ethel Cuff Black

Bertha Pitts Campbell

Zephyr J. Chisom Carter

Edna Brown Coleman

Jessie McGuire Dent

Fredericka Chase Dodd

Myra Davis Hemmings

Olive C. Jones

Jimmie Bugg Middleton

Pauline Oberdorfer Minor

Vashti Turley Murphy

Naomi Sewell Richardson

Mamie Reddy Rose

Eliza P. Shippen

Florence Letcher Toms

Ethel Carr Watson

Wertie Blackwell Weaver

Madree Penn White

Edith Motte Young

National Presidents

Sadie T. M. Alexander	1919–1923	Jeanne L. Noble	1958–1963
Dorothy Pelham Beckley	1923–1926	Geraldine Pittman Woods	1963–1967
Ethel LaMay Calimese	1926–1929	Frankie Muse Freeman	1967–1971
Anna Johnson Julian	1929–1931	Lillian Pierce Benbow	1971–1975
Gladys Byram Shepperd	1931–1933	Thelma Thomas Daley	1975–1979
Jeanette Triplett Jones	1933–1935	Mona Humphries Bailey	1979–1983
Vivian Osborne Marsh	1935–1939	Hortense Golden Canady	1983–1988
Elsie Austin	1939–1944	Yvonne Kennedy	1988–1992
Mae Wright Downs	1944–1947	Bertha Maxwell Roddey	1992–1996
Dorothy Irene Height	1947–1956	Marcia L. Fudge	1996–2000
Dorothy Penman Harrison	1956–1958	Gwendolyn E. Boyd	2000–2004

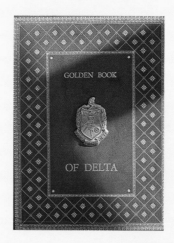

EXECUTIVE COMMITTEE

Gwendolyn E. Boyd, *National President*

Dr. Louise A. Rice, *National First Vice President*

Kasandra L. Scales, *National Second Vice President*

Dr. Doris McEwen Walker, *National Secretary*

Denise E. Gilmore, *National Treasurer*

Roseline McKinney, *Executive Director*

NATIONAL COMMISSION
ON ARTS AND LETTERS

Dr. Camille O. Cosby, *Honorary Chair*

Sharon J. Chapman, *Co-Chair*

Edna Lee Long-Green, *Co-Chair*

Judith T. Allen

LaShawn Amers-McConnell

Harriette Cole

Anitra Durand-Allen

Valeria A. Foster

Annesase C. Jones

Carolyn McClain Young

Virginia LeBlanc

Leslie Michelle Lee

Essie M. Jeffries

Orbra H. Porter

Q. Ragsdale

Stacy Nicole Smith

Jocelyn Walters-Brannon

Elaine Lewis

CONTENTS

Foreword, Camille O. Cosby, Ed.D.   **xiii**

Welcome to the Delta Table,
Gwendolyn E. Boyd   **xv**

1. Appetizers, Party Foods, and Beverages   1

A Leader for Her Time:
Frankie Muse Freeman, Esq.   **3**
An After-Theater Buffet (Jabberwock
Dinner)   **4**
Cocktails and Hors d'Oeuvres
for a Crowd (Reception to Honor
National Officers)   **10**

2. Salads   21

Women Helping Women to Make a Difference:
Keyana Mitchell   **23**
A Bridal or Baby Shower   **28**
Ladies' Night Out (New Members'
Celebration)   **32**
Luncheon for the Ladies (United Nations
NGO Luncheon)   **36**
Food for Thought: A Book Club Meeting
Meal   **40**

3. Soups, Stews, and Chilis   47

Style and Substance: A Conversation with
Essie M. Jeffries   **49**
A Wedding Reception Buffet   **58**
Dancing and Dining After-Dark Buffet
(Step Show Afterparty)   **64**

4. Poultry and Game   69

A Mother's Culinary Legacy:
Bishop Vashti Murphy McKenzie   **71**
A Formal Sit-Down Dinner
(Crimson and Cream Ball)   **78**
A Juneteenth Backyard Picnic   **84**

5. Beef and Pork   95

Memories of a Traveling Childhood:
Hortense Golden Canady   **97**
A Graduation Celebration   **98**

6. Fish and Shellfish   113

The Art of Fishing:
Dr. Floretta Dukes McKenzie   **115**
A Barbecue Bash
(Chapter Roundup Barbecue)   **122**
A Fiftieth (or Fortieth or Sixtieth)
Birthday Party   **128**

7. Vegetables and Side Dishes 135

Multitasking in the '50s:
   Dorothy Penman Harrison 137
A Formal Luncheon (Founders' Day) 140

8. Breads and Breakfast Foods 165

Shaped by Our Purpose:
   Stacy Nicole Smith 167
An Anniversary Celebration (Initiation
   Year Anniversary) 168
Tea for More Than Two (Delteen Tea) 178
A Celebration Breakfast (Prayer Breakfast) 188

Breakfast at Midnight (A Red-and-White
   Midnight Breakfast) 192

9. Desserts 197

Keeping the Connection:
   Dorothy I. Height Shares a Memory 199
A Summer Sit-Down Dinner with Friends
   (Installation Dinner) 218
Christmas Dinner for Family and Friends 266

*A Brief History of Delta Sigma Theta
   Sorority, Inc.* 273
Index 277

FOREWORD

Camille O. Cosby, Ed.D.

ccasions to Savor is not only a collection of recipes, menus, and meal memories but also a clear manifestation of the sisterhood that defines the women of the Delta Sigma Theta Sorority, Inc. Globally and historically, African-blooded women have prepared foods in communal settings while sharing experiences, information, and guidance. The women of Delta have continued that tradition of togetherness and positive reciprocity by living as paragons of unselfishness. Two words characterize the Delta's sound spirit . . . *education* and *service.*

One must be actively enrolled in a baccalaureate program or have graduated from a four-year program at an accredited academic institution to be considered for membership, yet a degree is not the only criterion for membership. One must also help others to know and achieve their potential. Deltas have provided academic and self-strengthening assistance for thousands of women since the organization's inception in 1913.

The women of Delta Sigma Theta are indeed the epitome of sisterhood—having the ability to listen attentively, creating an environment for meaningful interaction, and speaking clearly from

one's head and heart; engaging in positive reciprocity, which encourages mutual respect and honesty; thinking beyond oneself and being a caring person; and eating healthfully so that one can do all of the above!

Indeed, Deltas are women of goodwill, proponents of unification. In this book you will discover how the women of Delta Sigma Theta Sorority, Inc., successfully combine sisterhood, scholarship, and service.

WELCOME TO
THE DELTA TABLE

Throughout our history, as African-American women, and as Deltas, ingenuity has, without a doubt, helped us to survive and to thrive. Although our ancestors may have been required to "grow the fruit but eat the rind," they were able to transform those rinds into nutritious and delicious dishes. Now, as members of Delta Sigma Theta Sorority, Inc., we use our energy and enthusiasm to gather socially conscious people together at the meal table not only to celebrate our triumphs but also to promote activism and envision an even better future.

At Delta events like Jabberwocks, Step Shows, and Crimson and Cream Balls, we may pull out all the stops to be sure everyone is entertained and sustained but, at the same time, we use these opportunities for bringing people together as a way to reinforce our sense of community, raise funds for scholarships, and engender the desire to create a better community for all.

When Deltas wrap shower gifts, decorate wedding cakes, or dress party tables in our colors, we are reinforcing our sisterhood, but we are also reminding ourselves that we have a higher communal purpose—to use whatever success or privilege we may have achieved to work for positive change.

Sharing the recipes, menus, and stories in this book is yet another way through which we hope to use our God-given talents and skills in order to inspire others, to build a bridge not only between generations but also between those of us who created these dishes and those of you who will be preparing them to share with your family and friends. Many of these recipes have been handed down from mother to daughter; many of them are associated with a special occasion or a special bit of family lore. Sending them out into the world is our way of welcoming you to our table, where we hope that you, your friends, and your loved ones will join in our celebrations.

Delta Sigma Theta Sorority, Inc., was founded in 1913 by twenty-two dynamic and visionary young women at Howard University. Now our more than 200,000 members throughout the world continue to promote academic excellence; to provide meaningful, relevant programs in our communities; and to use our collective energy to make a positive connection not only at the meal table but also in corporate boardrooms, educational institutions and other organizations, and to make every event an Occasion to Savor.

GWENDOLYN E. BOYD,
22nd National President
Delta Sigma Theta Sorority, Inc.
Washington, D.C.
June 2003

1

APPETIZERS, PARTY FOODS, AND BEVERAGES

A LEADER FOR HER TIME
Frankie Muse Freeman, Esq.

Frankie Freeman's presidency (1967–1971) defines a special moment in time—a time when the entire world was in turmoil, when many foundational beliefs, particularly for African-American women, were coming unraveled, and when Deltas were wondering just what role the sorority should play in advancing the rights of all African-Americans.

Delta Sigma Theta required a strong and committed leader to shape our social-action and civil-rights agendas, someone who would make our activities relevant to the times, and we found her in Soror Frankie Freeman. One of the most prominent civil-rights attorneys of her day, she was appointed by President Johnson as the first woman to serve on the United States Commission on Civil Rights, a post she held for sixteen years.

Perhaps one of her most unexpected—and fortuitous—choices was the decision to enter Howard University School of Law as a young wife in 1941. The members of Howard's teaching faculty at that time were among the preeminent legal minds in the country, and their legacy is evident in all Soror Frankie Freeman has done since, both as an attorney and as the president most responsible for shaping Delta's political and social-action programs.

Ms. Freeman believed strongly that "in order to make a change, one must get involved." To that end, she initiated a program whereby Deltas at regional conferences wrote letters to their representatives in Congress on issues of importance to African-Americans and then marched as a group to mail them. Today, we have Delta Days in the Nation's Capital, when members pay personal visits to their representatives on Capitol Hill.

Doing things Delta style, however, means more than dedication to a political agenda; it also means having fun and enjoying social interchange with sorors, friends, and family.

As Soror Freeman explains it, her mother, Maud Beatrice Smith Muse, spent a lot of happy time in the kitchen. Soror Frankie particularly remembers the sweet potatoes her mother often cooked and kept on the stove for family members as well as friends and neighbors to snack on.

Keeping up the family tradition, Soror Freeman still enjoys cooking and entertaining. She finds the preparation of food to be very relaxing, and often, when she has a problem to solve, she says, she "gets out the pots and pans."

AN AFTER-THEATER BUFFET

(JABBERWOCK DINNER)

Ham Biscuits with Poppy Seeds (page 6)

Cheese Wafers (page 15)

Turkey Chili (page 66)

Seafood Gumbo, South Carolina Style (page 60)

White Rice

Stacy's Marinated Vegetable Salad (page 31)

Chocolate Cake à la Hicks (page 211)

Charlotte's Cheesecake (page 223)

Strawberry Delight (page 246)

THIS IS A great after-theater menu because all the dishes can be prepared in advance and either finished quickly or reheated just before serving.

TO PREPARE:

꙰ Make the cheese wafers a day or more in advance and store them airtight.

꙰ The day before, make all the desserts. Store the chocolate cake at room temperature and the cheesecake and strawberry delight in the refrigerator. Prepare the salad and refrigerate it to be drained just before serving.

꙰ Early in the day, cook the chili and gumbo. When they're done, cool and refrigerate them in their pots to be reheated before serving.

꙰ Before you go out, set up the ham biscuits in their pan and refrigerate them to be baked when you return.

A JABBERWOCK DINNER— DELTA STYLE

The Jabberwock got its name when the Iota Chapter in Boston was trying to raise money for a scholarship drive. One member of the chapter, Marion Conover Hope, came up with the idea of a variety show and suggested calling the show a Jabberwock. One can only assume that Mrs. Hope had been rereading *Alice's Adventures in Wonderland* and *Through the Looking-Glass* and was mindful of Lewis Carroll's delightful nonsense verse.

The nature of the performance has expanded over the years from a variety show that usually involved a competition to one that may concentrate on a particular discipline, be it ballet, music, or theater. The after-performance buffet is planned to reflect and extend the theme of the preceding event while showcasing the Delta colors.

If you're planning an after-theater supper, why not maintain the afterglow of a "shining" performance with a table covering that glitters and shines. The buffet table may be covered in satin or sheer organza. The china might be white and paired with colorful stemware.

Are there tables assigned to your guests? Instead of giving the tables numbers, why not name them—after classical ballets, famous Motown tunes, or plays? If you're printing or handwriting menus, get creative with the names of the dishes themselves—try "Cha Cha Cheese Wafers" or "A Raisin in the Sun Turkey Chili."

Whether or not it's a Delta event, you'll enhance the festive feeling by creating an atmosphere that reflects your chosen theme in as many ways as possible.

HAM BISCUITS WITH POPPY SEEDS

MAKES 72 SERVINGS

1 cup margarine (at room temperature)

3 tablespoons dry mustard

3 tablespoons poppy seeds

1 tablespoon Worcestershire sauce

1 onion, finely minced

36 party rolls

18 slices boiled ham, cut into quarters

9 slices Swiss cheese, cut into quarters

Preheat the oven to 350 degrees.

Combine the margarine, mustard, poppy seeds, Worcestershire sauce, and onion in a small bowl to make a soft spread. Cut rolls in half and spread the margarine mixture on both halves of the rolls. Start with the bottom half of the roll and layer a slice of ham, Swiss cheese, and then ham again. Replace the roll top, and repeat with the remaining rolls.

Ham Biscuits with Poppy Seeds

Bake the sandwiches in an aluminum pan for 12 to 15 minutes. Let cool for 5 minutes and cut in half.

CYNTHIA J. RODGERS
Clinton, Maryland
Prince George's County Alumnae Chapter

ROBIN'S BUFFALO WINGS

MAKES 12 SERVINGS

5 pounds split chicken wings

2 cups vegetable oil

½ cup butter

2 (0.7-ounce) packets Italian dressing mix

½ tablespoon dried basil

¾ cup hot sauce, or to taste

⅛ cup lemon juice

Wash and pat dry the wings. Heat the oil in a large skillet. When hot, place 12 to 15 wings in the pan, and fry for 8 to 10 minutes or until golden brown. Remove and drain well; keep warm. Continue cooking the remaining wings.

In a medium saucepan, melt the butter over low heat; add the dressing mix, basil, and hot sauce to taste. When the mixture begins to bubble, add the lemon juice; stir well. Pour over the chicken wings.

ROBIN PENNINGTON CRAWFORD
Hillsborough, North Carolina
Durham Alumnae Chapter

RUMAKI

MAKES 8 SERVINGS

RUMAKI IS a Japanese-originated appetizer. This recipe is from my husband, Carl O. Clark. Dr. Clark was among the first thirteen African-American students to integrate Baltimore Polytechnic Institute in 1952, and the first to graduate. He is also the first African-American to receive a Ph.D. in physics from the University of South Carolina in Columbia.

1 pound chicken livers, cut into bite-size pieces

1 (8-ounce) can whole water chestnuts, drained

1 pound lean bacon, cut in half

Soy sauce

Seasoned salt

Garlic powder

Greek seasoning

Preheat the oven to 325 degrees.

Wash the cut chicken livers, pat dry, and wrap each piece with a water chestnut in a half slice of bacon. Secure with a toothpick and place on a baking sheet. Sprinkle with the soy sauce and the seasonings. Place in the oven. After the first 10 minutes of cooking, pour off any excess grease. Continue cooking 20 minutes longer or until cooked through. Remove from the oven and discard the excess fat.

BARBARA RANDALL CLARK
Orangeburg, South Carolina
Orangeburg Alumnae Chapter

SEAFOOD NACHOS

MAKES 6 SERVINGS

½ pound crabmeat, shredded

½ pound cooked medium shrimp

½ cup sour cream

1 (4.5-ounce) can diced green chilies, drained

1 (4.5-ounce) can diced red chilies, drained

1 teaspoon hot chili powder

½ teaspoon ground cumin

¼ teaspoon salt

1 (8.5-ounce) bag tortilla chips

1 (8-ounce) bottle mild salsa

1 cup shredded pepper Jack cheese

½ cup chopped black olives, drained

2 green onions, sliced

Preheat the oven to 375 degrees.

Combine the crabmeat, shrimp, sour cream, chilies, chili powder, cumin, and salt in a large bowl.

Line the bottom and sides of a 13-by-9-inch baking dish with the chips. Spoon the crabmeat mixture evenly over tortilla chips. Cover with the salsa, cheese, olives, and green onion. Bake just until the cheese melts, so the chips remain crisp.

COOK'S TIP | *Serve with sour cream, if desired.*

IRIS INGRAM
Irvine, California
Rolling Hills–Palos Verdes Alumnae Chapter

TANGY BAKED PARTY WINGS

MAKES 8 SERVINGS

3 pounds chicken wings
Salt and black pepper, to taste
2 tablespoons lemon pepper, or to taste
½ (20-ounce) bottle barbecue sauce
1 tablespoon honey
2 tablespoons lemon juice

Preheat the oven to 350 degrees.

Wash and pat dry the wings. Season with salt, pepper, and lemon pepper to taste. Coat a shallow baking dish with nonstick cooking spray. Place wings in the dish in a single layer. Bake for 35 minutes, or until done (clear juices should run from the chicken when pierced).

Combine the barbecue sauce, honey, and lemon juice in a small bowl. Brush half the sauce over the wings. Bake 5 minutes longer. Flip the wings over and brush with the remaining sauce. Bake an additional 5 minutes.

DYANI SEXTON
Chicago, Illinois
Chicago Alumnae Chapter

FANCY PARTY SANDWICHES

MAKES 24 SERVINGS

1 (3-ounce) package cream cheese, softened
1 tablespoon milk
4 slices crisply cooked bacon, crumbled
1 teaspoon horseradish
½ teaspoon Worcestershire sauce
6 thin slices white bread
6 thin slices whole-wheat bread

Combine the cream cheese, milk, bacon, horseradish, and Worcestershire sauce in a medium bowl; blend well. Spread the mixture on each slice of white bread and top with the whole-wheat slices. Trim the crusts from the sandwiches and cut into long strips or quarters for serving.

ARTIS HAMPSHIRE-COWAN
Mitchellville, Maryland
Member-at-Large

SPICY ASIAN WINGS

MAKES 8 SERVINGS

THIS RECIPE HAS been with me since the seventies. It's a favorite that's easy and fast to make. I've taken it to potluck suppers, school events, and office meetings. My daughters learned to make it at an early age. It's so easy, even my husband prepares it!

½ cup soy sauce
¼ cup red wine vinegar
2 tablespoons honey
1 tablespoon prepared mustard
2 tablespoons olive oil
4 cloves garlic, minced
2 tablespoons minced, peeled fresh ginger
1½ teaspoons crushed red pepper flakes
4 tablespoons dark brown sugar
¼ teaspoon black pepper
4 pounds chicken wings

Whisk together all ingredients except the chicken in a medium bowl. Add the washed and dried chicken wings and turn to coat. Marinate, covered, in the refrigerator 2 hours or overnight.

Preheat the oven to 450 degrees. Place the wings on a rack in a broiler pan. Bake for 30 minutes or until the meat temperature registers 185 degrees. To crisp the skin, if desired, increase the oven temperature to broil after the wings are done baking, and broil for 2 minutes or until the skin is crisp.

HELEN J. NEWTON FOBI
Rolling Hills, California
Rolling Hills–Palos Verdes Alumnae Chapter

SHRIMP MOLD

MAKES 8–10 SERVINGS

1 (1-ounce) envelope plain gelatin
¼ cup cold water
1 (10¾-ounce) can condensed tomato soup
1 (8-ounce) package cream cheese
1 tablespoon chopped onion or onion juice
1 tablespoon butter or margarine
1 pound boiled, chopped shrimp
½ cup mayonnaise
1 tablespoon Worcestershire sauce
Salt, to taste
1 tablespoon Tabasco sauce
1 cup chopped green peppers
1 cup chopped celery
1 (4.25-ounce) can chopped olives, drained

In a small bowl, combine the gelatin and water; set aside. Heat the soup in the top of a double boiler. Add the cream cheese, onion, and butter. When the cheese is heated and the mixture is smooth, add the gelatin mixture, stirring well. Remove the mixture from the heat and cool. Stir in the shrimp and the remaining ingredients, and whip until creamy. Pour into a wet mold or a mold greased with mayonnaise. Refrigerate for at least 2 hours or overnight. This may also be frozen.

Serve with crackers. Decorate the tray with romaine lettuce leaves and additional boiled shrimp.

JESSIE W. FOSTER
Baton Rouge, Louisiana
Baton Rouge Sigma Alumnae Chapter

Red and White Wine

Nonalcoholic Beverages (pages 16–19)

Rumaki (page 7)

Spicy Asian Wings (page 9)

Platter of Assorted Cheeses and Crackers

Mexican Dip (page 15) *and*
Tortilla Chips

W HEN YOU'RE PLANNING a cocktail reception during which people will be mingling, it's important to provide foods that can be eaten out of hand. The wings on this menu will leave guests holding bones, so be sure there are receptacles strategically placed to discard them. You can set bowls of dip and chips in various locations to avoid overcrowding.

Whether or not there's a full bar is left up to the hostess, the occasion, and the makeup of the group, but red and white wines are generally expected, as are sparkling water, soda, and other nonalcoholic beverages.

TO PREPARE:

꒘ All the recipes on this menu can easily be adjusted to feed any number of people.

꒘ Prepare and marinate the wings a day in advance so that they're ready to go into the oven a half-hour before party time.

꒘ Prepare the rumaki an hour or so ahead of time so that they, too, are ready to bake.

꒘ The dip can be made at any time of day and refrigerated until serving.

꒘ Don't forget to take the cheeses out of the refrigerator about a half hour ahead of time to bring to room temperature.

RECEPTION TO HONOR NATIONAL OFFICERS

Deltas are required by protocol, and as a way of showing our respect, to stand when the National President enters the room. Deltas celebrate in grand style the election and installation of new National Officers.

A reception of this size requires several food stations as well as several service bars, but even at a much smaller party, it's often wise to offer food and drink at more than one location in order to keep your guests circulating and avoid unnecessary bottlenecks.

If you're passing hors d'oeuvres, such as the rumaki or wings on the menu, be sure that they're distributed throughout the room, so that one group doesn't empty the tray while another goes hungry. You might, for example, make one pass through the room from right to left and then reverse direction the next time around. Making certain that all guests receive appropriate attention, even at a large gathering, is always the responsibility of the person giving the party.

ITALIAN SHRIMP APPETIZER

MAKES 8–10 SERVINGS

1 tablespoon garlic powder

1 tablespoon ground thyme

1 tablespoon dried parsley flakes

1 tablespoon seasoned salt

½ tablespoon cayenne pepper

⅔ cup Italian dressing

2 pounds cooked jumbo shrimp, peeled and
  deveined, with tails left on

Combine all ingredients, except the shrimp, in a large bowl; mix well. Add the shrimp and stir to coat well. Cover and marinate in the refrigerator for 1 hour or more. Serve chilled on a serving tray with a side of cocktail sauce.

ANTOINETTE M. WARD
Cincinnati, Ohio
Cincinnati Alumnae Chapter

SPICY SPINACH DIP

MAKES 2½ CUPS

THE FIRST TIME I brought my Spicy Spinach Dip to a family gathering, it was such a big hit that I'm now required to bring it to every one of our get-togethers.

1 (10-ounce) package frozen chopped spinach,
  thawed

½ envelope vegetable soup mix

½ teaspoon lemon juice

1 pint sour cream

½ cup mayonnaise

½ cup chopped fresh hot peppers (red or green) or
  1 (4-ounce) can chopped hot peppers, to taste

1 loaf round sourdough bread

Drain all the water from spinach. Mix the spinach, soup mix, lemon juice, sour cream, and mayonnaise in a medium bowl. Add hot peppers to desired taste. Refrigerate 2 hours. Hollow out loaf of bread and spoon spinach dip into hollow. Cut up removed bread and serve with the dip.

CURLEY SPIRES-POTTER
Bronx, New York
Bronx Alumnae Chapter

DEVASTATING DELTA DIVA DIP

MAKES 8–10 SERVINGS

1 pound ground beef

1 pound ground sausage

1 small onion, chopped

1 (8-ounce) package Velveeta cheese

1 (8-ounce) package cream cheese, softened

1 (10¾-ounce) can cream of mushroom soup

1 (24-ounce) jar salsa

1 (8.5-ounce) bag tortilla chips

Brown the beef, sausage, and onion in a medium skillet over low heat in a pot with a tight lid. Drain. Add the cheese, cream cheese, soup, and salsa and stir well. Cook on high for 15 minutes; reduce the heat to low and cook for 5 minutes longer, stirring occasionally.

Serve when the cheese melts throughly. Serve with the tortilla chips.

TRACY STOKES MILLER
McBee, South Carolina
Hartsville Alumnae Chapter

PUMPKIN DIP

MAKES 7 CUPS

2 (8-ounce) packages cream cheese, softened
1 (16-ounce) box powdered sugar, sifted
1 (30-ounce) can pumpkin
1 tablespoon ginger
1 tablespoon cinnamon

Cream the cream cheese and sugar together in a large bowl. Fold in the pumpkin. Add the ginger and cinnamon. Scoop into a small hulled-out pumpkin or into a bowl. Serve with gingersnap cookies.

COOK'S TIP | *You may want to cut this recipe in half because it makes a huge amount.*

CAROLYN C. JOHNSON
Williamsburg, Virginia
Williamsburg Alumnae Chapter

CHICKEN DIP

MAKES 8–10 SERVINGS

1 (12.5-ounce) can chicken breast, drained
2 (8-ounce) packages cream cheese, softened
½ cup mayonnaise
½ teaspoon garlic powder
¾ cup chopped pecans or walnuts

Combine the chicken, cream cheese, mayonnaise, and garlic powder in a medium bowl. Stir in half the pecans. Press the mixture into a serving dish. Sprinkle the remaining pecans on top. Serve with spicy crackers.

COOK'S TIP | *Add hot sauce, if desired.*

CHARLOTTE Y. MARSHALL
Panama City, Florida
Panama City Alumnae Chapter

Chicken Dip

DELTA CHEESE BALL

MAKES 15–20 SERVINGS

A GREAT SNACK for a committee meeting or a small party. Cheese lovers adore it. It's easy to make, and it looks especially appetizing on a tray surrounded by crackers and fruit.

3 (8-ounce) packages cream cheese, softened
3 green onions, tops only, chopped
1 medium red bell pepper, chopped in small pieces
1 (2.25-ounce) jar dried beef, chopped in food processor or blender
1 (4-ounce) can mushrooms, drained and chopped
1 (2¼-ounce) jar pitted ripe olives, drained and chopped
1 teaspoon monosodium glutamate (optional)
2 cups ground pecans and walnuts

Mix together all the ingredients except the nuts. Roll the mixture into a ball or form into a rectangle. Cover the ball or rectangle with the ground nuts. Chill overnight.

Place the cheese ball on a silver tray and surround with melba rounds or wheat crackers.

MERLE ALLEN FRANKLIN
Atlanta, Georgia
Atlanta Suburban Alumnae Chapter

SWEET-AND-SOUR CHEESE BALL

MAKES 1 LARGE OR 2 SMALL CHEESE BALLS

I STARTED TAKING THIS to social gatherings at work, and then prepared it for a Delta potluck. It was an instant hit.

2 (8-ounce) packages cream cheese
2 cups shredded Cheddar cheese
2 teaspoons Worcestershire sauce
1 teaspoon lemon juice
1 tablespoon chopped onion
1 (8-ounce) can crushed pineapple, well drained
½ cup finely chopped pecans or walnuts

Combine the cream cheese, Cheddar cheese, Worcestershire sauce, and lemon juice in a large bowl until well blended. Add the onion and pineapple. Mix well and form into a ball. Roll in chopped nuts and refrigerate for at least 2 hours to set.

CAROLYN C. JOHNSON
Williamsburg, Virginia
Williamsburg Alumnae Chapter

MEXICAN DIP

MAKES 8 SERVINGS

1 (15-ounce) can refried beans

1 avocado

½ cup sour cream

1 (4-ounce) can sliced or chopped black olives, drained

1 medium tomato, chopped

1 (8-ounce) package shredded Cheddar cheese

Layer the refried beans on the bottom of a wide, clear-glass bowl. Peel and mash the avocado. Mix the mashed avocado with the sour cream in a small bowl. (Add additional sour cream at your discretion.) Layer the avocado/sour cream mixture on top of the refried beans. Cover with olives, then tomatoes, and sprinkle with the shredded cheese. Serve at room temperature or chilled, accompanied by tortilla chips.

COREY MINOR SMITH
Canton, Ohio
Stark County Alumnae Chapter

CHEESE WAFERS

MAKES 2½ DOZEN

1 cup shredded sharp Cheddar cheese

½ cup butter

1 cup all-purpose flour

Dash of salt

Dash of paprika

1 cup cornflakes, crushed

½ cup chopped blanched almonds

Preheat the oven to 350 degrees.

Process the cheese and butter in a food processor until blended. Add the flour, salt, and paprika. Process until the mixture forms a ball. Stop often to scrape down the sides. Add the cereal and almonds. Process until blended, stopping twice to scrape down sides. Shape the dough into 1-inch balls. Place balls about 2 inches apart on ungreased baking sheets. Flatten each ball in a crisscross pattern with a fork dipped in flour.

Bake for 12 to 14 minutes or until lightly browned.

Remove to wire racks to cool. Store in a sealed container.

MARY ALICE NEWTON
Rolling Hills, California
Rolling Hills–Palos Verdes Alumnae Chapter

Cheese Wafers

TACO DIP

2 (9-ounce) jars bean dip

2 (12-ounce) containers commercial guacamole

1 cup chopped green onions

3 chopped tomatoes

3 (2¼-ounce) cans sliced black olives, drained

1 pound sharp Cheddar cheese, shredded

1 cup sour cream

½ cup mayonnaise

1 (16-ounce) jar salsa

Layer the first 6 ingredients in a large glass dish in order. Mix the sour cream and the mayonnaise in a small bowl, and cover the layered dip with the mixture. Top with salsa before serving. Serve with tortilla chips.

MICHELLE RHODES BROWN
Chicago, Illinois
Glen Ellyn Area Alumnae Chapter

WATERMELON LEMONADE

WHENEVER I HOST book club meetings in the summer, nothing quenches the participants' thirst like homemade Watermelon Lemonade. My friends rave about my creative and refreshing spin on this summertime favorite.

½ seedless watermelon, cut into chunks (about 4 cups of chunks)

4 cups water

1½ cups sugar

1 cup bottled lemon juice or juice of 6 lemons

Lemon and watermelon wedges (optional)

Purée watermelon chunks in a blender to get 2½ cups juice. Remove foam (bubbles) from surface of juice and discard. Mix the water, sugar, and lemon juice in a large bowl, stirring until sugar has dissolved. Add the watermelon juice, mixing well.

Serve with lemon and watermelon wedges, if desired.

MICHELE COLLINS
Richton Park, Illinois
Chicago Alumnae Chapter

IDA'S HOMEMADE LEMON-RASPBERRY LEMONADE

MAKES 12-15 SERVINGS

I RECALL from my childhood that my dad would always drink something called Brackist lemonade. When I tasted Ida's delicious Lemon-Raspberry Lemonade, I felt as if I were with Dad again.

3 packets Kool-Aid unsweetened lemonade

3 cups sugar

3½ quarts water

1 (32-ounce) bottle chilled raspberry seltzer, or more to taste

1 lemon, thinly sliced, for garnish

Mix the first 3 ingredients in a large bowl. Freeze half the mixture in ice cube trays and store the remainder in a pitcher.

When ready to serve, add the lemonade ice cubes and seltzer to the lemonade mixture and garnish with lemon slices.

Ida's Homemade Lemon-Raspberry Lemonade

COOK'S TIP | *You can use water instead of the Kool-Aid to make the cubes. For a festive touch, add 1 whole raspberry to each ice cube before freezing.*

JEAN MCCRAY ASHE
Atlanta, Georgia
East Point/College Park Alumnae Chapter

BAPTIST PUNCH

MAKES 20-30 SERVINGS

SURPRISE THOSE BAPTISTS and non-Baptists with this flavorful punch.

8 tea bags

2 cups boiling water

1 lemon

2 cups sugar

1½ teaspoons almond flavoring

1½ teaspoons vanilla flavoring

4 quarts 7-Up

Add the tea bags to the boiling water and let steep for 20 minutes; remove tea bags. Place the tea in a bowl or pitcher. Roll the lemon until soft, and slice into round, thin slices. Add the lemon slices and the sugar to the tea; stir. Add the almond and vanilla flavorings; stir. Refrigerate overnight.

Add the 7-Up when ready to serve.

ALFREDIA BOYD
Columbia, South Carolina
Columbia, South Carolina, Alumnae Chapter

2

SALADS

WOMEN HELPING WOMEN
TO MAKE A DIFFERENCE

Keyana Mitchell

elta founder Florence Letcher Toms was an avid collector of elephants, and many sorority members have embraced her passion. Female elephants are known to form a complex matriarchal society, with the eldest female serving as the head of the family. The responsibility for raising the young is shared by all the females.

The support Keyana Mitchell received from her mother and godmother recalls the matriarchal society of female elephants. After her own mother died, Soror Keyana's teenage mother found a home with one of her high-school teachers, a Delta and fellow church member who became Keyana's godmother. They lived there while Keyana's mother finished college. She was determined to succeed for her own deceased mother, for her daughter's godmother, and for her daughter.

Her mother never gave up, and Soror Keyana learned at an early age never to give up on achieving any goal you set for yourself. "My mom's life made me realize," she says, "how hard it is for young Black mothers to make it. I desperately want to enrich the lives of young women like her and make it easier, because I could be one of them."

Growing up in Clarksdale, Mississippi, she says, gave her a sense of humility and helped her to understand the trials of everyday life in a rural town in an impoverished state. At the age of sixteen, Soror Keyana left home to attend the Mississippi School for Mathematics and Science, in Columbus, and from there she went on to the University of Mississippi, where she became a member of the Lambda Sigma chapter of Delta Sigma Theta.

She was always an outstanding student, and her academic record as an undergraduate won her a summer internship at the Yale University Medical School. "My mother had some health issues when I was young," she explains, "and she couldn't understand why the doctors treated her so poorly. I wanted to do something, but I wasn't sure how. The best thing I thought to do was to become a doctor myself. I figured that was the only way I could make a real difference in the way poor people were treated."

Now attending the Emory University School of Medicine as a Truman fellow, Soror Keyana plans to specialize in obstetrics and gynecology, an appropriate route for helping to build family relationships from the moment a child is born. She is determined to return to the Mississippi Delta to provide essential services to those who are least able to help themselves. She also realizes, however, that many of the changes she would like to make in her home state will require policy changes on the federal level, and she therefore hopes to work

AN INTERNATIONALLY ACCLAIMED soprano, Soror Harolyn Blackwell began her career on the Broadway stage in 1980, appearing in the first major revival of Leonard Bernstein's *West Side Story.* Her transition to opera occurred in 1994 when she was selected as a finalist for the Metropolitan Opera National Council Auditions and subsequently stepped in at the last minute to perform the entire run of *La Fille du Regiment.* Since then, she has enjoyed a reputation as one of the world's top touring sopranos. In 1997, however, she was again lured to Broadway by Bernstein, playing the role of Cunegunde in a revival of *Candide,* directed by Hal Prince. Her solo albums include *Strange Hurt* and *Blackwell Sings Bernstein: A Simple Song.*

A native of Washington, D.C., Soror Blackwell earned her bachelor's and master's degrees in music from the Catholic University of America, where she was inducted into Delta Sigma Theta in 1976.

for the United States Department of Health and Human Services, and eventually to be the secretary of health for the state of Mississippi—high goals, indeed, but, as she learned from her mother, high goals are worth fighting to achieve.

Even this hardworking scholar, however, takes time off from academic pursuits, and when she does, one thing she loves to do for relaxation is to bake! She says she's been baking caramel sticky buns for Christmas since she was ten. It became her contribution to the family's Christmas traditions, which also included listening to Temptations Christmas music while trimming the tree. You'll find her recipe on page 180.

"I'm grateful to Delta," she says, "for allowing me to become a member and to interact with women who are dedicated to public service. Becoming a Delta has helped me to develop my full personality. I've learned to work with groups, express my ideas, and develop trust in others. The skills I've learned in the sorority have helped me to plan my future in medicine. I have to go back to Mississippi. I feel it's something I have to do—that I'm supposed to do. My roots are there—and where else but at home could I hear the Temptations on Christmas and make my sticky buns."

Soror Mitchell is intent on completing the circle of love with her mother and her godmother.

Smoked Turkey Salad with Walnuts

MAKES 8 SERVINGS

A GREAT LUNCHEON OR BUFFET DISH, this salad is delicious and fun to make. You can use the salad dressing below or just use bottled salad dressing. Add a little sour cream if you want it thinner.

1½ cups salad dressing of your choice

½ cup chicken broth

Salt and white pepper, to taste

Lemon juice, to taste

4 cups smoked turkey, boned, skinned, and cut into small to medium chunks

½ medium red onion, chopped

⅔ cup chopped walnuts

½ cup raisins

1–2 stalks celery, chopped

1 cup seedless red grapes, cut in quarters

½ teaspoon crushed red pepper

Salt and black pepper, to taste

Romaine lettuce for garnish

Red and green grapes on vine for garnish

Small cherry tomatoes for garnish

Salad Dressing (see recipe below)

In a medium bowl, combine the salad dressing with the chicken broth, salt, white pepper, and lemon juice to taste.

Place the turkey in a large bowl and add the onion, walnuts, raisins, celery, and grapes. Add the crushed red pepper. Add salt and black pepper, to taste. Fold in 1 cup of the Salad Dressing mixture.

SALAD DRESSING

2 large egg yolks

½ teaspoon salt

1 teaspoon sugar

1 teaspoon Dijon mustard

4 tablespoons lemon juice or vinegar

1½ cups vegetable oil

To make the Salad Dressing, combine all the ingredients except the oil in the container of a food processor fitted with a steel or plastic blade. Process for a few seconds. Turn off the machine and scrape down the sides. With the machine running, add the oil through the tube in a thin stream. Blend until thick.

Place the Romaine lettuce leaves side by side on a shallow serving dish. Mound the salad in the center of the dish and garnish it with red and green grapes, and cherry tomatoes and serve with the remaining Salad Dressing mixture.

DEBORAH MARINA DOUGLAS
Chicago, Illinois
Chicago Alumnae Chapter

CRABMEAT AND VEGETABLE RICE SALAD

MAKES 6 SERVINGS

I WON FIRST PLACE with this recipe in the 1989 *Essence* Magazine/Uncle Ben's Good Eating Recipe Contest. The recipe appears in the December 1989 issue of *Essence*.

1½ cups uncooked converted rice

2 cups (8 ounces) flaked imitation crabmeat

1½ cups frozen green peas, thawed, or 1 (14-ounce) can baby green peas, drained

1 cup shredded carrots

2 small green onions, thinly sliced

1 cup low-calorie mayonnaise or salad dressing

¼ cup milk

1 tablespoon fresh lemon juice

¼ teaspoon ground black pepper

⅛ teaspoon garlic powder

½ head leaf lettuce or other greens

1 pint cherry tomatoes

In a medium saucepan, cook the rice according to package directions; let cool. In a large bowl, combine the rice, crabmeat, peas, carrots, and green onions; mix well. In a small bowl, combine the mayonnaise, milk, lemon juice, pepper, and garlic powder; blend until smooth. Stir into the rice mixture; toss to coat well. Chill the salad. Arrange a bed of lettuce on a salad plate and top with the salad. Garnish with the tomatoes.

MARY DUNCAN ROSE
Petersburg, Virginia
Petersburg Alumnae Chapter

JETT'S TACO SALAD

MAKES 15 SERVINGS

1 pound ground beef

1 (16-ounce) container sour cream

1 (1.25-ounce) packet taco seasoning

1 medium head lettuce

4 medium tomatoes

1 bunch green onions

1 (1-pound) bag nacho-cheese-flavored chips

1 medium block (10-ounce) mild Cheddar cheese

Brown the ground beef in a medium skillet; drain well and cool. Combine the sour cream and taco seasoning in a small bowl. Combine the ground beef with the sour-cream mixture and place in the refrigerator overnight.

Before serving, chop the lettuce, tomatoes, and green onions. Smash the chips. Shred the cheese. Mix all the ingredients together with the chilled ground-beef mixture in a large bowl. Place on a large tray to serve.

DEBORA L. JETT
Stockton, California
Stockton Alumnae Chapter

MOM'S CHICKEN SALAD

MAKES 8–12 SERVINGS

8 boneless, skinless chicken breasts

2 teaspoons each of poultry seasoning, dried sage, and celery seeds

Salt and pepper, to taste

4 stalks celery, diced

9 hard-boiled large eggs, diced

1 (10-ounce) jar sweet pickle relish

1 cup chopped pecans or walnuts

1 tablespoon sugar

2 cups Miracle Whip or other commercial salad dressing

1 hard-boiled large egg, sliced

Boil the chicken breasts in water in a Dutch oven, along with poultry seasoning, sage, celery seeds, salt, and pepper. When tender, drain and cool the chicken. Cut the chicken into bite-size pieces. Place in a large mixing bowl. Add the celery, diced eggs, relish, nuts, and sugar; add the Miracle Whip and mix well. Garnish with egg slices. Serve on lettuce or make a great sandwich on your favorite bread.

JEANETTE PERKINS WILLIAMS
Milwaukee, Wisconsin
Milwaukee Alumnae Chapter

CAROL PERKINS REID
Macon, Georgia
Macon Alumnae Chapter

KIMBERLY PERKINS JONES
Atlanta, Georgia
Atlanta Alumnae Chapter

SUPREME SPAGHETTI SALAD

MAKES 6 SERVINGS

THIS IS a great, easy-to-prepare side dish for grilled meats, especially chicken.

1 (8-ounce) package spaghetti, cooked according to package directions

1 (8-ounce) bottle Italian dressing

1 (0.7-ounce) packet Good Seasons dry Italian dressing mix

1 ounce salad herb mix

½ green bell pepper, chopped

½ red onion, chopped

2 medium tomatoes, chopped

1 (4-ounce) can ripe black olives, drained

Drain the spaghetti, and rinse with cold water; drain well. Combine the dressings in a small bowl. Combine the spaghetti, herbs, bell pepper, onion, tomatoes, and olives in a large bowl. Pour the dressing over the spaghetti mixture; toss well. Chill until serving time.

COOK'S TIP | *Serve over greens and top with grilled chicken or steak.*

BESSIE GREENE
Jackson, Mississippi
Jackson Alumnae Chapter

A BRIDAL OR BABY SHOWER

Baptist Punch (page 17)

Quiche Lavita (page 191)

*Smoked Turkey Salad
with Walnuts* (page 25)

Bellhouse Hot Rolls (page 170)

Peach Cream Trifle (page 250)

Almond Kisses (page 265)

HERE'S A SIMPLE but elegant menu to highlight a happy occasion. Whether the guest of honor is becoming a bride or a mother, she'll be thrilled to celebrate her imminent milestone with these distinctly festive dishes.

TO PREPARE:

❧ A day in advance, make the punch as the recipe directs; bake the almond kisses and store them airtight; make the trifle and refrigerate it.

❧ In the morning, make the quiche to be served at room temperature. Make the dressing, combine the salad ingredients, and refrigerate them separately. Make the dough for the rolls so that it will have time to rise.

❧ About a half hour before serving, put the rolls in to bake and finish the salad.

GIVING A SHOWER DELTA STYLE

Although Deltas would decorate, as always, in the sorority's colors, including the gift wrap on the packages, most of our shower traditions and rituals are the same as those for any bridal or baby shower. Two that you might choose to follow are to give each guest a disposable camera so that she can take home her own memories of the event, and also to make "predictions" about the future of the bride or mother-to-be. Ours are based on Delta lore, but yours might grow out of your own shared history with the guest of honor.

SPICY KALE SLAW

MAKES 4–6 SERVINGS

4–5 large stalks kale

4 green onions, very finely chopped

½ red bell pepper

½ orange or yellow bell pepper

1–1½ teaspoons Blanched Garlic Paste (see opposite)

Juice of ½ lemon

Pinch of seasoned salt

2 pinches of cayenne pepper

2 tablespoons white wine vinegar

⅓ cup extra-virgin olive oil

Salt, to taste

Freshly ground black pepper, to taste

Soak the kale in cold saltwater for at least 10 minutes; rinse and wash in plain water the second time. Remove the leaves from the stems and spin- or air-dry. Discard the stems. Finely chop the greens, the onions, and the peppers by hand or in a food processor. Place the chopped ingredients in a small bowl.

Whisk together the garlic paste, lemon juice, seasoned salt, cayenne pepper, vinegar, and olive oil in a small container. Pour the mixture over the chopped ingredients and toss well. Add salt and freshly ground pepper. Chill or set aside for at least 30 minutes.

COOK'S TIP | *Commercial garlic paste may be substituted for the Blanched Garlic Paste.*

BLANCHED GARLIC PASTE

MAKES ABOUT ½ CUP

25 cloves garlic, separated

⅓ cup olive oil

½ teaspoon sea salt

Place the garlic cloves flat in a small microwavable container. Microwave on High for 10 seconds. Peel by popping out garlic cloves. Put the garlic in a small saucepan filled with cold water, and simmer for 1 minute. Drain and repeat the previous step; let simmer 30 seconds. Drain and add the olive oil. Simmer 12 minutes, stirring frequently.

Purée the mixture in a blender until very smooth. Scrape down the sides to maximize the blending. Blend in the salt. Store paste in refrigerator and use when recipes call for garlic.

CHERYL L. DOBBINS
Washington, D.C.
Federal City Alumnae Chapter

STACY'S MARINATED VEGETABLE SALAD

MAKES 10 SERVINGS

THIS IS A NEW recipe that was passed on to me by a soror when I was in need of something a little different as a salad or side dish. It's easy and requires no cooking . . . just a little planning the night before it is served.

1 cup sugar

½ cup vinegar

½ cup vegetable oil

1 teaspoon salt

1 teaspoon black pepper

1 (15-ounce) can white shoepeg corn, drained

1 (15-ounce) can French-style green beans, drained

1 (14-ounce) can baby peas, drained

1 (4-ounce) jar pimientos, drained

1 small bunch green onions, peeled and chopped

Combine the sugar, vinegar, oil, salt, and pepper in a small saucepan, and boil over low heat, stirring constantly, until the sugar dissolves. Combine the corn, green beans, and peas in a medium bowl. Add the pimientos and green onions. Pour the dressing over the vegetables. Stir well. Refrigerate covered overnight. Drain and serve.

COOK'S TIP | *Instead of the canned vegetables, you can use frozen corn, beans, and peas, rinsed in hot water to thaw them, and drained.*

BEVERLY EVANS SMITH
Marietta, Georgia
Chair, Long-Range Planning Committee
Marietta-Roswell Alumnae Chapter

Stacy's Marinated Vegetable Salad

LADIES' NIGHT OUT

(NEW MEMBERS' CELEBRATION)

Lenora's Punch (page 18)

Delta Cheese Ball (page 14)

Marinated Asparagus (page 143)

Shrimp Pilau (page 127)

Mixed Green Salad

Supreme Lemon-Filling Cake (page 217)

WHEN THE "GIRLS" get together, there's always lively conversation and lots of laughter. This is a menu that will allow the hostess to join in the fun without spending too much time in the kitchen.

TO PREPARE:

☙ Make the cheese ball and the asparagus the day before and store them in the refrigerator. Early in the day, make the cake, wash and tear the greens for the salad, and mix the dressing if necessary. Refrigerate the greens and dressing separately and remove them from the refrigerator about a half hour before serving to bring to room temperature.

☙ Prepare the ingredients for the pilau in the afternoon and start cooking it about an hour before dinner.

☙ Just before the ladies are expected to arrive, combine the ingredients for the punch—with or without the champagne.

A NEW MEMBERS' CELEBRATION

Needless to say, there is always much excitement when new members join the sorority. A new members' celebration event is the time for Deltas to really show their stuff—and I do mean stuff. The room is generally filled with gifts: sweatshirts, T-shirts, jackets, pens, key chains, purses, jewelry, and a variety of interesting items bearing the Delta symbols.

The Delta colors are everywhere, and in some instances the entire room is actually swathed in crimson and cream tissue paper. The women sing songs, tell stories, and may videotape the event so that they can relive the celebration for years to come.

Whatever the reason for your own ladies' get-together, you, too, will want to make it a night to remember. You might even introduce a little game or a grab bag, to be anticipated and repeated when your group reconvenes.

DILL TUNA SALAD

MAKES 8 SERVINGS

GROWING UP IN THE SOUTH was such a pleasant, palatable experience. I was a very picky eater as a child and disliked sweet pickles very much. I had an older cousin who babysat me all the time who substituted dill pickles for sweet pickles in his tuna fish salad. I have loved it ever since. I've experimented with different condiments, but I find this recipe is best. My seven-year-old loves this meal. It makes a nice lunch when served with fresh fruit and crackers or a wonderful dinner served with vegetables and sourdough bread.

2 hard-boiled large eggs, finely chopped
2 Roma tomatoes, finely chopped
3 tablespoons dill pickle salad cubes
½ cup mayonnaise
1 teaspoon ranch dressing
1 (12-ounce) can water-packed tuna, drained
Lettuce (optional)

Combine the eggs, tomatoes, pickles, mayonnaise, ranch dressing, and tuna in a medium bowl. Mix thoroughly, and refrigerate until ready to serve. Serve on lettuce leaves, if desired.

WANDA N. MUHAMMAD
Minneapolis, Minnesota
Minneapolis–St. Paul Alumnae Chapter

BROCCOLI SALAD

MAKES 12–16 SERVINGS

2 bunches broccoli
½ pound bacon, cooked and crumbled
1 small red onion, chopped
½ cup currants
1 cup Miracle Whip or other commercial salad
    dressing or mayonnaise
½ cup sugar
¼ cup apple cider vinegar

Chop broccoli into small pieces, removing as much of the stem as possible. Mix with the bacon, onion, and currants in a medium bowl.

Combine the salad dressing, sugar, and vinegar in a small bowl. Add the dressing to the broccoli, and refrigerate until ready to serve, but not too far in advance of serving.

SABRINA POLOTE
College Park, Georgia
East Point/College Park Alumnae Chapter

Dijon Green Bean Salad

DIJON GREEN BEAN SALAD

MAKES 4 SERVINGS

½ pound small green beans, trimmed

2 tablespoons prepared Dijon vinaigrette

2 teaspoons Dijon mustard

1 cup cherry tomatoes, halved

½ cup slivered or chopped green or red bell pepper

¼ cup sliced or slivered almonds, toasted

Bring 3 quarts of salted water to a boil in a saucepan. Remove from the heat and add the green beans. Let stand 3 minutes, stirring occasionally, or until beans are crisp-tender. Using a slotted spoon, transfer beans to a bowl of ice water; cool. Drain and pat dry.

Whisk together the vinaigrette and mustard in a medium bowl. Add the green beans, tomatoes, bell peppers, and almonds; toss to coat evenly.

DORIS C. RICE REMBERT
Los Angeles, California
Rolling Hills–Palos Verdes Alumnae Chapter

LUNCHEON FOR THE LADIES

(UNITED NATIONS NGO LUNCHEON)

Broccoli and Cheese

Salad (page 44)

Chicken Croquettes (page 86)

Stuffed Baby Eggplant (page 148)

Lemon Pudding

Soufflé (page 252)

LADIES WHO LUNCH in celebration of a special occasion deserve a special menu, and this one is a cause for celebration in and of itself.

TO PREPARE:

❧ Make the salad in the morning and chill it until serving time. Make the chicken croquettes up to the point of breading and frying, and store them in the refrigerator. Prepare the eggplant, and store the shells and filling separately, to be combined and reheated just before serving.

❧ When everything else has been prepped, make the soufflé to go into the oven just as your guests arrive.

A LUNCHEON TO CELEBRATE NGO STATUS

In March 2003 Delta Sigma Theta was proud to be awarded Special Consultative Status as a Non-Government Organization with the Economic and Social Council of the United Nations in recognition of our long-standing commitment to political, social, and economic reform around the world.

Individual chapters celebrate this honor and commemorate our founders' determination toward social action by holding a luncheon and inviting a speaker to talk about issues relating globally to women and children.

A ladies' luncheon may be held in celebration of a particular milestone or accomplishment, or it might simply be an occasion for good friends or women of like mind to get together and enjoy good food along with lively conversation. But whatever the occasion, do show that you honor your guests by preparing this special meal and presenting it with care. If there is a particular occasion for celebration, you might want to use a centerpiece that reflects the reason for your gathering.

One way to be sure the memory doesn't fade is to commemorate it in a photograph. Buy matching picture frames for each of your guests and use them as place-card holders, with the name of the guest written on a card where the picture would go. When all the guests have arrived, have them gather for a group photo. Then be sure to send a copy of the photo to each of the ladies present to put in her frame. The frame size would vary according to the number of guests invited.

MARINATED CARROTS

MAKES 10–12 SERVINGS

2 pounds carrots, scraped and thinly sliced

1 medium red onion, thinly sliced

½ cup chopped green bell pepper

1 (10½-ounce) can condensed tomato soup

¾ cup sugar

½ cup vegetable or canola oil

½ teaspoon salt

Cook the carrots, covered, in a medium saucepan in salted boiling water for 5 minutes. Drain; let cool. Combine the carrots in a medium bowl with the remaining ingredients. Marinate for 2 to 3 days in the refrigerator. Serve cold or at room temperature.

BARBARA MOSELEY DAVIS
Mitchellville, Maryland
Washington, D.C., Alumnae Chapter

BROCCOLI SALAD WITH SUNFLOWER SEEDS

MAKES 8 SERVINGS

I ATTENDED A catered luncheon at a friend's house and loved the broccoli salad that was served. The hostess didn't know the recipe, so I found a broccoli recipe online and began tinkering with it until it had the zing I desired.

3 stalks broccoli (use the florets, breaking them into small pieces)

½ pound bacon, cooked and crumbled

1 medium purple (red) onion, diced

½ cup unsalted sunflower seeds

1 cup golden raisins

1 cup mayonnaise

¾ cup sugar

½ cup balsamic vinegar aged in wood

Combine the broccoli and next 4 ingredients in a medium bowl. Combine the mayonnaise, sugar, and vinegar in a small bowl. Pour over the broccoli mixture. Refrigerate overnight. Serve on a bed of lettuce.

JUNE G. PEMBROKE
Chicago, Illinois
Chicago Alumnae Chapter

Marinated Carrots

MANDARIN ORANGE AND ROMAINE SALAD

MAKES 4–6 SERVINGS

6 tablespoons olive oil

2 tablespoons wine vinegar

Pinch of salt

¼ teaspoon dry mustard

Pinch of pepper

1 teaspoon minced, dried tarragon, basil, chives, parsley, or other herbs

1 teaspoon minced or pressed garlic

1 head romaine or red-leaf lettuce

1 or 2 (8-ounce) cans mandarin orange sections, drained

½ green onion, minced (optional)

½ cup butter-toasted almond slivers

Combine the olive oil and the next 6 ingredients in a jar. Wash the lettuce and dry well. Tear into bite-size pieces and place in a large bowl. Add the mandarin oranges and, if desired, the minced green onions. Shake dressing and pour over the greens, tossing well to coat. Top with the toasted almond slivers.

MARGARET J. WASHNITZER
Washington, D.C.
Washington, D.C., Alumnae Chapter

JUDGE TRUDY'S SENSATION SALAD

MAKES 8–10 SERVINGS

PARSLEY ADDS A NICE FLAVOR to this simple but very tasty green salad.

½ cup vegetable oil

½ cup olive oil

2½ tablespoons lemon juice

2 cloves garlic, chopped

1 tablespoon vinegar

1 teaspoon salt

2–3 small heads lettuce

1 bunch parsley, chopped

1 cup grated Romano cheese

Ground black pepper and/or chopped jalapeño peppers (optional)

Mix the first 6 ingredients thoroughly in a medium bowl; set aside.

Wash the lettuce well and dry it. Break into bite-size pieces and place in a large salad bowl. Add the chopped parsley. Top with the reserved dressing. Toss the salad until the lettuce is well coated with dressing. Sprinkle with the Romano cheese and toss again. Add black pepper and/or jalapeño peppers, if desired.

JUDGE TRUDY M. WHITE
Baton Rouge, Louisiana
Baton Rouge Sigma Alumnae Chapter

FOOD FOR THOUGHT:
A BOOK CLUB MEETING MEAL

Watermelon Lemonade (page 16)

Chicken Dip (page 13) *and Crackers*

Heart-Smart Chili (page 67)

White Rice

Mandarin Orange and
Romaine Salad (page 39)

Chewy Chocolate Cookies (page 262)

EVERYTHING IN LIFE is a balance. This menu will feed your culinary appetite as lively discussion satisfies your mind. Do take care of your health with the heart-smart chili, but don't deny yourself the pleasure of a cookie at the end of the meal.

TO PREPARE:

❧ Make the cookies the day before your meeting and store them airtight.

❧ In the morning, prepare the salad ingredients and the dressing and refrigerate them separately. Make the dip and store it, covered, in the refrigerator. Make the lemonade and chill in the refrigerator.

❧ Time the chili so that it can cook for 2 hours before you're ready to serve. Cook the rice about a half hour before dinner.

WHEN DELTAS GATHER FOR DISCUSSION

Deltas always try to make every occasion just a bit special, and it's no different when the reason for gathering is to discuss a book. We might create a centerpiece of the books we've read together in the past. The hostess might have paper napkins imprinted with the title of the current book and provide small notebooks and pens—red, of course—to all members of the group. At the heart of the matter, however, are always the book and the food.

These dishes are all prepared in advance so that the person at whose home the group has gathered won't miss a moment of the conversation, and the cookies will provide continued sustenance for lively discussion long after the meal has concluded.

Heart-Smart Chili (page 67)

WALDORF SALAD

MAKES 4 SERVINGS

1 cup walnut halves

½ cup mayonnaise

¼ cup plain yogurt

1 teaspoon prepared mustard

Pinch of dry mustard

Juice of ½ lemon plus 1 tablespoon fresh lemon juice

4–6 tart apples, peeled, cored, and diced (about
   2 cups)

1–2 cups finely diced celery

Salt and freshly ground pepper, to taste

2 bunches tender mixed greens, washed and dried

2 tablespoons olive oil

Chopped celery leaves

Preheat the oven to 325 degrees.

Spread the walnuts in a single layer on a baking sheet. Toast 4 to 5 minutes until aromatic; let cool.

Combine the mayonnaise, yogurt, mustards, and lemon juice in a medium bowl. Fold in the apples and celery. Season with salt and black pepper.

Place the greens in a large bowl. Add the olive oil and the 1 tablespoon lemon juice; season with salt and pepper. Toss well. Divide the greens among four plates. Spoon the apple mixture on the greens; sprinkle with the toasted walnuts and celery leaves.

ALFREDIA BOYD
Columbia, South Carolina
Chair, National Nominating Committee
Columbia, South Carolina, Alumnae Chapter

Waldorf Salad

PICKLED BEETS

MAKES 10–12 SERVINGS

A LONG TIME FAVORITE OF MY FAMILY, for more than fifty years, Pickled Beets were generally used only for Thanksgiving and Christmas. However, they are delicious placed over some good collards or to enjoy along with greens or string beans.

½ cup vinegar

¼ cup packed brown sugar

½ cup granulated sugar

1 (16-ounce) can sliced beets, or 2 cups sliced, cooked fresh beets

2 teaspoons whole allspice

8 whole cloves

6 whole bay leaves

½ teaspoon salt

1 medium-size sweet onion, sliced (optional)

Heat ¼ cup of the vinegar in a small saucepan. Add the sugars, stirring to dissolve. Place the beets, spices, bay leaves, and salt in a bowl with the remaining ¼ cup vinegar. Pour the sugar/vinegar mixture over beets. Cover with the sliced onions, if desired. Refrigerate for 24 hours. Mix occasionally. Serve cold. May be used in salads.

COOK'S TIP | *After the beets are gone, slice white onions into the pickling juice. It makes a plain salad most succulent.*

CHARLOTTE CARTER-BURNETT
Orlando, Florida
Orange County Alumnae Chapter

DELTA OF DISTINCTION
Elizabeth Catlett: Sculptor

FOR SIXTY YEARS Soror Elizabeth Catlett has created from marble and wood powerful and sensuous images of women—workers, mothers, the oppressed. Her purpose, she has said, is "to present Black people in their beauty and dignity for ourselves and others to understand and enjoy." Now hailed as one of the greatest African-American artists of her generation, Soror Catlett is sustained by her conviction that artists should create work for all people, not just the elite, because, as she says, "it's important for everyone to see themselves reflected in art," and by a faith in art as a catalyst for social change.

Both of her parents, the children of slaves, became teachers in the Washington, D.C., public-school system. Soror Catlett received her B.A. from Howard University and her M.F.A. from the University of Iowa, where her career as a sculptor began. In the early 1940s, working and studying in New York, she met an extraordinary array of Black intellectuals, including W. E. B. DuBois, Ralph Ellison, Langston Hughes, and Paul Robeson, all of whom were driven by a similar sense of aesthetic and social purpose. In 1946 she traveled to Mexico, where she met and married Francisco Mora, a printmaker and painter. For the next fifty years Mexico was her home.

In April 2003, once more back in the United States, she received the Lifetime Achievement in Contemporary Sculpture Award from the International Sculpture Center.

BROCCOLI AND CHEESE SALAD

MAKES 6–8 SERVINGS

3 teaspoons rice wine vinegar

¾ cup mayonnaise

¼ cup sugar

4 cups raw broccoli, chopped

8 slices bacon, cooked and crumbled

½ medium red onion, or 3 green onions, chopped

1 cup Cheddar cheese, grated

Mix the vinegar, mayonnaise, and sugar in a small bowl. Mix the broccoli and the remaining ingredients in a medium salad bowl. Pour the mayonnaise mixture over the broccoli mixture; stir to mix well. Chill, then serve over a bed of lettuce.

DANETTE CARR
Oklahoma City, Oklahoma
Oklahoma City Alumnae Chapter

CRANBERRY RELISH

MAKES 8–10 SERVINGS

12 ounces fresh cranberries

1 cup orange juice

1 orange, peeled and chopped, or 1 (11-ounce) can mandarin orange sections, drained and chopped

1 cup sugar

1 large apple, chopped

1½ (¼-ounce) packets unflavored gelatin

1 (4-ounce) bag flaked coconut (optional)

Combine the cranberries and orange juice in a medium saucepan. Bring to a boil and cook until the cranberries have popped. Reduce the heat and add the other ingredients, stirring constantly until well mixed. Remove from the heat and transfer to a mold or other container; refrigerate until set.

COOK'S TIP | *This can be made days in advance of serving.*

SHEILA DEAN SHEARS
Silver Spring, Maryland
Co-Chair, Information and Communications
Washington, D.C., Alumnae Chapter

FOSTER'S CRANBERRY MOLD

MAKES 10 SERVINGS

1 (3-ounce) packet strawberry-flavored gelatin

1 (3-ounce) packet raspberry-flavored gelatin

2 cups boiling water

1 (16-ounce) can whole cranberries

1 (10-ounce) can crushed pineapple, drained

1½ tablespoons pineapple juice

Combine the contents of the gelatin packets with the water in a large bowl.

Add the cranberries, pineapple, and pineapple juice; mix well. Pour the mixture into a 12-cup mold. Cover and refrigerate for 4 hours or until firm. Turn out onto a lettuce-lined plate or serve in a compote dish as shown below.

ALYCE F. FOSTER
Riviera Beach, Florida
West Palm Beach Alumnae Chapter

Foster's Cranberry Mold

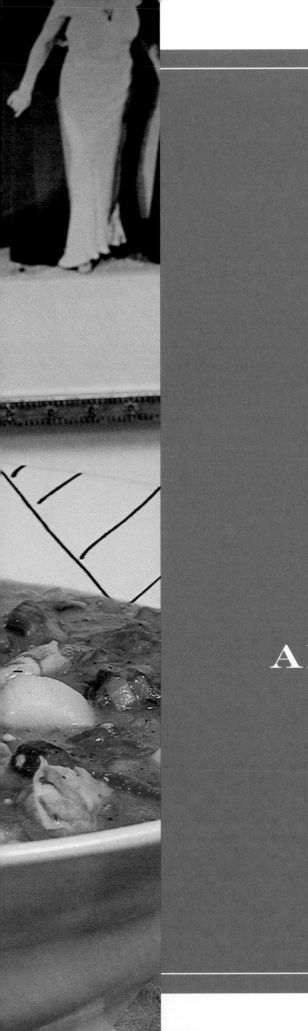

3

SOUPS,
STEWS,
AND CHILIS

STYLE AND SUBSTANCE

A Conversation with
Essie M. Jeffries

Hearing the words "Los Angeles," we immediately summon up images of Hollywood glamour, and California's Soror Essie M. Jeffries doesn't disappoint. A former retailer of women's clothing and the daughter of an accomplished seamstress, she has a knack for adding just the right touch—an interesting hat, a pair of fabulous pumps, or a special purse—to make whatever she's wearing unique. But for Soror Essie, beauty is more than skin-deep, and style is always based on a truly substantial foundation.

"As a little girl," she says, "I learned the importance of fabric, colors, cut, construction, and accessories—the whole package. I would sit and watch my mother create the most beautiful custom-made wedding gowns and evening dresses as well as both men's and women's coats and suits. I spent many days ripping out seams until they were sewn to her professional standards, but I always respected and treasured those times I spent with my mother. She taught me patience and the impor-

tance of sticking to a project until I got it right. The skills I learned all those years ago at her sewing machine are skills that have served me well in my twenty-five years as a Delta."

Soror Essie was inducted into the Los Angeles Alumnae Chapter in 1978, and since retiring after thirteen years as a probation officer and child abuse social worker in Los Angeles County, she has devoted virtually all her time to her church and an almost mind-boggling variety of Delta projects. She has served as her chapter's vice president, financial secretary, and two terms as chaplain, the position she says she has enjoyed the most. "It's just a part of me that on Sundays I belong in church. My spiritual foundation has been instrumental in all of the success I've experienced in my life, and I'll always be grateful for it."

In addition, Essie has served as a co-chair of the Arts and Letters committee in her chapter and the co-chair of the Spirit Awards fund-raiser. In 2001, having volunteered more than fourteen thousand hours of her time and served on thirteen different committees, she was named the Los Angeles chapter's Delta of the Year.

THE FOURTEENTH PRESIDENT of Bennett College for Women in Greensboro, North Carolina, Soror Johnetta B. Cole made history in 1987 when she became the first African-American female president of Spelman College. At her inauguration, Camille and Bill Cosby made a donation of $20 million to the college. At the time, it was the largest single gift ever given by an individual to any historically black college or university. In 1992, under her leadership, *U.S. News & World Report* ranked it the number-one liberal-arts college in the South. That same year, she was named to President-elect Bill Clinton's transition team as Cluster Coordinator for Education, Labor, and the Arts and Humanities.

Born in Jacksonville, Florida, Soror Cole completed her undergraduate work at Fisk University and Oberlin College and received her doctorate in anthropology from North-western University before embarking on a teaching career in the field of cultural anthropology.

An active participant in a number of community and civic organizations including the Carter Center and the TransAfrica Forum, Soror Cole is also a member of the Links, Inc., and the National Council of Negro Women, and she serves on the board of directors of the United Way of Greater Greensboro, Coca-Cola Enterprises, and Merck & Co., Inc. She has received numerous honors and awards, and holds more than thirty honorary doctorate degrees.

"People are surprised when they hear that number of hours, but I'm very well organized and I plan my time and use my resources wisely. I hope always to be a guide and role model for the younger sorors to continue the traditions and activities I've helped to establish as well as to add new ones of their own. Delta has helped me to develop a sense of who I am and where I can fit into the world to make a difference."

She is not only a devoted and tireless volunteer but also a consummate hostess, and in her entertaining as well as her committee work, Soror Essie M. Jeffries understands the importance of balancing style and substance.

"I enjoy cooking," she says, "but I love the presentation of food as much as I do its preparation."

In true Delta style, Soror Essie also knows how to combine business with pleasure, as she demonstrated when she held the Christmas meeting of the Mental Health Committee, which she was chairing at the time, in her home, and made it both a meal and a meeting to remember.

"It was a sit-down dinner, and I asked the thirty sorors in attendance to dress in formal attire. The tables were draped with white chiffon cloths, the napkins were bright red silk, and red and white candles floated in the centerpieces. The main course was Billy Bob's Black-Eyed Peas with Attitude (page 62) over rice. I also served homemade rolls, and for dessert I offered both apple cake and pecan pie. Oh, and of course there was champagne as well as cider. Many sisterhood bonds were strengthened that evening as we conversed around the table and several members said they wanted to remain on the committee just so they could attend the Christmas meeting again."

Whether it's planning her next project to help the community or the next fabulous dinner party, Soror Essie M. Jeffries epitomizes what it means to be a Delta. No one understands better than she that "of those to whom much is given much is expected," and that, however substantive one's contribution, it's important to accomplish it with style.

AN HONORARY member of Delta Sigma Theta, Dr. Camille O. Cosby has been responsible for bringing to the American public a variety of projects that advance an appreciation of the rich and diverse cultures of African-Americans. In 1995 she co-produced the Tony Award–nominated Broadway production of *Having Our Say,* based on the book of the same name by Sarah and Elizabeth Delaney, two centenarian African-American sisters. In 1999 she and her co-producer, Judith Rutherford James, received the Peabody Award for significant and meritorious achievement in broadcasting and cable for the made-for-television film of the play, which was broadcast on CBS.

Along with the award-winning broadcast journalist Renee Poussaint, she is a co-founder of the National Visionary Leadership Project, a program whose mission it is to unite elder African-American leaders from all walks of life with new generations of emerging leaders.

The mother of five and the wife of Bill Cosby, Soror Camille received a doctorate in education from the University of Massachusetts and is the author of *Television's Imageable Influences: The Self-Perceptions of Young African-Americans,* which grew out of her doctoral dissertation. In addition to her own numerous achievements, she continues to be involved in her husband's career and is actively involved in a number of national organizations.

BEEF AND VEGETABLE SOUP

MAKES 8–10 SERVINGS

THIS DELICIOUS, filling soup recipe is from my mother, Soror Barbara Jean Spearman Anderson.

1 (2-pound) beef roast

Salt and black pepper, to taste

2 (28-ounce) cans chopped tomatoes

1 cup barley

½ bay leaf

Pinch of rosemary

Pinch of basil

2 cloves garlic, chopped

4 potatoes, grated

4 carrots, grated

3 onions, grated

⅓ head cabbage, grated

1 (15-ounce) can peas, drained

1 (16-ounce) package frozen corn

1 teaspoon chili powder

Place the beef roast in a large stockpot and cover with water; add salt and black pepper. Boil until tender; remove the meat from the bone (if necessary) and chop into chunks. Place back in the stockpot. Add the tomatoes and next 9 ingredients. Turn heat to low, and simmer for 1 hour. Add more seasonings to taste. Add the remaining ingredients. Simmer for 30 minutes or so. Serve with homemade rolls.

ROSANNE A. SMITH
Knoxville, Tennessee
Oak Ridge Alumnae Chapter

OLD-FASHIONED VEGETABLE SOUP

MAKES 4–6 SERVINGS

CUT FROM A newspaper during World War II, this soup recipe is more than fifty years old. It is a favorite of my family.

1 pound ground beef

1 cup chopped onion

1 cup diced raw peeled potatoes

1 cup sliced carrots

1 cup sliced celery

2 (16-ounce) cans whole tomatoes, coarsely chopped

5 cups water

1 tablespoon salt

¼ teaspoon crushed basil

¼ teaspoon crushed thyme

1 bay leaf

¼ teaspoon black pepper

2 tablespoons instant beef bouillon

1 (8.5-ounce) can whole-kernel corn, undrained

1 (8.5-ounce) can green beans, undrained

1 (8.5-ounce) can sweet peas, undrained

Cook the ground beef and onion in a large skillet until the meat is slightly browned; drain. Add the remaining ingredients, except the corn, beans, and peas. Simmer for 30 minutes or until the raw vegetables are tender. Add the canned vegetables and continue heating for 5 minutes.

WILLIE PEARL JONES
Monticello, Mississippi
Pike County Alumnae Chapter

VICTORY GARDEN CHICKEN-VEGETABLE SOUP

MAKES 8–10 SERVINGS

THIS RECIPE FROM THE 1940s, given to me by my grandmother, is one that she often served in winter to beat the Chicago chill. My brother and I always loved having a bowlful when we came home from school. "Victory Garden" refers to a neighborhood in Chicago.

1 (3½-pound) chicken, cut into 8 pieces

8 cups water

¾ cup dry white wine

2 teaspoons salt

2 teaspoons olive oil

1 medium onion, finely chopped

1 pound red-skinned potatoes, peeled and cut into ½-inch pieces

1 pound tomatoes, coarsely chopped

3 medium carrots, peeled and sliced

4 ounces green beans, trimmed and cut into 1-inch pieces

2 medium zucchini, peeled and cut into ½-inch pieces

1 cup fresh or frozen whole-kernel corn

2 cups thinly sliced fresh spinach leaves

⅓ cup thinly sliced fresh basil

Salt and black pepper, to taste

Bring the chicken, water, wine, and 1 teaspoon of the salt to a boil in a large stockpot, skimming the surface to remove any fat. Simmer, covered, until the chicken is cooked through, about 25 minutes. Transfer the chicken breast and thigh pieces to a platter (leave the remaining chicken and stock in the pot).

Remove the meat from the bones and cut into ½-inch pieces. Cover and chill meat. Return scraps and bones to the stockpot. Simmer, covered, 1 hour. Strain. Cool stock slightly. Chill overnight. Spoon fat off top and discard.

Heat the oil in large pot over medium heat. Add the onion; sauté until golden, about 6 minutes. Add the stock, and bring to a boil. Add the potatoes, tomatoes, carrots, green beans, and the remaining 1 teaspoon salt. Simmer 10 minutes. Add the zucchini and corn; simmer until the vegetables are tender, about 15 minutes. Stir in the spinach and reserved chicken. Simmer until the chicken is heated through, about 3 minutes. Stir in the basil. Season with salt and pepper. Serve.

COOK'S TIP | *For convenience, you can skip the "return scraps and bones . . . simmer . . . chill" part of the recipe and use 6 cups canned chicken stock.*

EDNA LEE LONG-GREEN
Washington, D.C.
Co-Chair, National Commission on Arts and Letters
Washington, D.C., Alumnae Chapter

African Chicken-Peanut Soup

MAKES 6–8 SERVINGS

1½ cups cubed peeled sweet potato (1 medium)
½ cup chopped onion
½ cup diced red bell pepper
2 cloves garlic, minced
1 jalapeño pepper, seeded and minced
2 cups chopped cooked chicken breast
  (about 8 ounces)
1 cup bottled chunky salsa
½ teaspoon ground cumin
2 (16-ounce) cans fat-free, low-sodium
  chicken broth
2 (15-ounce) cans chicken-with-rice soup
1 (15-ounce) can black beans, drained
Salt and pepper, to taste
⅓ cup creamy peanut butter

Coat a large Dutch oven with cooking spray. Heat over medium-high heat until hot. Sauté the sweet potato, onion, bell pepper, garlic, and jalapeño pepper for 5 minutes. Stir in the chicken, salsa, cumin, soups, and black beans; bring to a boil. Reduce heat and simmer for 10 minutes. Whisk in the peanut butter; cook for 2 minutes.

COOK'S TIP | *Crunchy peanut butter gives the dish extra texture.*

MARGARET C. STOCKTON
Williamsburg, Virginia
Delta Omicron Chapter

Kielbasa Soup

MAKES 8–10 SERVINGS

½ cup butter
½ cup coarsely chopped carrots
½ cup minced celery
3 cups thickly sliced leeks
2 cups shredded cabbage
2 quarts (64 ounces) chicken broth
5 tablespoons all-purpose flour
2 cups peeled, cubed potatoes
½ teaspoon dried marjoram
¾ pound lean Polish kielbasa, thinly sliced
Salt and black pepper, to taste
Fresh parsley and dill for garnish (optional)

Melt ¼ cup of the butter in a large stockpot over low heat. Add the carrots and celery; sauté until softened. Add the leeks and cabbage, and sauté for 3 minutes. Stir in the chicken broth. Bring to a boil. Reduce the heat and simmer for 15 minutes. Melt the remaining ¼ cup butter in large skillet over low heat. Add the flour, stirring constantly for 3 minutes. Remove from the heat and whisk in 2 cups hot soup. Pour the flour mixture into the stockpot, stirring constantly. Add the potatoes and marjoram. Simmer for 10 minutes. Stir in the kielbasa and simmer for 15 minutes or until the vegetables are tender. Add salt and black pepper, and garnish each serving with parsley and dill, if desired.

JUDITH WILLIAMSON
Battle Creek, Michigan
Battle Creek Alumnae Chapter

CRAB BISQUE

MAKES 4–6 SERVINGS

1 pound fresh lump crabmeat, picked over to remove shell fragments

1 (10¾-ounce) can cream of celery soup

1 (10¾-ounce) can cream of mushroom soup

1 (4-ounce) can mushrooms, drained

1 soup can of milk

½ cup butter

Salt and black pepper, to taste

Combine all the ingredients in a heavy saucepan; cook over low heat, stirring constantly, until mixture comes to a slow boil.

COOK'S TIP | *You can use low-fat soups for this recipe. You can also add 2 tablespoons sherry for additional flavor.*

SABRINA POLOTE
College Park, Georgia
East Point/College Park Alumnae Chapter

Crab Bisque

BOYD'S CLAM CHOWDER

MAKES 6–8 SERVINGS

4 quarts littleneck clams (or about 1⅔ cups cooked, chopped canned clams)

1 clove garlic, chopped

1 cup water

2 ounces salt pork, finely chopped

2 cups chopped onions

3 tablespoons all-purpose flour

4½ cups clam broth

3 cups fish stock, chicken stock, or vegetable broth

1½ pounds potatoes, peeled and cut into ½-inch cubes

2 cups light cream

Oyster crackers (optional)

Clean the clams and place them in a large pot. Add the garlic and water and steam the clams just until opened, about 6 to 10 minutes, depending on their size. Drain and shell the clams, reserving the broth. Mince the clam flesh and set aside. Strain the broth through coffee filters or cheesecloth; set aside. (Skip this first part if using canned clams.)

Sauté the salt pork in a large heavy pot. Remove the cracklings and set aside. Slowly cook the onion in the fat about 6 minutes, stirring frequently, until cooked through but not browned. Stir in the flour and cook, stirring constantly, about 3 minutes. Add the reserved clam broth and the fish stock; whisk to remove any flour lumps. Bring to a boil, add the potatoes, lower the heat, and simmer until the potatoes are cooked through, about 15 minutes.

Stir in the reserved clams, salt pork cracklings, and cream. Heat through. Serve in large soup bowls with oyster crackers on the side, if desired.

ALFREDIA BOYD
Columbia, South Carolina
Chair, National Nominating Committee
Columbia, South Carolina, Alumnae Chapter

MOMMADOT'S EASY CREAM OF CRAB SOUP

MAKES 4 SERVINGS

½–¾ pound jumbo lump crabmeat

1 small onion, diced

½ green bell pepper, diced

1 small carrot, shredded

Minced fresh garlic (optional)

2 tablespoons vegetable oil

2 (10¾-ounce) cans cream of mushroom soup

2 cups 2% milk (add more or less, depending on desired thickness)

Salt and black pepper, to taste

Old Bay seasoning, to taste

Rinse the crabmeat, removing shell. Sauté the vegetables, and garlic, if desired, in the vegetable oil in a small skillet until semisoft. Combine the soup and milk in a large Dutch oven; stir to smooth. Add the vegetables. Stir in the crabmeat, add seasonings to taste, and simmer 15 minutes. Sprinkle a little more Old Bay on top for color.

COOK'S TIP | *If desired, add a few drops of hot sauce.*

DOROTHY L. HAIRSTON
Ocean Pines, Maryland
Delta-Tau Chapter, Cheyney University

SLUMGULLY

MAKES 10–12 SERVINGS

1 tablespoon vegetable shortening

3 pounds okra, sliced

1 large onion, chopped

3 cloves garlic, chopped

Salt and black pepper, to taste (or use garlic and
  onion salt)

1 (28-ounce) can whole tomatoes, coarsely chopped

1 (4-ounce) can tomato sauce

1 (15-ounce) can whole-kernel corn, drained

1 (15-ounce) can butter beans, drained

2 pounds smoked pork or beef sausage, sliced

2½ pounds shrimp, peeled and deveined

Hot cooked rice

Place the shortening in a deep skillet or Dutch oven; heat until hot. Add the okra, onion, and garlic. Season with salt and pepper. Cook over medium heat until the okra is tender. Add the tomatoes, tomato sauce, corn, and butter beans. Cook about 5 minutes. Add sausage and let this cook about 20 minutes. Add shrimp last and cook, covered, about 15 minutes. Serve over rice.

JESSIE W. FOSTER
Baton Rouge, Louisiana
Baton Rouge Sigma Alumnae Chapter

FLOURNOY'S NORTH LOUISIANA GUMBO

MAKES 8–10 SERVINGS

6 tablespoons vegetable shortening

6 tablespoons all-purpose flour

1 pound chicken or other meats

2 (14.5-ounce) cans tomatoes

1 cup chopped onions

2 cups chopped okra

1 clove garlic

1 red bell pepper, chopped

1 green bell pepper, chopped

½ teaspoon dried thyme

1 bay leaf

1 tablespoon salt

6 cups stock or water

1 pound shrimp, peeled and deveined

Hot sauce, to taste (optional)

Heat the shortening in a large stockpot over medium heat. Add the flour, a tablespoonful at a time, stirring constantly, until browned. Add the meat and the tomatoes. Cook 8 minutes. Add the vegetables, garlic, seasonings, the stock, and the shrimp. Add hot sauce, if desired. Cook over high heat until the meat is done, about 10 minutes. Serve with rice, if desired.

GLORIA COBB FLOURNOY
Dubberly, Louisiana
Minden Alumnae Chapter

A WEDDING RECEPTION BUFFET

Italian Shrimp Appetizer (page 12)

Crabmeat Quiche (page 133)

Sweet-and-Sour Cheese Ball (page 14) *and Crackers*

Curried Chicken (page 82)

Flournoy's North Louisiana Gumbo (page 57)

White Rice

Green Salad

Wedding Cake

Almond Biscotti (page 270)

Butter Nut Cookies (page 264)

EVERY DISH for a wedding reception buffet needs to be perfect, and yet everything must be done in advance and set out for guests to help themselves. This menu meets every criterion for such a joyous and festive occasion.

TO PREPARE:

❧ Make the biscotti a day in advance and store them airtight. Make the cheese ball and refrigerate it.

❧ In the morning, pick over the crabmeat for the quiche, and then prepare the shrimp. When they're in the refrigerator marinating, bake the Butter Nut Cookies. Prepare the greens and dressing for the salad and refrigerate them separately.

❧ The curried chicken and the gumbo can be cooked in the afternoon and reheated before serving.

❧ Make the quiche as close to serving time as possible. It can be set out at room temperature. The rice can cook while the quiche is baking. Finish the salad.

WHEN A DELTA GETS MARRIED

When the bride is a Delta, you can usually tell by the flowers she carries (stunning white roses), the dresses of the bridal party (deepest crimson for the maid of honor, and variations for the bridesmaids), and the decorations in the reception room (cream damask linen and dark red flowers). Traditionally, Deltas who have gathered for the occasion encircle the bride and serenade her. You, too, no doubt, have traditions that will help to make any wedding celebration personal and special.

While it is likely to be a formal occasion, modern times are less formal than times past. Raised daises are often done away with in favor of tables at floor level to create a greater sense of intimacy between the bridal party and other guests. Weddings are held in elaborate cathedrals and elegant sanctuaries or at home in a beautiful backyard setting, weather permitting, and the reception buffet might range from a formal sit-down catered dinner to a very informal reception for family and friends.

The dishes on this menu are certainly elegant enough for a wedding, but they are also designed to be prepared in advance and set on the buffet table at room temperature or in chafing dishes. If tables are assigned, guests can help themselves before finding their places. For an even less formal feeling, have the tables beautifully decorated and set, but allow guests to seat themselves.

Whatever degree of formality you choose, careful planning is always the key to flawless presentation.

SEAFOOD GUMBO, SOUTH CAROLINA STYLE

MAKES 4 SERVINGS

¼ cup olive oil

½ cup all-purpose flour

1 cup chopped onion

2 cloves garlic, chopped

1 cup chopped celery

1 large bell pepper, chopped

1 (16-ounce) can whole tomatoes

1 (13-ounce) can chicken broth

½ teaspoon dried sweet basil

½ teaspoon dried thyme or parsley

1 teaspoon ground black pepper

2 bay leaves

1 teaspoon hot sauce

1 pound medium shrimp, peeled and deveined

½ pound crabmeat or scallops or mussels

1 (10-ounce) package frozen okra, thawed (optional)

½ teaspoon gumbo filé powder

Heat the olive oil in a large pot. Add the flour gradually, stirring until the mixture turns light brown, then add the onion, garlic, celery, and bell pepper and cook until the vegetables soften, for about 6 to 8 minutes. Add the tomatoes, broth, basil, thyme, pepper, bay leaves, and hot sauce. Cook over low heat for 30 minutes. Add the seafood and the okra, if desired, and simmer for 15 minutes. Just before serving stir in the gumbo filé and remove the bay leaves. Serve over fluffy rice.

COOK'S TIP | *This recipe can be doubled or tripled to serve more people.*

MARY E. FAULKNER
Yonkers, New York
Westchester Alumnae Chapter

RACHEL'S TO-DIE-FOR SHRIMP GUMBO

MAKES 8–10 SERVINGS

SHRIMP GUMBO is one of the specialties in Cajun cooking. My grandmother, who grew up in the Louisiana bayou, told this specific recipe to me. Her grandmother was a freed slave and cooked for the family she worked for. Back then, shrimp was not plentiful for the slaves. Through the passing of time, fresh herbs and seasonings have been added to the recipe in place of some of the pork and excess salts. Each person has his or her own rendition. I hope that this will be to the liking of others, just as it has been for my family.

⅓ cup plus 1 tablespoon vegetable oil

½ cup all-purpose flour

2 medium stalks celery, chopped

2 cloves garlic, minced

1 medium green bell pepper, chopped

1 medium onion, chopped

2 (14½-ounce) cans chicken broth

1 (14.5-ounce) can stewed tomatoes

1 pound boneless, skinless chicken thighs, cut into thin strips

½ pound chorizo sausage, cut into ¼-inch slices

6 ounces okra, cut into ½-inch-thick slices
1 cup loosely packed fresh parsley, chopped
1 tablespoon minced fresh thyme
1 tablespoon minced fresh sage
¾ teaspoon salt
½ teaspoon coarsely ground black pepper
4 cups water
1 pound medium shrimp, peeled and deveined, with
    tail part of shell left on
1 cup long-grain white rice, cooked

In a 6-quart saucepan, heat the ⅓ cup oil over medium-low heat until hot. Gradually stir in the flour until blended and cook 15 minutes or until mixture is dark brown, stirring constantly.

Meanwhile, in a nonstick 12-inch skillet, heat the remaining 1 tablespoon oil over medium heat until hot. Add the celery, garlic, green pepper, and onion, and cook until vegetables are tender, 4 to 5 minutes, stirring occasionally.

When the flour mixture is ready, gradually stir in broth until blended and smooth. Add the stewed tomatoes, chicken, sausage, okra, herbs, salt, black pepper, cooked vegetables, and water; heat to boiling over high heat. Reduce heat to low; simmer, uncovered, 40 minutes. Skim off fat and discard.

Add the shrimp and cook, uncovered, 5 minutes longer, or until shrimp turn opaque throughout.

Serve the gumbo in large bowls with a scoop of hot rice in center.

RACHEL R. DAVIS
Tyler, Texas
Member-at-Large

WILMA'S JAMBALAYA

MAKES 10–12 SERVINGS

2 tablespoons olive oil
1 cup chopped onion
1 cup chopped celery
1 cup chopped green bell pepper
1 clove garlic, pressed
1 (28-ounce) can crushed tomatoes (3½ cups)
2 cups diced cooked ham
1 pound diced smoked sausage
1 cup diced boneless, skinless chicken breast
2 tablespoons paprika
½ teaspoon salt, or to taste
¼–½ teaspoon crushed red pepper flakes
¼ teaspoon black pepper
5 cups chicken stock or broth
3 cups rice, uncooked
10 ounces medium shrimp, peeled and deveined

Heat the oil in a large Dutch oven until hot but not smoking. Sauté the onion, celery, bell pepper, and garlic until tender. Add the tomatoes, ham, sausage, chicken, paprika, salt, red pepper flakes, and black pepper. Cook over low to medium heat, stirring frequently until the vegetables are very soft, about 3 to 4 minutes. Add chicken stock, rice, and shrimp; bring to a boil. Reduce heat, cover, and simmer 10 to 15 minutes or until the liquid is absorbed. Stir with a fork, cover, and let stand 5 minutes.

Serve with corn bread, if desired.

WILMA WAMBLE
Edmond, Oklahoma
Oklahoma City Alumnae Chapter

BILLY BOB'S BLACK-EYED PEAS WITH ATTITUDE

MAKES 8–10 SERVINGS

A LONGTIME FRIEND shared this recipe with me. He makes this dish as he travels across the country visiting his Delta friends. It's even better the second day.

½ medium green bell pepper

1 (1-pound) package mild all-beef links

1 (1-pound) package hot all-beef links

1 (16-ounce) bag frozen cut okra

Cajun seasoning, to taste

2 cups water

2 (14.5-ounce) cans diced tomatoes

1 (1-pound) package peeled cooked baby shrimp

6 (15-ounce) cans black-eyed peas, rinsed well and drained

Cut the bell pepper half in half again. Dice one quarter and slice the other quarter. Cut the mild links crosswise and the hot links lengthwise. In a large stockpot, layer the meat, bell pepper, and okra. Sprinkle with Cajun seasoning and add water. Cook over high heat for 10 minutes, stirring constantly. Add the tomatoes and the shrimp; sprinkle with Cajun seasoning. Simmer for 15 minutes. Add the black-eyed peas, sprinkle with Cajun seasoning, and simmer for 10 minutes. Serve over rice, if desired.

ESSIE M. JEFFRIES
Los Angeles, California
Los Angeles Alumnae Chapter

WORLD'S BEST CHILI

MAKES 10–12 SERVINGS

A PERFECT SUPER BOWL PARTY DISH. The men love it.

4 (10-ounce) cans chicken broth

3 (10-ounce) cans tomato sauce

2 (4-ounce) cans diced green chilies with liquid

2 cloves garlic, minced

3 teaspoons ground oregano

3 teaspoons ground cumin

½ teaspoon monosodium glutamate (optional)

3 teaspoons finely ground black pepper

4 teaspoons salt

5 tablespoons chili powder, or to taste

1 teaspoon dried cilantro

1 teaspoon dried thyme

8 ounces light beer

8 teaspoons vegetable oil

5 pounds thinly sliced center pork chops, diced into ¼-inch cubes

4 pounds beef flank steak, diced into ⅜-inch cubes

3 medium Spanish onions, diced

2 green bell peppers, diced

Juice of 1 lime

Shredded Cheddar cheese

Small round crackers

Combine the chicken broth, tomato sauce, and green chilies in a 2-gallon pot; heat on low. Combine the garlic, oregano, cumin, monosodium glutamate, pepper, salt, chili powder, cilantro, thyme, and beer in a medium bowl; add to the chicken broth mixture. Heat 4 teaspoons of the oil in a large skillet. Add the pork, half at a time, and cook lightly on all sides; do not overcook. Add the pork to the chicken broth mixture and boil for 30 minutes. Add the remaining 4 teaspoons oil to the skillet, and lightly brown the steak; do not overcook. Add the beef to the chili pot, and cook at a slow boil for about 1 hour. Add the onions and bell peppers. Cook at a slow boil for about 2 to 3 hours, stirring with a wooden spoon every 10 to 20 minutes.

Cool for 1 hour, then refrigerate for 24 hours. Reheat before serving.

Sprinkle with the lime juice and shredded cheese, and serve with small round crackers.

COOK'S TIP | *Add 2 (16-ounce) cans kidney or pinto beans to the chili or serve over a dollop of rice to thicken.*

LENORA PARRISH
Fairfield, California
Solano Valley Alumnae Chapter

LAVITA'S SLAMMIN' CHILI

MAKES 4–6 SERVINGS

I ORIGINATED THIS dish about twenty-five years ago. Married with a child and little money, I began to make chili mostly because it lasted more than one day and tasted even better the second or third day. Well, my husband got into the game because he fancied himself as a good cook, and he wanted to outdo me. Of course, he never did.

1 tablespoon vegetable oil
1 pound ground round (good hamburger meat), chicken, or turkey
1 pound Italian sausage, chopped
Black pepper, to taste
1 teaspoon seasoned salt
½ teaspoon cumin
1 tablespoon chili powder
2 teaspoons garlic powder, or 2 cloves garlic, chopped
1 cup chopped celery
½ cup chopped yellow onion
½ cup chopped sweet onion
1 small red bell pepper, chopped
1 small green bell pepper, chopped
1 (8-ounce) can sliced mushrooms, drained
1 (8-ounce) can tomato paste
1 teaspoon all-purpose flour
1 (16-ounce) can stewed tomatoes
1 (32-ounce) can kidney beans, rinsed and drained
Pinch of sugar
3–4 bottled hot peppers, or more if desired

Heat the oil in a large skillet. Brown the meat with the black pepper; drain well. Add the seasoned salt, cumin, chili powder, and garlic. Stir in the celery, onion, peppers, and mushrooms. Add the tomato paste with the flour and the stewed tomatoes. Spoon the mixture into a slow cooker. Simmer on High for 1 hour and then turn to Low. (Add water if chili gets too thick.) Add the kidney beans. Stir and taste. Add a pinch of sugar and more seasoned salt if needed. Add the hot peppers. Cook for 20 to 30 minutes.

Serve with rice and corn bread.

LAVITA ALSTON EMERSON
Seattle, Washington
Seattle Alumnae Chapter

DANCING AND DINING
AFTER-DARK BUFFET

(STEP SHOW AFTERPARTY)

Tangy Baked Party Wings (page 8)

Shrimp Mold (page 9)

Wilma's Jambalaya (page 61)

Stacy's Marinated Vegetable Salad (page 31)

Chocolate-Sour Cream
Pound Cake (page 203)

Mary McLeod Bethune's
Sweet Potato Pie (page 233)

Atlanta Lemon Whip Lush (page 254)

THERE WILL BE plenty of time for you to dance with your guests, because all these dishes are prepared ahead and are either served as is or quickly reheated. Just set everything out on the buffet table and join in the fun.

TO PREPARE:

❧ The day before, make and refrigerate the shrimp mold, the salad, and the lemon dessert. Make the pound cake and store it, covered airtight, at room temperature.

❧ Bake the sweet potato pie.

❧ In the afternoon, cook the jambalaya and prepare the wings up to the point of final baking.

DINING AND DANCING AT A DELTA STEP SHOW AFTERPARTY

A step show is a series of performances given by members of the various African-American Greek organizations competing against one another, usually for prizes. The performances themselves consist of groups, dressed alike in the sorority or fraternity's colors, doing intricately synchronized steps, claps, chants, and songs they've practiced long and hard to perfect.

The afterparty buffet would be decorated in colors associated with each of the participating organizations, and both the atmosphere and dress would be casual. The overarching theme of these evenings is to reflect the unity among Greeks that underlies the friendly competition.

Deltas, however, don't have to wait for an "official" occasion to enjoy a night of dining and dancing after dark, and neither should anyone else. By all means, make your buffet table festive and colorful and ask your guests to wear their favorite "dancin' duds." If you'll be dancing to a particular kind of music or tunes from a particular time, attire reflecting that theme would be both appropriate and fun.

Winners of a 1996 North Jersey Alumnae Chapter Delta Step Show

TURKEY CHILI

MAKES 8–10 SERVINGS

1 pound ground turkey

1 (8-ounce) can tomato sauce

1 (6-ounce) can tomato paste

1 tablespoon sugar

1 (16-ounce) can chicken broth

½ cup water

1 medium green bell pepper, finely chopped

1 medium onion, finely chopped

2 teaspoons dried Italian seasoning

Salt and black pepper, to taste

2 tablespoons chili powder

1 teaspoon garlic powder

2 (16-ounce) cans, rinsed and drained, or 1 pound
   fresh-cooked, kidney beans

Brown the ground turkey in a large skillet sprayed with nonstick cooking spray. Drain any liquid and add all the remaining ingredients, except the kidney beans. Simmer at least 30 minutes over low heat. Add more water, if necessary. Add the beans and heat until warm. Serve over warm steamed rice with corn bread.

CHRISTINE MARTIN
Queens Village, New York
Nassau Alumnae Chapter

DEL RIO TURKEY CHILI

MAKES 6–8 SERVINGS

WHILE PREPARING a repast for a committee meeting I was hosting, I realized that I was out of kidney beans for my turkey chili. I didn't have time to run to the grocer, so I added black-eyed peas and zucchini, which I had on hand. When served to my Delta sisters, the chili received rave reviews, and it has become one of my signature dishes.

2 tablespoons canola oil

1 medium white onion, chopped

2 tablespoons chopped garlic

1 medium zucchini, chopped

2 pounds ground turkey

1 pound smoked turkey sausage or turkey
   kielbasa, chopped

2 (⅜-ounce) packets onion soup mix or 1 (⅜-ounce)
   packet onion soup mix plus 2 tablespoons salt

1 (15-ounce) can regular or low-sodium black-eyed
   peas, undrained

1 (12-ounce) can diced tomatoes

1 (24-ounce) can tomato purée

1 packet chili mix

2 tablespoons cayenne pepper, or to taste

OPTIONAL TOPPINGS
(PER SERVING)

1 ounce reduced-fat Cheddar cheese, shredded

1 ounce reduced-fat sour cream

1 ounce chopped scallions

Heat the canola oil in a large skillet. Add the onion, garlic, and zucchini. Sauté until the vegetables are translucent, for about 2 or 3 minutes. Then add the ground turkey, chopped turkey sausage, and onion soup mix. Stir well and cook, covered, until the meat is browned. Drain the excess liquid. Add the black-eyed peas, diced tomatoes, and tomato purée; stir well. Add the chili mix and the cayenne pepper. Simmer for 30 minutes. Serve in large mugs or soup bowls. Add the optional toppings of your choice.

KIMBERLEY REED THOMPSON
Detroit, Michigan
Detroit Alumnae Chapter

WHITE CHILI

MAKES 6 SERVINGS

MY GOOD FRIEND John Burrill gave me this recipe. We share a love of cooking.

2 cups chopped white onion

2 tablespoons minced garlic

1 teaspoon vegetable oil

1 (8-ounce) can chopped green chilies, drained

2 cups cubed cooked chicken breast

2 (14-ounce) cans Great Northern beans, rinsed and drained

3 (14-ounce) cans clear chicken broth

2 teaspoons ground cumin

2 teaspoons ground oregano

¼ teaspoon cayenne pepper, or more to taste

Shredded Monterey Jack cheese for garnish

Corn chips for garnish

Sauté the onion and garlic in the oil in a large, heavy saucepan. Add the chilies, chicken, beans, chicken broth, and seasonings. Bring to a boil; reduce heat and simmer for 20 minutes. Serve with shredded Monterey Jack and corn chips.

JUDITH WILLIAMSON
Battle Creek, Michigan
Battle Creek Alumnae Chapter

HEART-SMART CHILI

MAKES 18–20 SERVINGS

2 (15-ounce) cans diced tomatoes, with their juice

1 (15-ounce) can tomato sauce

1 (15-ounce) can kidney beans, undrained

7 (15-ounce) cans butter beans, undrained

3 (15-ounce) cans black beans, undrained

3 (15-ounce) cans garbanzo beans, undrained

4 cups diced onions

2 cups diced carrots

Black pepper, garlic powder, onion powder, chili powder, and cumin, to taste

Combine all the ingredients in a large stockpot. Bring to a boil, then reduce heat and simmer for 2 hours.

DORIS MCEWEN WALKER
Lakewood, Washington
National Secretary
Seattle Alumnae Chapter

4

POULTRY

AND GAME

A Mother's
Culinary Legacy
Bishop Vashti Murphy McKenzie

When the National Chaplain, Bishop Vashti Murphy McKenzie, delivers a sermon, it is an awe-inspiring experience. There is an intimacy in her delivery, even when the auditorium is filled with thousands of Deltas, that allows each person to feel that Bishop McKenzie is speaking directly to her.

Two decades ago, Soror Vashti felt that God had something in mind for her life beyond an already successful career in journalism and broadcasting, and, once she acknowledged her calling, she found doors opening that allowed her to fulfill her purpose.

In 1990, she was appointed senior pastor of the 103-year-old Payne Memorial AME Church, becoming the first woman of her denomination to lead a congregation of that size. The assignment, however, was as challenging as it was prestigious. The church was located in the city's urban core, surrounded by drugs, crime, and violence. She was, nevertheless, able to increase its membership from 300 to 1,700 and the value of its holdings

from $1.6 to $5.6 million by instituting a concept of ministry that emphasized numerous innovative community outreach programs.

On Tuesday, July 17, 2000, Bishop McKenzie became the first woman to be elected bishop in the 213-year history of the African Methodist Episcopal Church. Her first assignment was in southern Africa, where she took over the church's

Eighteenth Episcopal District, a territory with two hundred churches and 10,000 members in Lesotho, Botswana, Swaziland, and Mozambique. She is, however, well prepared for the post, having already spent significant time in Africa over the past decade. Familiar with the conditions, she has focused on economic development, human rights, church growth, and the fight against AIDS.

In addition to her many religious titles, Bishop McKenzie proudly wears the titles of soror, wife, and mother. To the sorority, she is known as National Chaplain and the granddaughter of Founder Vashti Turley Murphy. "For me she was Grandmother," Bishop McKenzie says. "She taught my cousins and me to count in French and

SUNDAY-AFTERNOON ROASTED CHICKEN

MAKES 4 SERVINGS

THIS MAKES A perfect Sunday-afternoon meal, especially in fall and winter. It's easy to make and perfect to serve with broccoli and rice, a tossed salad, and hot corn-bread muffins. A traditional family meal.

1 (4- to 5-pound) whole chicken
Salt and black pepper, or seasoned salt, to taste
Italian seasoning
¼ cup butter or margarine, melted
¼ lemon

Preheat the oven to 400 degrees.

Rinse the chicken inside and out; pat dry. Season the chicken, inside and out, with salt and pepper or seasoned salt. Then sprinkle entire chicken with Italian seasoning. Place the chicken breast side up on a baking rack inside of a shallow roasting pan. Roast for about 45 minutes; remove and baste with the melted butter and the juice from the lemon. To prevent browning too quickly, cover the top only with aluminum foil. Place chicken back in oven and continue roasting until juices run clear, about 45 minutes more (total cooking time for the chicken should be about 20 minutes per pound).

DENISE E. GILMORE
Kansas City, Missouri
National Treasurer
Kansas City Alumnae Chapter

Sunday-Afternoon Roasted Chicken, surrounded by Skillet Greens (page 144)

CHICKEN BREAST SUPREME

MAKES 10–12 SERVINGS

8 whole chicken breasts

¼ cup butter

Salt and black pepper, to taste

½ cup slivered almonds

1 (10¾-ounce) can cream of chicken soup

1 (10¾-ounce) can cream of mushroom soup

1 (10¾-ounce) can cream of celery soup

½ cup dry white wine

Freshly grated Parmesan cheese

Preheat the oven to 350 degrees.

Place the chicken breasts in a 9-by-12-inch baking dish. Dot with butter. Add salt and black pepper. Sprinkle with almonds. Combine the soups and wine in a medium saucepan; mix well. Heat until warm. Pour over the chicken breasts; sprinkle with the Parmesan cheese. Bake, uncovered, for 1 hour.

LORRAINE W. DABNEY
Palo Alto, California
San Francisco Peninsula Alumnae Chapter

CHICKEN BREASTS À L'ORANGE

MAKES 4 SERVINGS

4 large chicken breasts, with skin on

Salt and black pepper, to taste

¼ cup butter or margarine

¼ cup orange marmalade

¼ cup Worcestershire sauce

Preheat the oven to 450 degrees.

Wash the chicken thoroughly and pat dry. Season with salt and black pepper. Place chicken skin side up in a baking pan. Bake for 20 minutes.

Melt the butter in a saucepan. Add the marmalade and stir until heated. Remove the pan from the heat and stir in the Worcestershire sauce. Pour the sauce over the chicken evenly. Reduce the oven temperature to 300 degrees. Bake for about 12 to 15 minutes, or until well browned. Baste the chicken three times during the last half of the cooking process.

MERLE ALLEN FRANKLIN
Atlanta, Georgia
Atlanta Suburban Alumnae Chapter

Chicken Breasts à l'Orange

SMOTHERED CHICKEN

MAKES 4–6 SERVINGS

¾ cup all-purpose flour

1 teaspoon poultry seasoning

1 teaspoon paprika

1 teaspoon black pepper

1 (2½-pound) broiler-fryer chicken, cut in half

6 tablespoons unsalted butter

2 medium stalks celery, chopped

3⅓ cups chicken broth

Preheat the oven to 350 degrees.

Combine ¼ cup of the flour, ½ teaspoon of the poultry seasoning, ½ teaspoon of the paprika, and ½ teaspoon of the black pepper in a shallow bowl. Lightly dredge the chicken halves in the seasoned flour mixture.

Melt 2 tablespoons of the butter in a large skillet over medium-high heat. Sauté the celery in the butter for 1 to 2 minutes. Place the chicken in the skillet, skin side down. Sauté on each side for 5 to 7 minutes, or until the chicken is golden brown. Transfer the chicken, skin side up, to a rectangular baking dish.

Deglaze the skillet with ⅓ cup of the chicken broth, scraping the browned bits from the bottom of the pan. Add the remaining 4 tablespoons butter to the skillet, stirring constantly to blend. Sprinkle the remaining ½ cup flour over the mixture. Whisk to make a roux. Cook the roux for 3 to 5 minutes over medium heat. Add the remaining chicken broth, a little at a time, whisking well after each addition.

Season with the remaining poultry seasoning, paprika, and pepper. Pour the thickened gravy over the browned chicken halves. Bake for 30 minutes, or until there is no pink flesh next to the bone. Serve with rice.

HORTENSE GOLDEN CANADY
Lansing, Michigan
Past National President (1983–1988)
Lansing Alumnae Chapter

CHICKEN BREAST SCALOPPINE

MAKES 4 SERVINGS

4 boneless, skinless chicken breasts

1 large egg, beaten

1 cup milk

1 tablespoon Dijon mustard

3 dashes of hot sauce

1 cup Italian bread crumbs

1 teaspoon chopped fresh parsley

⅔ tablespoon vegetable oil

⅔ tablespoon butter

1 lemon, cut into 4 wedges

Pound the chicken breasts with a wooden mallet until about ½ inch thick. Combine the egg, milk, mustard, and hot sauce in a medium bowl. Soak the chicken breasts in the egg mixture for 15 minutes.

In a small bowl, combine the bread crumbs and parsley. Dredge the chicken breasts in the bread-crumb mixture.

Heat the oil and butter in a large skillet until sizzling. Sauté the chicken about 5 minutes on each side or until done. Serve with the lemon wedges.

ALFREDIA BOYD
Columbia, South Carolina
Chair, National Nominating Committee
Columbia, South Carolina, Alumnae Chapter

MOROCCAN CHICKEN BREASTS

MAKES 18–20 SERVINGS

⅓ cup all-purpose flour

1 tablespoon ground cumin

1 teaspoon paprika

1 teaspoon turmeric

½ teaspoon salt

8 (8-ounce) skinless chicken breast halves
   with bone

4 teaspoons olive oil

4 teaspoons minced garlic

4 teaspoons fresh diced, peeled ginger

1 (14.5-ounce) can fat-free chicken broth

16 Kalamata olives, pitted and cut in half

3 navel oranges, peeled, white part (pith) removed
   and flesh cut into ¾-inch chunks

⅓ cup finely chopped fresh cilantro

Preheat the oven to 350 degrees.

In a wide, shallow bowl, mix the flour, cumin, paprika, turmeric, and salt. Add the chicken and turn to coat; shake off the excess coating.

Heat 2 teaspoons of the oil in a large nonstick skillet over medium heat. Add half the chicken; cook 2 minutes per side or until browned. Place in a shallow 3-quart baking dish in a single layer. Repeat with the remaining oil and chicken.

Add the garlic and ginger to the skillet; sauté over medium heat 1 minute to cook slightly. Add the broth and olives; bring to a boil and pour over the chicken. Top with the oranges and cover with foil. Bake for 25 minutes or until cooked through. Sprinkle with cilantro before serving.

COOK'S TIP | *To make ahead, prepare the oranges up to three days in advance. Bag and refrigerate. Bake the chicken up to two days ahead. Cool, cover, and refrigerate. Reheat, covered, at 350 degrees for 1 hour. Chop cilantro 30 minutes before using.*

FLAXIE FLETCHER, M.D.
Los Angeles, California
Rolling Hills–Palos Verdes Alumnae Chapter

Crab Bisque (page 55)

Judge Trudy's
Sensation Salad (page 39)

Moroccan Chicken Breasts (page 77)

Minted Onions (page 146)

Copper-Penny Carrots (page 152)

Sassy Fruit 'n' Sauce (page 251)

Perfect Pound Cake (page 202)

SPECIAL OCCASIONS require special foods and special attention to detail. Get out the best china, polish your silver, and welcome your guests with a menu that's truly memorable.

TO PREPARE:

❧ Make the pound cake the day before, wrap it airtight, and store it at room temperature. The evening before your dinner, mix up the fruit (except the bananas and fresh strawberries) and refrigerate it. Make the salad dressing and store it in the fridge. In the morning, slice the carrots, wash and tear the lettuce, and grate the cheese for the salad. Prepare the oranges for the chicken and pick through the crabmeat. Store everything in the refrigerator.

❧ About an hour before your guests arrive, prepare the chicken up to the point of baking, get the onions into their pan ready to go into the oven, and precook the carrots.

❧ Cook the bisque just before serving.

A CRIMSON AND CREAM DELTA EXTRAVAGANZA

The Crimson and Cream Ball, usually a black-tie function with women in long gowns and men in tuxedoes, is held by various chapters at different times of the year, usually as a fund-raiser. The elegance of the venue and decor must match that of the guests, with round tables

Deltas dressed for a Crimson and Cream Ball

for ten clad in floor-length damask cloths and damask napkins in silver napkin rings.

The floral centerpieces are intended to make a bold and beautiful statement, and the ambience is enhanced either by candles placed in silver candelabra or small votives surrounding the flowers. Service is formal as well, and the music is supplied by a live band, also dressed in formal attire.

The color scheme of a Delta Crimson and Cream Ball would, of course, reflect both the sorority's colors and the theme of the event. If, for example, tables are covered in cream-colored cloths, the centerpieces might be deep crimson flowers. Or, the color scheme might

be reversed, with crimson damask cloths and cream-colored roses. The final effect is intended simply to make the room absolutely breathtakingly beautiful.

While this is, obviously, a catered event, there's no reason not to replicate the elegant setting and service at home, albeit on a smaller scale. The recipes on this menu are ones that you can easily prepare in a home kitchen. Just ask your guests to "dress up" and get out your best linen, china, flatware, and glasses. Make sure there are beautiful flowers, and light the candles before everyone sits down to dinner so that they will be flattered and bedazzled by their dancing light.

DELTA EXECUTIVE MEETING CASSEROLE

MAKES 10–12 SERVINGS

THIS IS AN EXCELLENT ONE-DISH MEAL for a committee meeting. You can make it ahead and freeze it before baking.

2 (2- to 3-pound) chickens

1 cup chopped onion

1 cup chopped green bell pepper

Salt and black pepper, to taste

1 (8-ounce) package thin spaghetti

1 (8-ounce) can chopped Mexican or Italian
   tomatoes, drained

1 (8-ounce) can green peas, drained

1 (8-ounce) can mushrooms, drained

8 ounces Velveeta or other cheese, shredded

Place the chickens in a large stockpot with the onion and bell pepper. Season with salt and pepper. Cover with water. Bring to a boil, reduce heat, and cook until the chicken is tender.

Remove the chicken from the liquid and debone. Save 1½ quarts of the chicken broth in the stockpot.

Preheat the oven to 350 degrees.

Boil the pasta in the broth until fully cooked; do not drain. Add the tomatoes, peas, and mushrooms. Add the chicken and cheese. Pour into a 13-by-9-inch baking dish.

Bake for 20 to 30 minutes or until the edges are brown.

JOY M. THOMAS
Fort Worth, Texas
Fort Worth Alumnae Chapter

CURRIED CHICKEN

MAKES 4 SERVINGS

1 (3- to 4-pound) chicken, cut up

Salt and black pepper, to taste

2 tablespoons curry powder

1 tablespoon ground cumin

2 tablespoons olive oil

1 medium onion, chopped

4 cloves garlic, chopped

3 medium potatoes, peeled and cut into
    medium-size chunks

2 green onion tops, chopped

Juice of ½ lemon

Wash the chicken thoroughly and remove the skin. Season with the salt and pepper. Mix the curry powder and cumin into a paste with a few drops of water; spread over the chicken.

Heat the olive oil in a large skillet. Sauté the onion and garlic lightly in the olive oil. Add the chicken. Fry over low heat for 10 to 15 minutes. Add the potatoes to the pan, along with the green onion tops and the lemon juice. Continue cooking until the chicken and the potatoes are tender.

RITA BENN
Maywood, Illinois
Glen Ellyn Area Alumnae Chapter

STACEY'S BODACIOUS BUTTERMILK FRIED CHICKEN

MAKES 8–10 SERVINGS

⅓ cup ground black pepper

1 tablespoon paprika

⅓ cup garlic powder

⅓ cup onion powder

⅓ cup seasoned salt

3 whole fryer chickens, cut up

6 large eggs

¾ cup buttermilk

4 tablespoons water

1 (1-pound) bag all-purpose flour

1 teaspoon each of black pepper, seasoned salt,
    garlic powder, and onion powder

Canola oil for frying

Stacey's Bodacious Buttermilk Fried Chicken

Combine the first 5 ingredients in a small bowl; mix well. Sprinkle each piece of chicken heavily with the seasoning mixture. Refrigerate for an hour or two to allow the seasonings to marinate.

Beat the eggs, buttermilk, and water in a large mixing bowl. Dip the chicken pieces in the egg mixture, turning a couple of times to coat thoroughly.

Mix the flour, black pepper, seasoned salt, garlic powder, and onion powder in a large grocery bag. Shake to mix well. Drop the chicken pieces into the bag of seasoned flour. Seal and shake the bag carefully in order to coat each piece of chicken with flour. You may want to drop only a few pieces at a time into the bag. When you are ready to cook, heat about ¼ inch of oil in a large, deep skillet to approximately 350 degrees. Fry the chicken until brown and crispy on all sides (about 8 to 15 minutes per side; white meat does not have to cook as long as dark meat). Remove the chicken and place it in a paper towel–lined pan to drain.

STACEY J. BROWN
South Euclid, Ohio
Greater Cleveland Alumnae Chapter

CHICKEN POTPIE

MAKES 6–8 SERVINGS

4–5 chicken pieces, cooked and deboned
2 (15-ounce) cans mixed vegetables, drained
2 (10½-ounce) cans cream of chicken soup
2 (10½-ounce) cans cream of celery soup
1 cup all-purpose flour
½ cup mayonnaise
1 cup milk

Preheat the oven to 350 degrees.

Layer the chicken and the next 3 ingredients in the order listed in a 13-by-9-inch casserole dish.

Combine the flour, mayonnaise, and milk in a small bowl. Pour over the casserole. Bake for 55 minutes or until brown.

CHARLOTTE Y. MARSHALL
Panama City, Florida
Panama City Alumnae Chapter

A Juneteenth Backyard Picnic

Ida's Homemade Lemon-Raspberry Lemonade (page 17)

Stacey's Bodacious Buttermilk Fried Chicken (page 82)

Dirty Rice (page 157)

Easy Fried Corn (page 149)

Dijon Green Bean Salad (page 35)

Deep-Dish Apple Crumb Pie (page 236)

Gooey Squares (page 257)

JUNETEENTH DATES BACK TO THE YEAR
1865, when Major General Gordon
Granger led his Union Army troops into the
city of Galveston and on June 19 officially proclaimed freedom for slaves in Texas. Granger's
arrival in Galveston was the culmination of a
two-and-a-half-year journey through the Deep
South. Many states, parishes, and counties had
been excluded from learning of President Lin-
coln's Emancipation Proclamation, and count-
less African-American slaves denied their
freedom. On this date, though, the Proclamation was announced to Texas and other parts of
the South, to grant them their freedom forever.

TO PREPARE:

🐾 Be sure to make the lemonade far enough
in advance to give the ice cubes time to
freeze. Finish it just before serving so that
the cubes don't melt before everyone has a
chance to see them.

🐾 Both desserts can be made a day in advance.
Keep the pie in the refrigerator until just
before serving. Bring to room temperature
or serve warm, if you wish. Store the squares,
tightly covered, at room temperature.

🐾 In the morning, prepare the green beans and
the Dijon dressing and refrigerate them separately to be combined just before serving.

🐾 Fry the chicken before your guests arrive
and serve it at room temperature.

🐾 Both the rice and the corn are easy to put
together and quick to cook.

JUNETEENTH DONE
THE DELTA WAY

This is an occasion when Deltas turn to family
and remember our history. Juneteenth is always
a multigenerational celebration, a day to bring
out cameras and video recorders, and to talk
about those who have gone before us.

Children, in particular, love to hear stories
about their ancestors. Is there a name that's been
passed down through the generations in your
family? Why not tell the child who now bears
that name about the one who gave it to him or
her? Every family has its own lore, and this is a
time to share it with the youngest among you,
who may not have heard it before, as well as to
tell them about the meaning of the holiday itself. But Juneteenth is by no means a solemn
occasion, so also be sure to include lots of
games, contests, and activities to keep everyone
involved and entertained as they enjoy the
picnic fare.

JERK CHICKEN DRUMS

MAKES 2–4 SERVINGS

WHILE ON LINE, pledging my beloved DST, I made jerk chicken drums for my line sisters. My Line Sister Number 7 raved about the chicken because the meat was falling off the bones and she placed it between two pieces of bread. She loved the taste and asked over and over again when I was making that lovely jerk chicken. This goes out to Line Sister Number 7: When you cook, you cook with love from the soul! (Oh, and by the way, she couldn't believe I made it in a slow cooker.)

8–10 chicken drumsticks or more, depending on the size of the slow cooker

2 cups white cooking wine with lemon flavoring

Seasoned salt, to taste

Black pepper, to taste

1 tablespoon Jamaican jerk seasoning paste, or more for spicier drumsticks

1 cup peeled and quartered potatoes or other vegetables (optional)

Place the drumsticks in a large dish. Pour 1½ cups of the wine over the chicken. Then lightly coat chicken on both sides with seasoned salt and pepper. Marinate in the refrigerator overnight.

Remove the chicken from the marinade and spread the jerk seasoning over the chicken.

Pour ½ cup water and the remaining ½ cup white wine in the bottom of a slow cooker. Add the drumsticks. Also add peeled quartered potatoes, if desired. Cook on Low for 7 to 9 hours. You can add green beans or any other vegetable during the last 1 to 2 hours, if desired.

COOK'S TIP | *For healthier cooking, remove the skin from the drumsticks before marinating.*

DONNA MARIA WILKERSON
Bloomfield, Connecticut
Hartford Alumnae Chapter

CHICKEN CROQUETTES

MAKES 2–4 SERVINGS

3 tablespoons butter or margarine

5 tablespoons all-purpose flour

1 cup milk

2 cups chopped, cooked chicken

½ teaspoon celery salt

½ teaspoon black pepper

½ teaspoon salt

1 tablespoon chopped onion

2 teaspoons chopped fresh parsley

½ tablespoon all-purpose (combination) seasoning

About 2 cups fine dry bread crumbs

1 large egg, lightly beaten

Canola oil for frying

Chicken Croquettes

Melt the butter in a medium skillet; add the flour and blend to a smooth paste. Add the milk gradually and cook until mixture thickens, stirring constantly. Add the chicken and next 6 ingredients; cook for several minutes over medium heat. Remove from the heat; cool and shape into croquettes or cutlets. Roll in fine bread crumbs, dip in lightly beaten egg, and roll in crumbs again. Fry in oil until browned; drain on paper towels.

CARNIECE BROWN-WHITE
Denver, Colorado
Denver Alumnae Chapter

CHICKEN ALL-IN-ONE

MAKES 3–4 SERVINGS

FAMILIES TODAY ARE always on the run, so it's hard to consistently provide them with wholesome meals. This recipe gives all the good nutrients of a well-balanced meal—and it takes only an hour.

4 boneless, skinless chicken breast halves
Seasoned salt and black pepper, to taste
2 large potatoes, peeled
2 (16-ounce) cans French-style or whole green beans, drained
½ cup butter or margarine
¼ cup water
1 (0.07-ounce) packet dry Italian seasoning

Preheat the oven to 350 degrees.

Rinse the chicken breasts with cold water and pat dry. Season them with seasoned salt and pepper. Place the chicken in one side of a medium-size roaster pan. Cut the potatoes into medium-size cubes and place on the opposite side of the roaster. Place the green beans in the center.

Melt the butter in a small saucepan; add the water, then the Italian seasoning. Stir the mixture well and pour it over the chicken, beans, and potatoes. Bake, covered, for about 1 hour or until the chicken is tender and the potatoes are soft.

Serve with a fresh garden salad and crescent rolls.

COOK'S TIP | *Experiment with other seasonings to spice up the chicken. Carrots can be substituted for one can of the beans.*

SANDRA K. PARKER
Saginaw, Michigan
Saginaw Alumnae Chapter

CHICKEN AND BROCCOLI CASSEROLE

MAKES 8 SERVINGS

THIS DISH WAS a staple of law school study sessions at my house. If there were leftovers everyone went home with her own "study-later food bag."

4–6 chicken breasts
2 (10-ounce) packages frozen broccoli spears
1 medium onion, chopped
1 teaspoon butter or margarine
3 cloves garlic, crushed
1 (10¾-ounce) can cream of mushroom soup
1 (10¾-ounce) can cream of chicken soup
1 cup mayonnaise
1 small can water chestnuts, drained and chopped
1 teaspoon lemon juice
1 teaspoon curry powder
1 cup shredded sharp Cheddar cheese
½ cup seasoned bread crumbs of choice

Cover the chicken with water in a large saucepan. Cook over medium heat until tender; drain and cool. Shred into large pieces.

Cook the broccoli according to the package directions. Drain and layer on the bottom of a 12-by-8-inch baking dish. Lay the shredded chicken over the broccoli.

Preheat the oven to 350 degrees.

Sauté the onion in the butter in a small skillet until it begins to turn golden; then add the garlic and cook 2 more minutes. Combine the soups, mayonnaise, water chestnuts, onion mixture, lemon juice, and curry powder in a large bowl. Pour over the chicken and broccoli and top with cheese. Sprinkle the bread crumbs evenly over the top. Bake for 35 to 40 minutes or until bubbly.

EDNA LEE LONG-GREEN
Washington, D.C.
Co-Chair, National Commission on Arts and Letters
Washington, D.C., Alumnae Chapter

GLADYS'S CHICKEN AND RICE CASSEROLE

MAKES 4–6 SERVINGS

1 cup uncooked long-grain rice
1 cup boiling water
1½ pounds boneless, skinless chicken breasts
Seasoned salt, to taste
1 (10¾-ounce) can cream of chicken soup
1 (10¾-ounce) can cream of mushroom soup
1 (10¾-ounce) can French onion soup

Preheat the oven to 350 degrees.

Wash the rice and place in the bottom of a well-greased 13-by-9-inch baking dish. Cover the rice with the boiling water. Place the chicken on top of the rice. (If the chicken breasts are large, cut in half before cooking.) Sprinkle with a small amount of seasoned salt.

Mix the soups in a medium bowl. Pour the soup mixture over the chicken. Cover with foil and bake 1½ to 2 hours.

Serve with a green salad and rolls.

DORIS FLACK BROOME
Missouri City, Texas
Suburban Houston–Fort Bend Chapter

DELTA OF DISTINCTION
Alexis Herman

IN MAY 1997, the Honorable Alexis Herman was sworn in as the nation's first African-American secretary of labor, the position she held until 2001. During that time she oversaw the revision and simplification of the department's skills programs, allowing people to move more quickly from welfare to work.

A native of Mobile, Alabama, she graduated from Xavier University in New Orleans and worked for Catholic Charities before entering government service as director of the Women's Bureau under President Carter. She reentered the private sector in 1980 as an entrepreneur and labor relations expert. In 1993, President Clinton appointed her assistant to the president and director of the White House Public Liaison Office.

Today she chairs the Coca-Cola Company's Diversity Task Force; is a senior advisor to Toyota Motor Sales, USA; and is a contributing writer for Monster.com. Soror Herman is Honorary Chair of the Sorority's Social Action Commission.

CHICKEN MACARONI OR SPAGHETTI

MAKES 4–6 SERVINGS

1 (4- to 5-pound) chicken, cooked

1 small green bell pepper, chopped

2 stalks celery, chopped

2 medium onions, chopped

2 cups chicken broth

1 (4-ounce) can chopped mushrooms, drained

1 (6-ounce) jar pimientos, drained

½ pound Cheddar cheese, shredded

1 (8-ounce) package macaroni or spaghetti, cooked and well drained

Preheat the oven to 350 degrees.

Shred or cut the chicken into bite-size pieces. Cook the bell pepper, celery, and onions in the chicken broth in a large saucepan until tender. Add the mushrooms, pimientos, and cheese. Combine the chicken and sauce with the macaroni in a 12-by-9-inch baking dish. Bake for about 30 to 45 minutes or until well heated and cheese is melted.

VIENNA M. JEFFERSON
Calumet City, Illinois
Chicago Alumnae Chapter

PYRAMID PENNE RIGATE

MAKES 4–6 SERVINGS

THIS EASY RECIPE IS dedicated to the busy Pyramids who do not have a lot of time to plan and prepare a meal. Pyramids are women who are inducted into the first level of seeking membership in the sorority. Women who are inducted together share a special bond.

1 medium red onion, chopped

1 red bell pepper, chopped

1 tablespoon butter or margarine

½ pound sliced button mushrooms, or 1 (8-ounce) can sliced button mushrooms, drained

2 cups diced cooked chicken

1 (12-ounce) jar Alfredo sauce

2 chicken bouillon cubes

1 (12-ounce) package penne rigate

Sauté the onion and bell pepper in the butter in a large skillet until soft. Stir in the mushrooms. Add the diced chicken and Alfredo sauce. Simmer for 10 minutes. While the sauce simmers, bring 4 quarts of water to a rapid boil in a large saucepan. Add the bouillon cubes and stir in the penne rigate. Return the mixture to a rapid boil, stirring frequently. Cook for 10 to 12 minutes or until tender. Drain. Pour the pasta into a serving dish. Pour the chicken and sauce over it and toss lightly.

JOYCE WHITE
Jackson, Mississippi
Jackson Alumnae Chapter

CHICKEN CHOW MEIN

MAKES 4–6 SERVINGS

1 pound skinless chicken breasts

2 teaspoons salt

2 teaspoons black pepper

4 (3-ounce) packages Chinese ramen chicken-flavored soup noodles

2 tablespoons olive oil

4 cloves garlic, chopped

1 medium white onion, chopped

2 tablespoons soy sauce

2 cups frozen mixed vegetables

2 large eggs

Chopped green onions for garnish

Wash the chicken thoroughly; cut into small pieces and season with the salt and black pepper. Boil the noodles in a large pot per package directions. Drain and rinse with cold water.

Heat the oil in a large skillet. Fry the chicken, garlic, and onion with the soy sauce until tender. Add the frozen vegetables, and cook for 5 minutes or until tender. Beat the eggs in a small bowl, and prepare a thin omelet in a small skillet. Cut the omelet into strips for garnish. Mix the noodles and the chicken in the pot; turn off the heat. Garnish with egg and green onion; cover and let stand for 5 minutes before serving.

RITA BENN
Maywood, Illinois
Glen Ellyn Area Alumnae Chapter

TURKEY DUMP BEANS

MAKES 10 SERVINGS

WITH THE FIRST BITE, the sweetness of this dish surprises the taste buds.

6–8 slices bacon, cooked and crumbled

1 pound ground turkey or turkey sausage, browned and drained

1 (16-ounce) can dark kidney beans, drained

1 (16-ounce) can light red kidney beans, drained

1 (32-ounce) can pork and beans, drained

1 (16-ounce) can yellow wax beans, drained

1 (16-ounce) can butter beans, drained

1 cup catsup

½ cup packed brown sugar

1 medium onion, diced

5 tablespoons cider vinegar

3 drops liquid smoke

Combine all the ingredients in a slow cooker; stir well. Cook on High for 1 hour; reduce heat and cook on Low for 5 hours.

PAMELA SMITH
Maple Heights, Ohio
Co-Chair, Program Planning and Development
Greater Cleveland Alumnae Chapter

TANGY TURKEY-SPINACH LASAGNA

MAKES 8–10 SERVINGS

2–3 medium tomatoes, thinly sliced

Italian spices, to taste

½ cup balsamic vinegar

½ (8-ounce) package lasagna noodles

1 pound ground turkey (or ground beef)

Salt and black pepper, to taste

1 (26-ounce) jar three-cheese pasta sauce

1 cup ricotta cheese

1 (10-ounce) package frozen spinach, thawed

1½ cups shredded Italian cheese mixture (or
   mozzarella only)

Place the tomatoes in a large bowl. Sprinkle with Italian spices, and pour the vinegar over them, covering completely. Cover and set aside in the refrigerator. Before using, remove from the vinegar and shake off any excess liquid.

Boil the noodles according to the package directions. Drain and set aside.

Brown the ground turkey in a large skillet; season with salt, pepper, and Italian spices to taste. Drain and add the pasta sauce. Bring to a boil, cover, and let simmer over low heat for 5 minutes.

Preheat the oven to 375 degrees.

Spray a 13-by-9-inch baking dish with nonstick spray. Spoon a small amount of meat sauce over the bottom of the dish. Arrange one layer of noodles over the sauce. Spread half the ricotta cheese on the noodles. Spread more sauce over the ricotta. Place the sliced tomatoes on the sauce in straight rows, covering as much area as possible. Spoon a small amount of sauce on top of each tomato. Place the spinach over the tomatoes. Cover with half the Italian cheese mixture. Repeat layers, ending with the cheese mixture. Bake, uncovered, for 35 to 40 minutes or until the lasagna is bubbly and the cheese is beginning to brown. If necessary, cover the casserole later in the baking process so the cheese does not burn or dry out.

DYANI SEXTON
Chicago, Illinois
Chicago Alumnae Chapter

FRIED WILD RABBIT

MAKES 4 SERVINGS

1 (2-pound) wild rabbit, skinned

Salt and black pepper, to taste

All-purpose flour

Oil for deep frying

Grated onion

Parboil the rabbit for 20 minutes. Reserve the liquid from the parboil. Cut the rabbit into pieces for serving. Sprinkle with salt and pepper and dip in flour.

Pour oil into a heavy skillet to a depth of ½ to 1 inch. When the oil is hot, gently lower the pieces of rabbit into it. Do not crowd them. Turn the pieces to brown them on all sides. When completely browned and cooked through, remove the pieces from the skillet.

Make the gravy by skimming the fat off the drippings in the skillet, retaining 3 tablespoons (or 1 tablespoon for each cup of gravy required) in a saucepan. Add 1 to 2 tablespoons flour for each tablespoon oil, stirring the oil and flour over low heat until the mixture is blended and rich brown in color. Stir frequently. Season with a small amount of salt and black pepper to taste, and add a little grated onion. Be careful not to scorch the mixture. Complete the browning before adding any liquid.

Place the rabbit pieces back in the skillet with the flour mixture. Gradually pour in cooled liquid from the parboil. Raise the heat until the gravy is thick and smooth, stirring constantly. Add more liquid if necessary.

MERLE ALLEN FRANKLIN
Atlanta, Georgia
Atlanta Suburban Alumnae Chapter

VENISON ROAST

MAKES 4 SERVINGS

1 (2-pound) venison roast
½ cup vinegar
2 medium onions, sliced
Black pepper, to taste
1 (10¾-ounce) can cream of mushroom soup
½ pound ground pork sausage

Soak the roast in the vinegar mixed with 2 quarts water, or enough to cover the roast. Refrigerate overnight.

Preheat the oven to 350 degrees.

Make slits in the roast and place onion slices in the slits and on top of the roast. Pepper the roast generously and spoon the soup over it. Sprinkle the pork sausage on top. Bake for 2 hours or until the venison is tender when tested with a fork.

ALFREDIA BOYD
Columbia, South Carolina
Chair, National Nominating Committee
Columbia, South Carolina, Alumnae Chapter

5

BEEF

AND

PORK

MEMORIES OF A TRAVELING CHILDHOOD
Hortense Golden Canady

I t's a Delta tradition to stand and applaud when one of our national presidents, past or present, enters the room. To stand is a time-honored sign of respect, and Soror Hortense Canady, who was elected at our thirty-seventh national convention in 1983, usually receives numerous accolades.

Vivacious and engaging, she is quick to speak of her own encounter with Founder Bertha Pitts Campbell in 1981, during the reenactment of the Woman's Suffrage parade of 1913. Delta Sigma Theta, Sorority Inc., had been founded only two months before the original parade, and Ms. Campbell had marched back then in what was Delta's first social-action activity. In the '81 march, at the age of ninety-two, Soror Campbell was expected to ride along the route, but she had other ideas. "I walked it the first time," she said, "and I'll walk it this time." Which is how she came to be walking down Pennsylvania Avenue directly behind Hortense Canady, and how Hortense heard a polite but impatient voice over her shoulder, saying, "Walk faster, or I'll step on your heels." There is laughter but also admiration in her tone as she repeats those words.

Anyone who spends even a brief time with her is likely to hear stories about her beloved grandparents, Joseph Henry and Anna Elizabeth Atwa-ter. "My grandfather," she begins, "was a fireman on the Gulf, Mobile, and Ohio Railroad, which, in the 1920s and 1930s was a great job for an African-American man.

"One of the best perks of the job was that any railroad employee could ride free of charge anywhere in the country. I got to accompany my grandfather riding the great streamliners of the day.

"During the years my grandfather was traveling for the railroad, my grandmother owned and operated the Atwater Café, which was located directly across the street from the Lane College campus.

"I remember the fried chicken and fried apricot pies my grandmother used to pack for my grandfather and me when we were going on our journey. No sooner would the train leave the station than my grandfather would insist that I *must* be hungry. And it didn't matter that I told him I wasn't because he'd immediately open that basket and eat everything in it.

"Now, when I look into my recipe box, it's like taking a trip down memory lane. There's Mrs. Orr's Filé Gumbo, Aunt Cora's Ice Cream, Aunt Pearl's Sweet Potato Pie, and Mrs. Beverly's Rolls. I love having names attached to those recipes because whenever I read the title I can not only taste the food, I can also picture those women in my mind."

Two of Anna Elizabeth Atwater's own recipes, for Beef Pot Roast and Smothered Chicken can be found on pages 100 and 76, respectively.

DELTA OF DISTINCTION
Shirley Ann Jackson

FROM THE TIME she was a young girl, Soror Shirley Ann Jackson expressed a keen interest in why things work. She took that interest to the Massachusetts Institute of Technology, where she was the only Black of forty-three women in a freshman class of nine hundred. In 1973 she became the first African-American to receive a doctorate from MIT in any subject.

In her current role as president of Rensselaer Polytechnic Institute, the oldest technological university in the United States, she presides over 4,800 undergraduates and 4,300 graduate students. Before taking up her post at Rensselaer, Soror Jackson served as the first African-American to head the Nuclear Regulatory Commission, crisscrossing the country to inspect troubled nuclear facilities and solving knotty environmental-safety problems.

She considers her parents her ultimate role models, saying that "the best thing parents can do for children is to provide the environment and opportunity for their children to pursue their interests—whether in science, the humanities or any other field." Soror Jackson was the 2002 recipient of the Mary Church Terrell Award, the Sorority's highest honor.

BEEF POT ROAST

MAKES 6–8 SERVINGS

3–4 pounds chuck, shoulder, top or bottom round, brisket, blade, or rump
1 clove garlic
Garlic salt or garlic powder, to taste
All-purpose flour
2 tablespoons vegetable oil
2 cups beef broth
2 carrots, slivered
1 onion, quartered
2 stalks celery, slivered
½ green bell pepper, chopped (optional)
1 bay leaf
Salt and black pepper, to taste
Dash of Worcestershire sauce

Rub the meat with the garlic clove; add the garlic salt or powder. Dredge the meat in flour on all sides. Heat the oil in a heavy stockpot. Brown the meat. Spoon off any excess oil. Add the beef broth. Add the vegetables and seasonings. Simmer, covered, 3 to 4 hours.

HORTENSE G. CANADY
Lansing, Michigan
Past National President (1983–1988)
Lansing Alumnae Chapter

POT ROAST WITH VEGETABLES AND GRAVY

MAKES 10–12 SERVINGS

LISA SAWYER, my special friend from the 1989 New York Alumnae Chapter line fondly named "The Untouchables," hated pot roast until she attended a dinner party at my house. Her mother had made it many times while she was growing up, and she would never eat it. When she tasted mine, she not only enjoyed it but also went back for seconds.

2 (3- to 4-pound) seven-bone beef roasts
Salt, black pepper, and any other seasonings of your
  choice, to taste
4 large Vidalia onions, sliced diagonally
4 large red potatoes, sliced diagonally
4 large white potatoes, sliced diagonally
4 stalks celery, halved down the middle
4 large carrots, sliced diagonally in 4 pieces
1 large red bell pepper, sliced
1 large green bell pepper, sliced
1 large yellow bell pepper, sliced
3 tablespoons all-purpose flour

Season the meat and let stand in the refrigerator overnight.

Preheat the oven to 325 degrees.

Place the roasts on a rack in a large roaster. Pour 1 cup water into the pan. Cook, covered, for about 1½ hours. Add the vegetables. Season with salt and black pepper. Cook, covered, for an additional hour. Remove the pot roasts from the pan. Carefully slice the meat and place it on a large platter with the vegetables. Pour the drippings into a medium saucepan.

In a small jar with a tight-fitting lid, combine ¼ cup cold water and 3 tablespoons all-purpose flour; shake well. Gradually stir the flour mixture into the pan drippings. Cook, stirring constantly, over medium heat until the mixture boils and thickens. Add salt and pepper, if needed. Pour a small amount over the meat and serve the rest on the side.

VIRGINIA R. TOOMER
New York, New York
New York Alumnae Chapter

EVERYDAY MEAT LOAF

MAKES 8 SERVINGS

WHEN I DON'T have time to make "Fancy Meat Loaf," I make this version.

⅔ cup dry bread crumbs

1 cup milk

1½ pounds ground beef

2 large eggs, lightly beaten

¼ cup grated onion

1 teaspoon salt

⅛ teaspoon black pepper

½ teaspoon sage

Piquant Sauce (see recipe below)

Preheat the oven to 350 degrees.

Soak the bread crumbs in the milk in a large bowl. Add the meat, eggs, onion, and seasonings; mix well. Form into a 12-by-8-inch loaf pan. Cover with some of the Piquant Sauce; bake 45 minutes. Spread with more Piquant Sauce and bake 1 hour.

PIQUANT SAUCE

3 tablespoons packed light brown sugar

¼ cup catsup

¼ teaspoon ground nutmeg

1 teaspoon dry mustard

Combine the ingredients in a small bowl; mix well.

EDNA LEE LONG-GREEN
Washington, D.C.
Co-Chair, National Commission on Arts and Letters
Washington, D.C., Alumnae Chapter

FANCY MEAT LOAF

MAKES 8–10 SERVINGS

MEAT LOAF WAS one of my mother's "Sunday" dishes and one of the first things I learned to cook. When I make it now, it still reminds me of home, and when I want to make a fancy meal, I make this recipe with three different meats.

1 pound ground beef

½ pound ground pork

½ pound ground veal or ground turkey

¼ cup finely chopped onion

2 tablespoons finely chopped celery

2 teaspoons salt

¼ teaspoon black pepper

¼ teaspoon dried sage

¼ teaspoon dry mustard

¼ teaspoon poultry seasoning

4 slices soft bread, cubed

1 cup warm milk

2 large eggs, lightly beaten

1 tablespoon Worcestershire sauce

½ cup dry bread crumbs

½ cup chili sauce

½ cup boiling water

Preheat the oven to 350 degrees. Thoroughly mix the meats in a large bowl. Add the onion, celery, salt, pepper, sage, dry mustard, and poultry seasoning; mix well.

Soak the bread cubes in the milk in a medium bowl. Add the eggs and Worcestershire sauce; beat with an electric mixer. Add the egg mixture to the meat mixture, blending well. Form into two loaves.

Roll the loaves in bread crumbs and place in greased loaf pans. Spread chili sauce over each loaf. Set loaf pans in a large baking pan. Pour the water around the loaves, and bake, uncovered, for 1 hour. Baste with liquid in pan at 15-minute intervals. Serve hot or cold.

EDNA LEE LONG-GREEN
Washington, D.C.
Co-Chair, National Commission on Arts and Letters
Washington, D.C., Alumnae Chapter

ONE-POT DINNER

MAKES 4 SERVINGS

1 pound ground beef

1 pound bacon, cut into small pieces

1 cup chopped onion

2 (31-ounce) cans pork and beans

1 (16-ounce) can kidney beans, drained

1 (16-ounce) can butter beans, drained

1 cup catsup

¼ cup packed light brown sugar

1 tablespoon liquid smoke

3 tablespoons distilled white vinegar

1 teaspoon salt

Dash of black pepper

Brown the ground beef in a medium skillet; drain well and place in a slow cooker. Brown the bacon and onion; drain well and add to the slow cooker. Pour in the remaining ingredients, stirring well. Cook, covered, on Low for 4 to 6 hours.

LORRAINE W. DABNEY
Palo Alto, California
San Francisco Peninsula Alumnae Chapter

STUFFED CHEESE (KESHI YENÁ)

MAKES 10–12 SERVINGS

THIS RECIPE IS unique to the island of Curaçao, where I was born and raised. It is one of my favorite traditional Curaçao dishes. Since I don't get to go home often anymore, my mom makes sure it's prepared and ready to be eaten whenever I do get to visit. I offer this to preserve for future generations the traditional recipe, which has been handed down through the ages among Curaçao families.

And now . . . as we say in old Papiamentu (the native language of the island of Curaçao): *Zjanta ku zjeitu!* Enjoy!

1 Edam cheese (about 2 to 2½ pounds)

½ cup butter or margarine

2 pounds ground beef

3 tomatoes, peeled and chopped

1 tablespoon tomato paste

2 onions, sliced

1 small clove garlic, chopped

1 green bell pepper, chopped

2 teaspoons Worcestershire sauce

¼ cup raisins or prunes

¼ cup sliced olives

1 tablespoon capers

1 tablespoon chopped fresh parsley

2 tablespoons catsup

2 tablespoons piccalilli or any highly seasoned
   pickled-vegetable relish (optional)

¼ teaspoon minced hot pepper, or hot sauce,
   to taste (optional)

Salt and black pepper, to taste

5 large eggs

Preheat the oven to 350 degrees.

Line a deep, greased baking dish or individual custard cups with overlapping slices of cheese, reserving several slices for the top.

Heat the butter in a large skillet until hot. Add the remaining ingredients, except the eggs, and sauté until the tomatoes are reduced and the meat is no longer pink, about 20 minutes.

Beat 4 of the eggs in a small bowl, and blend into the meat mixture. Beat remaining egg.

Transfer the mixture to the prepared baking dish and cover it with the reserved cheese. Brush with the remaining egg, beaten, to seal. Bake 25 to 35 minutes or until the cheese is melted. Serve with rice on the side.

COOK'S TIP | *Substitute cleaned and deboned tuna or salmon for the beef. Replace the Edam cheese with mozzarella, if Edam is not available.*

CESSNA VEERIS
Alpharetta, Georgia
Tau Eta Chapter (Brenau University)

SPAGHETTI CRUST PIE

MAKES 6–8 SERVINGS

FOR TEN YEARS, as Team Mom of the Greenville Senior High Academy varsity boys' basketball team, I prepared this dish for "my boys" and the coaches. It was a regular battle between the coaches and the boys, as the coaches told the boys to eat less, while they themselves ate more and more.

5 cups Meat Sauce (see following recipe)
½ pound spaghetti
2 tablespoons margarine, melted
2 large eggs, beaten
½ cup freshly grated Parmesan cheese
¾ cup grated sharp Cheddar cheese
2 slices mozzarella or sharp Cheddar cheese, cut in quarters

Prepare the Meat Sauce and keep warm.

Preheat the oven to 350 degrees.

Cook the spaghetti according to package directions; drain and place the spaghetti in a large bowl. Add the melted margarine and beaten eggs. Stir in the grated Parmesan cheese and mix well. Pour spaghetti mixture into a 4-quart dish and press with back of a spoon to form a crust, building up the sides. Sprinkle the grated Cheddar cheese over the crust.

Spread the meat sauce evenly on top of spaghetti and bake for 40 to 50 minutes. Remove from the oven when bubbly.

Add the quartered cheese slices and bake for an additional 5 minutes or until the cheese melts. Let stand for 5 minutes before cutting.

MEAT SAUCE

1 pound ground chuck
1½ pounds Italian sausages, sliced
½ green bell pepper, chopped
1 medium onion, diced
1 stalk celery, diced
½ teaspoon each of salt, dried sage, parsley flakes, ground cinnamon, crushed red pepper, black pepper
2 (28-ounce) cans peeled tomatoes
2 (16-ounce) cans tomato sauce
1 (16-ounce) can stewed tomatoes

Cook the ground chuck in a large skillet and drain. Sauté the sausages. Place the beef and sausage in a large pot. Add the bell pepper, onion, and celery; stir well. Add the seasonings; cook until bubbly. Add the peeled tomatoes, tomato sauce, and stewed tomatoes and cook for 10 minutes more.

COOK'S TIP | *Freeze any unused meat sauce for a smaller pie or to serve over rice or noodles.*

DELORES "DEE DEE" W. CANTY
Greenville, South Carolina
Greenville Alumnae Chapter

TAMALE PIE

MAKES 12 SERVINGS

THIS RECIPE HAS a Mexican flavor; however, the cornmeal topping also gives it an Afro-American touch. The recipe has proven to be a popular dish because it provides a complete, one-dish meal.

2 tablespoons vegetable oil
1 clove garlic, chopped
1½ cups chopped green bell pepper
1 cup chopped onion
1 pound ground beef
1 (15-ounce) can black olives, drained
1 (15-ounce) can tomato sauce
1 (16-ounce) can tomatoes
1 (12-ounce) can whole-kernel corn, drained
2 tablespoons chili powder, or more to taste
1 tablespoon sugar
1½ cups grated sharp Cheddar cheese
¾ cup yellow cornmeal
½ teaspoon salt
2 cups cold water
Sour cream (optional)

Heat the vegetable oil in a large skillet. Sauté the garlic, bell pepper, and onion until tender. Add the ground beef and cook until browned. Stir in the olives. Add the tomato sauce, tomatoes, corn, chili powder, and sugar; stir well. Simmer for 20 minutes. Remove from the heat; cool. Stir in the cheese. Pour the mixture into a 13-by-9-inch baking dish.

Preheat the oven to 375 degrees.

Combine the cornmeal, salt, and water in a small saucepan. Cook until thickened, stirring continuously. Spread over top of mixture in the baking dish, sealing edges. Bake for 40 minutes.

Serve with dollops of sour cream on top, if desired.

EUGENIA B. HARDAWAY
Chicago, Illinois
Chicago Alumnae Chapter

SIMPLE MARINADE FOR GRILLED STEAKS

MAKES ABOUT 1 CUP

MY HUSBAND CREATED this recipe. If you don't eat beef, use chicken or shrimp.

½ cup water
¼ cup liquid smoke
½ teaspoon garlic powder
2 teaspoons parsley flakes
½ teaspoon onion powder
¼ cup mixed chopped green onion and bell pepper

Mix all the ingredients together in a large bowl. Add steaks and marinate for at least 1 hour in the refrigerator before grilling or baking.

CHERYLANN FOSTER-WESTERFIELD
Harvey, Louisiana
New Orleans Alumnae Chapter

SPAGHETTI PIZZA

MAKES 6-8 SERVINGS

½ cup skim milk

1 large egg, beaten

1 (7-ounce) package spaghetti, cooked

Vegetable cooking spray

½ pound lean ground beef or turkey

1 medium onion, chopped

1 medium green bell pepper, chopped

2 cloves garlic, minced

1 (15-ounce) can tomato sauce

1 teaspoon Italian seasoning

¼ teaspoon ground black pepper

2 cups sliced mushrooms

2 cups shredded mozzarella cheese

Blend the milk and egg in a medium bowl. Add the spaghetti and toss to coat. Spray a 15-by-10-inch baking pan with vegetable cooking spray. Spread the mixture evenly in the pan.

Preheat the oven to 350 degrees.

Cook the beef, onion, bell pepper, and garlic in a large skillet until the meat is no longer pink; drain. Add the tomato sauce and seasonings. Spread evenly over the spaghetti. Top with the mushrooms and cheese. Bake for 20 minutes. Let stand for 5 minutes before cutting into squares.

DELORES L. CONNOR
Fort Worth, Texas
North Dallas Suburban Alumnae Chapter

DELTA OF DISTINCTION
Judith Jamison
Dancer and Director

MADE AN HONORARY Delta in 1975, Soror Judith Jamison was born in Philadelphia and made her New York debut with the American Ballet Theatre, appearing in *The Four Marys*. In 1965 she joined the Alvin Ailey American Dance Theater, where, recognizing her extraordinary talent and captivating stage presence, Mr. Ailey created some of his most enduring roles especially for her.

She has performed on Broadway in *Sophisticated Ladies* and as a guest artist with ballet companies all over the world.

In 1988 she established her own company, the Jamison Project, and in 1989 was named the artistic director of the Alvin Ailey American Dance Theater. At our Fortieth National Convention in 1990, Delta Sigma Theta awarded her the first Keeper of the Flame Award.

Judith Jamison (seated, center)

LASAGNA CASSEROLE

MAKES 8–10 SERVINGS

MY MOTHER, Jessie, of Cincinnati, Ohio, passed this recipe down to me. With a few additions, it has become a favorite of my husband, Rickey, and Sorors Lesa, Lisa, and Tracy.

1 pound lean ground beef or turkey

½ teaspoon seasoned salt

2 pinches of black pepper

1 (16-ounce) jar Italian sausage spaghetti sauce

1 (16-ounce) jar tomato, basil, and garlic spaghetti sauce

Pinch of salt

1 (16-ounce) package wide egg noodles

1 (8-ounce) package shredded mozzarella cheese

1 (8-ounce) package shredded Cheddar cheese

Brown the ground beef in a large skillet over medium heat. Add the seasoned salt and pepper to the meat. Remove the meat from the skillet and drain the grease. Remove the excess grease from the pan. Return the meat to the skillet and stir in the sauces. Simmer over low heat for 20 minutes.

Boil 4 quarts of water over high heat in a large saucepan. Add salt. Reduce the heat and add the noodles. Cook for 7 or 8 minutes or until done. Drain and rinse the noodles in a colander.

Preheat the oven to 300 degrees. Place the noodles in a 13-by-9-inch greased baking dish. Add the meat sauce and stir together to mix. Stir in additional sauce, if needed.

Combine the cheeses in a bowl. Sprinkle over the top of the casserole. Bake for 30 minutes. Serve with garlic bread.

RENÉE JOHNSON
Canton, Michigan
Inkster Alumnae Chapter

FAYE'S MEATY BAKED BEANS

MAKES 10–12 SERVINGS

THIS IS AN easy make-ahead baked-bean casserole. It can be a meal of its own or a zesty addition to a buffet.

1 pound lean ground beef

4 (15-ounce) cans baked beans or pork and beans

1½ cups frozen yellow whole-kernel corn

1 cup finely chopped green bell pepper

1 cup finely chopped onion

3 tablespoons distilled white vinegar

½ cup packed light brown sugar

Preheat the oven to 350 degrees.

Brown the beef in a large skillet. Add the beans, corn, green pepper, and onion; mix well. Stir in the vinegar. Spoon the mixture into a 13-by-9-inch baking pan. Sprinkle with the brown sugar. Bake for 20 to 25 minutes.

FARELLA ESTA' ROBINSON
Kansas City, Missouri
Kansas City, Missouri, Alumnae Chapter

PORK CHOPS AND CABBAGE

MAKES 4 SERVINGS

THIS IS A family recipe that has been passed down through the years. As children, we would look forward to the first matured cabbage from my mother's spring garden. We knew we were in for a treat.

4 (½-inch-thick) pork loin chops
¼ teaspoon ground black pepper
3 tablespoons seasoned salt
½ teaspoon minced garlic
2 tablespoons lemon juice
1 tablespoon olive oil
¼ cup diced green onion
¼ cup diced green bell pepper
¼ cup diced red bell pepper
1 (10¾-ounce) can condensed cream of mushroom soup
2 cups shredded cabbage
¼ teaspoon freshly grated nutmeg

Preheat the oven to 350 degrees.

Season the chops with the pepper, seasoned salt, garlic, and lemon juice.

In an ovenproof skillet, brown the chops on both sides in the olive oil. Remove from the pan and set aside. Add the onion and peppers to the drippings in the pan; sauté for a few minutes. Add the soup; bring to a boil. Return the chops to the skillet; add the cabbage. Top with nutmeg.

Bake, covered, for 1 hour.

MILDRED HOUSE
Rancho Palos Verdes, California
Rolling Hills–Palos Verdes Alumnae Chapter

COUNTRY HAM WITH RED-EYE GRAVY

MAKES 4 SERVINGS

4 (¼-inch-thick) slices country ham
1 cup water
1 tablespoon black coffee

Cook the ham slices in a heavy skillet over low heat about 15 minutes or until tender and lightly browned. Remove to a plate. Add the water to the skillet, stirring to loosen all the browned bits. Continue cooking for about 3 to 5 minutes, adding coffee to darken. Serve the gravy over the ham.

ALFREDIA BOYD
Columbia, South Carolina
Chair, National Nominating Committee
Columbia, South Carolina, Alumnae Chapter

IN JANUARY 2003, Soror Stephanie Tubbs Jones (D-OH) made history by becoming the first Black woman to serve on the Ways and Means Committee of the United States House of Representatives, which deals with such weighty issues as Social Security, tax law, international trade, and health care.

A former judge, Soror Jones will use her position as a platform for speaking out on Social Security and prescription drug benefits for senior citizens. She believes that "Economic empowerment is the civil rights of today," and considers it her responsibility to serve as "the voice for the voiceless."

SAUSAGE AND RICE CASSEROLE

MAKES 4 SERVINGS

1 pound mild ground sausage

½ cup uncooked rice

½ cup diced onion

½ cup diced celery

2 (10¾-ounce) cans chicken and rice soup

1 cup shredded Cheddar cheese

¾ cup water

Preheat the oven to 325 degrees.

Brown the sausage in a medium skillet; drain. Layer the sausage in a 9-by-9-inch baking dish. Combine the rice, onion, celery, soup, and cheese in a medium bowl. Spread over the sausage. Pour the water over the top. Bake, covered, for 1 hour. Increase the oven temperature to 350 degrees; bake, covered, for 1 hour longer or until ingredients are tender.

COOK'S TIP | *Reduce baking time to 1 hour by using instant rice.*

MARY HAMMOND
Oklahoma City, Oklahoma
Oklahoma City Alumnae Chapter

MICKEY'S RED BEANS AND RICE

MAKES 12 SERVINGS

MY GRANDMOTHER, MRS. Tommie Jordan, cooked Red Beans and Rice on a regular basis because this is the family's favorite dish. Now that my granny is deceased, my family asks me to make the recipe. The Jordan clan loves this Deep South dish, and we love to share this meal with friends. When you serve this dish prepare yourself for the delicious taste of beans and meat smothered in tomato paste.

1 pound smoked sausage

1 pound ground pork sausage, hot or mild

1 pound ground beef

1 (16-ounce) package dried kidney beans, soaked overnight

1 tablespoon drippings from cooked meat

1 ham hock

½ medium onion, chopped

1 clove garlic, chopped

1 tablespoon sugar

Salt, to taste

Dash of chili powder

1 (6-ounce) can tomato paste

Brown the sausages and beef in a large skillet; drain, reserving 1 tablespoon of the drippings. Refrigerate meat until ready to use.

Place the soaked beans in a large stockpot; add water to fill three-fourths of the pot. Add the reserved drippings, the ham hock, onion, garlic, sugar, salt, and chili powder. Bring to a boil; reduce heat to low and cook for 2 hours. Add the browned meats and the tomato paste. Simmer for 30 minutes. Serve with rice.

VICTORIA "MICKEY" EASTERLING
Hattiesburg, Mississippi
Hattiesburg Alumnae Chapter

6

FISH

AND

SHELLFISH

THE ART OF FISHING
Dr. Floretta Dukes McKenzie

D r. Floretta Dukes McKenzie, a member of Delta Sigma Theta for more than fifty years, says that the woman she has become and the focus of her life in education were based on her early indoctrination into the sorority and the members who were her teachers.

She remembers the joy of joining the sorority at Miners Teachers' College (now D.C. Teachers' College) in 1953, Delta's fortieth anniversary, at a ceremony that was attended by renowned suffragist and civil rights activist Mary Church Terrell and included a program honoring Founder Eliza P. Shippen, who had been on the staff of Miners. In the 1950s, when it was still very much a privilege to attend college, and teaching was considered a noble profession, the Delta chapter at Miners had the highest scholastic average of any Black sorority, and each new member felt it was her personal responsibility to uphold that tradition.

Beginning her career as a teacher in Maryland, Dr. McKenzie moved on to hold administrative positions on the city and county levels before serving in the federal government and being named superintendent of the Washington, D.C., school system. As a deputy assistant secretary in the United States Department of Education's Office of School Improvement, she oversaw fifteen discretionary education programs and initiatives and

supervised a staff of 100 employees with a budget of $67 million.

Now vice chair of the Board of Trustees of Howard University, Dr. McKenzie is the most senior member of Delta Sigma Theta on the university's administrative board, following in the tradition of past national presidents Geraldine Pittman Woods and Frankie Muse Freeman, who also served as Howard trustees.

When asked what it was that motivated her to devote so much of her professional life to the education of children, Soror McKenzie answers without hesitation, "It's what I was trained to do. My formal education in institutions of higher learning and my informal training as a member of Delta Sigma Theta always focused on scholarship, service, and leadership. My family valued and respected people who brought value to their community, and I believe that I have a responsibility to the people who may not have been as fortunate as I to provide, to the extent I am able, educational opportunities. Equity and exposure for all children has been a goal for my entire life."

Quietly determined, she is not one to be denied when requesting money for a cause that is close to her heart. Those who were in the room remember a Delta meeting at which there was a request on the floor for $200 to purchase books for children. The hat was passed and Soror McKenzie quietly counted the contributions, which didn't

BORN IN HOUSTON, Texas, in 1936, Soror Barbara Jordan rose to become the first African-American woman from the South ever elected to the United States Congress, where she served from 1972 until 1979 sponsoring bills and promoting legislation to help the poor, Blacks, and the disadvantaged.

Her renowned oratorical skills as a debater at Texas Southern University took her first to the Texas State Senate, where, in 1967, she became the first Black woman to serve in the legislature of that state. As a United States congresswoman she gained national prominence for both her position and statement during President Nixon's impeachment hearings and was subsequently tapped to give the keynote speech at the Democratic National Convention in 1976 and again in 1992.

Soror Jordan retired from politics in 1978 because of poor health but remained a forceful advocate for the causes in which she believed. She served as an unpaid adviser on ethics for Texas Governor Ann Richards and was one of the most eloquent voices raised in opposition to the nomination of Robert Bork to the Supreme Court in 1987. Her career was sadly cut short when she died in 1996.

In 1997 the Austin City Council voted to name the passenger terminal at Austin-Bergstrom International Airport in her honor and commissioned a sculpture of her to be placed in the terminal. The seven-foot-tall bronze statue by Bruce Leslie Wolfe was unveiled in 2000.

quite meet expectations. At that point, she began to speak about the children, about the importance of reading, and about how fortunate those attending the meeting were to have books to read. In conclusion, she said that, in the true spirit of giving, she was certain her fellow Deltas would show more respect and support for the program and contribute far more than the $200 originally requested. The hat was passed again, and, when Soror McKenzie recounted, the sum had more than doubled. She just smiled and quietly took her seat.

That quiet patience and determination may also be why she so enjoys her favorite hobby, which happens to be fishing. "I enjoy the peace and quiet," she says. "The water is calm and the outdoors allows me to relax and dream. It also seems a fair game of nature and woman. I put bait on the hook and wait for the fish to bite. Sometimes it happens quickly and others it takes a long time. I figure my part of the game is to be patient and not become angry with the fish for not biting.

Nor should the fish be angry that what he thinks is food is actually a hook and a line. The game of skill is between the fish and me. We each must try to figure the other one out. The fish must determine how long he will fight and try not to run out of patience. Sometimes the fish wins and sometimes I win. The sport has taught me a lot about patience. It also has helped me to judge when it is no longer good to hold on and to throw in the rod and give up. In many of the dealings in my life, this ability has served me well.

"The other advantage of fishing is that the quality of the fish I catch is so much better than that of any fish I've ever purchased in a store. The freshness of the fish when cooked is superior to any other fish I've ever tasted, even in the finest restaurants, and my fish taste buds, having tasted the difference, are forever spoiled.

"The art of fishing is to respect the challenge you face each time you throw your bait into the water."

DELTA OF DISTINCTION
Julianne Malveaux

A TRUE PIONEER in the field of economics, Soror Julianne Malveaux, who holds bachelor's and master's degrees from Boston College and a doctorate in economics from MIT, has focused her research and attention on the labor market and the impact of public policy on women and people of color.

The author of several books and now a syndicated weekly columnist, her opinions on national affairs, the American workplace, and the economy appear in more than twenty newspapers. She is well known for her appearances on a wide variety of television programs, including *Politically Incorrect* and *The News-Hour with Jim Lehrer,* and on CNN, Fox News, MSNBC, and CNBC, among others.

As president and CEO of Last Word Production, a multimedia production company, she has designed educational and issue-based seminars and diversity-training programs for Fortune 500 companies. Her colleague Dr. Cornel West has described her as the most provocative, progressive, and iconoclastic public intellectual in the country.

SAVORY BAKED FISH

MAKES 4–6 SERVINGS

½ cup chopped celery

1½ pounds flounder or sole fillets

½ teaspoon salt

½ teaspoon ground white pepper

¼ teaspoon dried rosemary, crushed

¼ teaspoon paprika

1 large tomato, sliced

½ cup chopped green onions

¼ cup Chablis or other dry white wine

Preheat the oven to 350 degrees.

Arrange the celery evenly in the bottom of a baking dish. Arrange the fillets on top of celery. Sprinkle the fillets evenly with salt, white pepper, rosemary, and paprika. Place the tomato slices over the fillets; top with green onions. Pour the wine into the baking dish. Bake for 25 minutes or until the fish flakes easily when tested with a fork.

HAZEL H. BRISTOW
Reston, Virginia
Potomac Valley Alumnae Chapter

BAKED FISH CREOLE

MAKES 8 SERVINGS

I LOVE CREOLE dishes, and this is one of my favorites because you can use any type of fish. My college roommate lives in Slidell, Louisiana, and when I visit, she serves this dish. We usually prepare it together and "catch up" while enjoying each other's company and the food!

3 cups water

1½ cups uncooked white rice

¼ cup butter

1 onion, chopped

1 clove garlic, minced

2 stalks celery, chopped

¼ cup all-purpose flour

2 cups milk

1 (20-ounce) bottle chili sauce

½ teaspoon hot sauce

1 teaspoon salt

1 teaspoon black pepper

1 pound ocean perch, cod, or catfish fillets

2 tomatoes

Preheat oven to 400 degrees. Lightly coat a 13-by-9-inch baking dish with nonstick cooking spray.

In a saucepan, boil the water; add the rice and stir. Reduce heat to low, cover, and simmer for about 20 minutes.

In a heavy pot or Dutch oven, melt the butter over medium heat; add the onion and garlic. Cook until tender, about 3 to 5 minutes. Add the celery; cook for about 4 to 5 minutes. Add the flour and stir until very well blended, about 3 minutes. Stir in the milk; bring to a boil. Stir in the chili sauce and hot sauce; add salt and black pepper. Spoon the rice into the bottom of prepared baking dish. Place the fish over the rice in a single layer. Slice the tomatoes over fish, and pour the sauce over the top. Bake for about 20 minutes, or until the fish flakes when tested with a fork.

COOK'S TIP | *Serve with a green salad and garlic bread.*

ROBIN SILAS
Jackson, Mississippi
Jackson Alumnae Chapter

ROZCHEL'S
RED-HOT
CHOWDER HALIBUT

MAKES 4 SERVINGS

ONE EVENING WHILE trying to think of another way to prepare halibut, my sister, Rosalind Morgan, suggested that I throw a soup on top of it. Her suggestion was New England clam chowder. I happen to enjoy spicy food; but this dish can be enjoyed with or without the additional spices. It is a fast, simple, and healthy dish that will definitely delight your taste buds.

1½ pounds halibut steaks
Seasoned salt, to taste
1½ teaspoons garlic powder
½ teaspoon ground white pepper
1 tablespoon butter or margarine
1 (10¾-ounce) can New England clam chowder
Cayenne pepper, to taste
Louisiana hot sauce, to taste

Sprinkle the halibut with the seasoned salt, garlic powder, and ground white pepper. Melt the butter in a medium skillet. Sauté the halibut for about 1 minute on each side. Pour the soup over the halibut. Add the cayenne pepper and hot sauce to taste. Cook until the fish is tender.

RACHELLE HOLLIE GUILLORY
Los Angeles, California
Inglewood Alumnae Chapter

SANDRA'S SPICY SALMON

MAKES 2 SERVINGS

1 teaspoon seafood seasoning

½ cup chopped green onions

Juice of 1 small lemon

1 teaspoon crushed red pepper

Freshly ground pepper, to taste

¼ cup diced onion

¼ cup chopped green bell pepper

1 sprig fresh cilantro, chopped

1 sprig fresh basil, chopped

¼ cup raisins

5 ounces balsamic vinaigrette salad dressing

1 (10-ounce) salmon fillet

¼ cup chili sauce (optional)

Combine the seafood seasoning with the next 10 ingredients in a zip-top bag; mix well. Place the salmon in the marinade in the bag. Close the bag, and refrigerate for 2 hours. Preheat the grill for about 5 minutes. Place the salmon, skin side down, on the grill. Grill until flaky. Serve with chili sauce, if desired.

COOK'S TIP | *Salmon may also be baked. Just spray a baking pan with some garlic-flavored cooking spray. Place the salmon, skin side down, in the pan. Drain the vegetables from the marinade and place on and around the salmon. Bake at 350 degrees for 30 minutes or until flaky. Serve the salmon with the vegetable mix. Use the chili sauce for dipping, if desired.*

SANDRA PHILLIPS
Mansfield, Louisiana
Lambda Chapter, Chicago

GRILLED SALMON STEAKS

MAKES 6 SERVINGS

6 (8-ounce) salmon steaks, about 1 inch thick

½ cup olive oil

¼ cup chopped fresh dill

3 tablespoons minced green onions

3 tablespoons lime juice

1 tablespoon champagne mustard

½ teaspoon salt

¼ teaspoon ground white pepper

Place the salmon steaks in a shallow dish. Combine the oil and the remaining ingredients, stirring well. Pour the marinade over steaks. Cover and marinate in refrigerator for at least 1 hour or overnight. Remove the salmon from the marinade, reserving the marinade.

Grill the salmon over hot coals for 7 minutes on each side or until the fish flakes easily when tested with a fork. Baste frequently with the marinade while grilling.

HAZEL H. BRISTOW
Vienna, Virginia
Potomac Valley Alumnae Chapter

FRIED CATFISH WITH HOMEMADE TARTAR SAUCE

MAKES 4 SERVINGS

MY DAD'S FAVORITE meal was fish with home-made tartar sauce. Red snapper was his favorite fish for this recipe when we lived in Galveston, Texas, but my Delta mom, Sammie Williams, adapted the recipe for catfish in Los Angeles. Dad liked it spicy, and so does my family.

1 cup mayonnaise

2 tablespoons chopped capers

Zest and juice of 1 lemon

1 tablespoon grated onion

2 tablespoons chopped fresh tarragon

Salt, pepper, and hot sauce, to taste

2 pounds catfish

Whole milk

2 teaspoons each of paprika, cayenne pepper, salt, and black pepper

2 cups white or yellow cornmeal

Oil for frying

Lemon wedges for garnish

Blend the mayonnaise, capers, lemon zest and juice, onion, tarragon, salt, pepper, and hot sauce together in a small bowl to make a tartar sauce; refrigerate for at least 1 hour.

Soak the catfish in milk (enough to cover) in a flat container for 30 minutes.

Mix together the paprika, cayenne pepper, salt, and black pepper. Remove the fish from the milk and season it with the paprika mixture. Dredge the seasoned fish in the cornmeal. Heat the oil in a large cast-iron skillet. Fry the fish in the oil until it flakes easily with a fork.

Serve the fish on a platter with lemon wedges and the tartar sauce on the side. Cole slaw and fried potatoes make good accompaniments.

PEGGY BELCHER-DIXON
Los Angeles, California
Inglewood Alumnae Chapter

A BARBECUE BASH

(CHAPTER ROUNDUP BARBECUE)

Robin's Buffalo Wings (page 6)

Grilled Salmon Steaks (page 120)

Grilled Steaks with Simple Marinade (page 106)

Lucy and Ethel's Baked Beans (page 139)

Broccoli Salad (page 34)

Watermelon Lemonade (page 16)

Dump Cake (page 221) *with*
Vanilla Ice Cream

Modern Marble Cake with Chocolate
Never-Fail Icing (pages 216 and 222)

CASUAL AL FRESCO dining is what barbecue is all about. This menu combines traditional favorites with a nod to the health conscious in the grilled salmon and broccoli salad—maybe not classic barbecue fare, but delicious nevertheless.

TO PREPARE:

- Make and frost the cakes the day before and store them, well covered, at room temperature. In the evening, place the salmon steaks in the marinade and refrigerate them. Prepare the lemonade so that half can be frozen as the recipe directs.

- In the morning, prepare the broccoli and the dressing and refrigerate them separately. Get the beans in the oven early enough to have them ready when you're ready to eat.

- Marinate the steaks for an hour before grilling. Once the steaks are in the marinade, begin frying the wings and making the sauce.

- Fire up the grill and you're ready to get cooking.

A DELTA-STYLE ROUNDUP BARBECUE

Each fall, while the weather is still warm, individual Delta chapters "round up" and reclaim members for another exciting sorority year. The traditional barbecue is an informal, outdoor event involving lots of good food, games, and contests.

Plan your own roundup barbecue in the spring to corral and say farewell to friends who might be going away for the summer, in July to welcome back summer visitors from the previous year, or in early fall, as we do, to round up returning travelers for the new sorority year.

Keep everything as simple and disposable as possible. Checkered tablecloths—red or otherwise—are always appropriate. And this is one time when paper and plastic plates and utensils will certainly be acceptable. Pick the ones you'll be using to set the theme and color scheme of the day—just make sure they're colorful and that napkins are plentiful.

SEAFOOD VELVET

MAKES 6–8 SERVINGS

½–1 pound skinless flounder fillets, poached or
steamed
1 pound medium shrimp, cooked, peeled, and
deveined
2 tablespoons finely sliced green onions, including
tops
1 cup mayonnaise
½ cup grated Parmesan cheese
1 tablespoon spicy brown mustard
½ cup plus 2 tablespoons half-and-half
2 tablespoons bread crumbs
Paprika
Fresh parsley sprigs
1 lemon, sliced, for garnish

Preheat the oven to 425 degrees.

Break the fish into large chunks. Cut the shrimp
in half. Combine the green onions, mayonnaise,
cheese, mustard, half-and-half, and bread crumbs
in a medium bowl. Mix well and fold in the seafood.
Spoon the mixture into 6 or 8 greased individual
baking dishes. Bake 15 minutes or until golden.
Garnish with paprika, parsley, and lemon slices.

Serve with a green salad and rice.

BEVERLY EVANS SMITH
Marietta, Georgia
Chair, Long-Range Planning Committee
Marietta-Roswell Alumnae Chapter

JAZZY PIQUANT SHRIMP WITH ANGEL HAIR PASTA

MAKES 4 SERVINGS

I CREATED THIS dish when I was asked to make
something with shrimp for my cousin's birthday. I
had no access to recipe books, so I made this up,
and everyone loved it.

1 large green bell pepper, chopped
1 large red bell pepper, chopped
1 yellow bell pepper, chopped (optional)
1 large onion, chopped
2 tablespoons light olive oil
1 pound medium shrimp, peeled and deveined
1 tablespoon chopped fresh basil
1 tablespoon chopped fresh parsley flakes
1 tablespoon chopped fresh chives
1 tablespoon Italian seasoning
¼ cup red wine vinegar
1 cup cocktail sauce
1 (12-ounce) package angel hair pasta
Grated Parmesan cheese (optional)

Sauté the peppers and onion in 1 tablespoon of the
olive oil in a medium skillet over low heat; when
soft, set aside. Heat the remaining tablespoon olive
oil in the skillet over medium heat. Add the
shrimp. Cook until pink. Remove the shrimp from
the skillet and add to sautéed peppers and onion.
Sprinkle the basil, parsley flakes, chives, and Italian
seasoning over the mixture. Pour red wine vinegar

dressing over the mixture. Add the cocktail sauce. Simmer just until heated.

While cooking the sauce, cook pasta according to package directions. Rinse well and drain. Place the pasta on a large platter. Top with the shrimp and pepper/onion mixture. Serve immediately with grated Parmesan cheese, if desired, and crusty garlic bread.

HURLENE SCOTT
Akron, Ohio
Akron Alumnae Chapter

CURRIED SHRIMP

MAKES 4 SERVINGS

I HAVE ENJOYED cooking this shrimp curry for close friends and family through the years. One Christmas I even served it as a side dish with turkey and stuffing. There were no leftovers. I pride myself on being a thirty-minute gourmet. This dish is simple and fast—and spicy!

2 dozen jumbo shrimp

½ cup butter

2 cloves garlic, finely chopped

6 tablespoons hot (or mild) curry powder, or to taste

1 teaspoon celery salt

Dash of seasoned salt

1 medium red onion

4 green bell peppers

Boil the shrimp very gently just until pink, 2 or 3 minutes. Peel, devein, and set aside.

Melt the butter in a large frying pan and sauté the chopped garlic for 1 minute. Be careful not to overheat the butter. Let the butter cool, and add the curry powder, celery salt, and seasoned salt. Stir until the sauce has a very smooth consistency.

Add the shrimp. (You may have to add additional butter to make the curry sauce like a gravy.)

Slice the vegetables lengthwise so that the strips of onion and bell pepper are about 3 inches long and ½ inch wide. Ten minutes before serving, sauté the vegetables slowly in the shrimp and curry mixture so that the onions are not wilted and the bell peppers are crisp. Cook for 5 to 7 minutes only, or until the sauce is bubbling slightly.

Serve immediately over brown or yellow rice with steamed broccoli and a Caesar salad.

CHARISSE R. LILLIE
Philadelphia, Pennsylvania
Philadelphia Alumnae Chapter

SHRIMP WITH VEGETABLES ON ANGEL HAIR PASTA

MAKES 4 SERVINGS

I LOVE SEAFOOD and am constantly finding things at restaurants that I go home and re-create. This dish is one of them. Of course, I made some modifications and included my favorite vegetables.

1 pound angel hair pasta

½ cup Italian salad dressing

1 pound medium to large shrimp, peeled and deveined

1 medium onion, chopped

1 cup chopped green bell pepper

½ zucchini, sliced

1 cup chopped broccoli

1 (15-ounce) can diced tomatoes

½ teaspoon chopped fresh basil

½ teaspoon chopped fresh oregano

1 teaspoon chopped garlic

¼ teaspoon salt

¼ teaspoon black pepper

Grated Parmesan cheese

Prepare the pasta according to package directions; drain well and set aside.

Pour the Italian dressing into a large skillet over medium heat; add the shrimp and cook until it turns pink. Add all other ingredients except the pasta and cheese. Mix well; simmer, covered, 10 minutes.

Serve over the prepared pasta, sprinkle with grated Parmesan cheese before serving.

CAROL E. WARE
Westerville, Ohio
Columbus Alumnae Chapter

SHRIMP CASSEROLE

MAKES 8–10 SERVINGS

THIS RECIPE WAS passed on to me by my late cousin, Willie Mae Bowen Ashmore. She was the owner and cook of the Angier Avenue Tearoom in Atlanta during the 1950s and 1960s.

2 cups rice or noodles, cooked

1½ pounds shrimp, peeled and deveined

1 pound fresh crabmeat

2 (4.25-ounce) cans crabmeat

2 (10¾-ounce) cans cream of mushroom soup

1 cup chopped onions

½ cup finely chopped green bell pepper

1 cup evaporated milk

2 large eggs, beaten

1 teaspoon finely chopped cooked beets

Salt and black pepper, to taste

Bread crumbs or crushed saltines for garnish

Preheat the oven to 350 degrees.

Mix all the ingredients except the bread crumbs in a large bowl. Spoon into a 9-by-9-inch greased baking dish. Bake, covered, 30 to 35 minutes. Sprinkle with bread crumbs. Bake for 5 to 10 minutes until light brown.

CAROLYN ROBERSON
Maplewood, Minnesota
Minneapolis–St. Paul Alumnae Chapter

SHRIMP PILAU

MAKES 6–8 SERVINGS

THIS SPICED-RICE DISH, called Pilau in Swahili, is traditionally made with a blend of spices (including black pepper, allspice, nutmeg, and cardamom) that is sold widely in East Africa and known as pilau spice. However, curry substitutes nicely, creating a taste similar to that obtained with the spices that are normally used.

¼ cup olive oil

1 medium onion, chopped

1 medium green bell pepper, chopped

2 cloves garlic, diced

1 jalapeño pepper, diced

1 medium tomato, diced

1 pound large shrimp, peeled and deveined

2 cups uncooked long-grain rice (basmati or jasmine rice may be substituted)

¼ cup chopped fresh cilantro

1 cup diced carrots

2 teaspoons salt

¼ teaspoon black pepper

3 tablespoons pilau spice or curry powder

2 cups vegetable stock

2 cups water

2 large eggs, beaten

Heat olive oil in a large pot over a medium-high flame. Sauté onion and green pepper for 5 minutes or until the onion turns golden brown. Add garlic, jalapeño pepper, and tomato. Cook for another 3 to 5 minutes, until tomato becomes stewlike in consistency. Add shrimp and stir. Cook for 5 minutes, until shrimp turn pink in color. Add rice, cilantro, carrots, salt, pepper, and pilau spice or curry powder; stir thoroughly. Add vegetable stock and water, cover pot, and reduce flame to low. Cook without uncovering pot for 25 to 30 minutes, until liquid is absorbed and rice grains are tender.

Fluff the rice with fork, keeping the pot warm. Pour the eggs over the rice and re-cover the pot. Keep the pot on a warm burner an additional 5 minutes, until the eggs are cooked.

COOK'S TIP | *Excellent as either an entrée or side dish.*

KHALIAH A. JOHNSON
New York, New York
North Manhattan Alumnae Chapter

Spicy Spinach Dip (page 12)

Assorted Cheeses and Crackers

Shrimp Scampi (page 130)

Arborio Rice

Green Salad

Ricotta, Lighter-Textured
Cheesecake (page 226)

WHATEVER THE YEAR, a birthday calls for a real celebration. This Italian-flavored menu is festive enough for any special occasion.

TO PREPARE:

❧ Bake and refrigerate the cheesecake a day in advance.

❧ On the morning of the party, peel and clean the shrimp. Store them in the refrigerator until you're ready to cook the scampi. Prepare the greens and salad dressing and refrigerate them separately.

❧ In the afternoon, make and refrigerate the dip, but don't cut or fill the bread until just before serving. Remember to take out the cheese to come to room temperature about a half hour before your guests arrive.

❧ Put up the rice 20 to 25 minutes before you're ready to serve. While the rice cooks, make the scampi.

A DELTA BIRTHDAY

One distinctive way a Delta birthday celebration is set apart from any other is by the presence of the celebrant's sorority sisters. Birthday parties are always fun and, no matter how old we are, they seem to bring out the youthful exuberance in us. We can celebrate that inner child by asking guests to bring a photo of the person whose birthday it is at the age when they met.

Use the photos to create a collage on a large piece of corkboard or oak tag. Decorate the border or frame in advance with streamers, ribbons, and other festive items so that it becomes a focal point around which guests will gather to discuss happy memories.

The hostess can also put together a slide show composed of old family photographs. Set up the screen so that the slides can be projected during the birthday dinner and viewed by the group.

Very often invitations include the words "No gifts, please," but there will always be some who refuse to heed that admonition. To avoid any embarrassment, those presents should remain unopened until all the guests have gone home.

SHRIMP SCAMPI

MAKES 4 SERVINGS

I GOT THIS basic recipe from the seafood department of my local grocery store about five years ago. I have varied it with onions, tomato, different seasonings, and burgundy instead of the original white wine. It's a great meal to prepare if you like shrimp.

1 pound raw headless shrimp with the shells on

½ cup butter or margarine

1 large clove garlic, minced

2 teaspoons chopped fresh parsley

¼ cup finely chopped green bell pepper

¼ cup finely chopped onion

¼ cup lemon juice

⅓ cup Burgundy

1 tablespoon Worcestershire sauce

1 tablespoon soy sauce

Seasoned salt and black pepper, to taste

Ground ginger, to taste

1 plum tomato, chopped

Peel and devein the shrimp; rinse under cold water. Melt the butter in a large skillet or wok. Add the garlic, parsley, green pepper, and onion; brown lightly. Add the lemon juice, wine, Worcestershire sauce, soy sauce, seasoned salt, pepper, and ginger; stir well. Add the shrimp and sauté, stirring, for 4 to 5 minutes, or until shrimp are tender. Sprinkle the chopped tomato on top of mixture and simmer, covered, for 5 minutes. Serve over rice with a green salad.

JARITA MOORE
Schaumburg, Illinois
Schaumburg–Hoffman Estates Alumnae Chapter

WEST INDIAN SHRIMP SCAMPI

MAKES 4–6 SERVINGS

A TRIBUTE TO my Caribbean Delta sisters

3 pounds fresh shrimp

½ fresh lemon

½ teaspoon black pepper

¼ teaspoon garlic powder

½ teaspoon hot sauce

½ teaspoon poultry seasoning

½ teaspoon dried thyme

½ teaspoon curry powder

1 cup butter

All-purpose flour

Cook the shrimp in boiling salted water with the lemon half for about 3 minutes or until shrimp turn pink. Cool slightly, peel, and devein. Combine the pepper, garlic powder, hot sauce, poultry seasoning, thyme, and curry powder in a small bowl. Marinate the shrimp in this mixture for about 25 minutes. Melt the butter in a skillet. Dip the shrimp in flour and fry until golden brown.

LASHAWN AMES-MCCONNELL
Brooklyn, New York
Member, National Commission on Arts and Letters
Brooklyn Alumnae Chapter

SHRIMP CREOLE PRONTO

MAKES 4 SERVINGS

Our "Circle of Girlfriends" has enjoyed this dish as we "convene" during the winter months to discuss men and good food! The two seem to go hand in hand!

2 tablespoons olive oil

1 cup chopped onion

1 cup chopped celery

1 green bell pepper, chopped

2 cloves garlic, minced

2 cups fresh or canned chopped, peeled tomatoes

1 (8-ounce) can tomato sauce

½ cup Marsala cooking wine

¼ teaspoon freshly ground black pepper

½ teaspoon red pepper flakes

1 pound shrimp, peeled and deveined

¼–½ teaspoon hot sauce

4 cups cooked rice

Heat the oil in a large saucepan over medium-high heat. Add the onion, celery, bell pepper, and garlic; cook 2 to 3 minutes. Add the tomatoes; cook 2 to 3 minutes, stirring occasionally. Add the remaining ingredients, except the rice; cook 2 to 3 minutes or until the shrimp turn pink. Serve over hot cooked rice.

OLA HILL
Upper Marlboro, Maryland
Prince George's County Alumnae Chapter

MAMA RUTH'S CRAB CAKES

MAKES 2–3 SERVINGS

1 pound crabmeat

1 tablespoon mayonnaise

1 tablespoon dry mustard

1 teaspoon parsley flakes

1 tablespoon Worcestershire sauce

½ teaspoon cayenne pepper

½ teaspoon seasoned salt

1 tablespoon lemon juice

1 teaspoon Old Bay seasoning

2 large eggs, beaten

Bread crumbs

Vegetable oil for frying

Remove all shell fragments from the crabmeat. Combine all the ingredients except the bread crumbs and oil in a medium bowl. Shape into cakes and coat lightly with bread crumbs. Fry quickly in hot oil in a skillet until golden brown or broil until golden.

COOK'S TIP | *A rémoulade or roasted red pepper sauce would be a nice finishing touch for this dish.*

RUTH BERRY DYSON
Washington, D.C.
Washington, D.C., Alumnae Chapter

FRIED CRAB FINGERS

MAKES 4 SERVINGS

THIS RECIPE IS always a favorite at my annual family reunion and a nice change from shrimp and crawfish. It's also quick to prepare.

1 pound crab fingers
Salt, black pepper, and garlic powder, to taste
1 large egg
1 teaspoon baking powder
1 teaspoon distilled white vinegar
¼ cup water
¼ cup all-purpose flour
¼ cup unflavored bread crumbs
Vegetable oil for frying

Season the crab fingers with the salt, pepper, and garlic powder; set aside for 1 hour or more.

Beat the egg, baking powder, and vinegar together in a large bowl, then add the water. Add the crab fingers to the mixture.

In a plastic bag, combine the flour, bread crumbs, and salt and pepper to taste. Drain the crab fingers slightly, add them to the flour mixture, and shake to coat evenly. Drop the coated crab fingers into a deep pot of hot oil and fry for 2 to 3 minutes, until they are golden brown and crisp.

JULIA BRADFORD MOORE
Baton Rouge, Louisiana
Baton Rouge Sigma Alumnae Chapter

CRAB CASSEROLE

MAKES 4 SERVINGS

A FAVORITE MEAL served with a green salad at a sorority committee meeting.

1 teaspoon butter
1 small onion, finely chopped
2 tablespoons finely chopped green bell pepper
1 tablespoon Creole seasoning
1 teaspoon dry mustard
1 tablespoon lemon juice
4 tablespoons mayonnaise
1 pound chopped backfin crabmeat or imitation
    crabmeat
Dash of red pepper
Dash of Worcestershire sauce
1 large egg, beaten
¼ cup bread crumbs or cracker crumbs
Salt and black pepper, to taste

Preheat the oven to 350 degrees.

Melt the butter in a large skillet. Sauté the onion and green pepper in the butter. Combine the Creole seasoning, mustard, lemon juice, mayonnaise, and sautéed onion and pepper with the crabmeat in a medium bowl. Add red pepper and Worcestershire sauce to the egg in a small bowl; mix with the crumbs. Add to the crabmeat; add salt and black pepper. Pour into an 8-by-8-inch greased baking dish. Bake about 45 minutes.

BARBARA D. MORGAN
Washington, D.C.
Washington, D.C., Alumnae Chapter

CRABMEAT QUICHE

MAKES 6–8 SERVINGS

THIS QUICHE IS versatile and elegant. It is perfect for lunch or a light dinner with a salad or cut into smaller servings for hors d'oeuvres.

4–5 ounces shredded Swiss cheese

1 (9-inch) baked pie shell

8 ounces crabmeat, picked over to remove shell fragments

3 green onions with tops, sliced

3 large eggs, beaten

1 cup half-and-half

½ teaspoon salt

½ teaspoon grated lemon peel

¼ teaspoon dry mustard

Pinch of ground mace

¼ cup sliced almonds

Preheat the oven to 325 degrees.

Arrange the cheese evenly over the bottom of pie shell. Arrange the crabmeat evenly over the top of the cheese. Sprinkle with the green onions. In a mixing bowl, combine the beaten eggs, half-and-half, salt, lemon peel, dry mustard, and mace. Pour the mixture evenly over the crabmeat. Top with sliced almonds. Cover the edges of the crust with foil. Bake for about 45 to 50 minutes, or until set. Remove from the oven and let stand for 10 minutes before serving.

COOK'S TIP | *Substitute ham or shrimp for the crabmeat, or use Cheddar or Monterey Jack cheese instead of Swiss.*

RITA L. BROWN
Tallahassee, Florida
Tallahassee Alumnae Chapter

7

VEGETABLES

AND SIDE

DISHES

MULTITASKING IN THE '50S
Dorothy Penman Harrison

ow that Soror Dorothy Harrison has no special timetable or duties to perform, she is able to arrange her time to suit her leisure, and, she says, one of the ways she likes to indulge herself is to enjoy breakfast—her favorite meal— at whatever hour she chooses.

Before being elected national president (1956–1958), Soror Harrison served as grand treasurer, an office she took up when it was vacated by her sister, Beatrice Penman.

"Of course, being the president following Soror Dorothy Height, who held the post from 1947 to 1956, was easy in some ways. We were close friends, allies, and national officers together, and she had done an excellent job of expanding the sorority by implementing many new programs, which put us on a sound, organized track. The hardest part of the job was that my husband became president of Langston University in Oklahoma at the same time, so I was also the First Lady of the university. Luckily, I had a small staff that helped me balance the university agenda with the Delta agenda. And often the sorors on campus would come to my aid when I needed help with an event. Looking back, I wonder how I did it, but since I was young, I suppose I didn't mind the hectic pace. And my positions allowed me to meet and interact with many world leaders who visited the campus and to introduce my sorors to them. I felt that it always served both Delta and Langston University that I was associated with them both."

Soror Harrison was often asked to entertain visitors to the university on very short notice, but her competent staff was usually able to whip up a delicious meal in almost no time at all, and she enjoyed the fine linens, china, crystal, and silver that were always brought out for such formal occasions.

"Over the dinner table," she remembers, "we discussed sensitive multicultural issues, and our guests often seemed surprised by my enthusiastic participation in those conversations. It pleased my husband that I could be both a gracious hostess and an informed contributor to our dinner-table discussions. We may not have solved the problems of the world, but the dining table allowed us a neutral forum in which to exchange ideas.

"When we retired and moved to Chicago, we continued to entertain diverse groups of people. My husband was charming and had a wonderful sense of humor that always made everyone feel at home. He liked breakfast foods as much as I do, and one of our favorite recipes—which everyone seemed to enjoy—was Au Gratin Grits. They're really good as a side dish any time of day."

You'll find Soror Harrison's versatile grits recipe on page 156.

SAUTÉED VEGETABLES

MAKES 4 SERVINGS

1 tablespoon canola oil

1 tablespoon grapeseed oil

½ teaspoon chopped garlic

1 medium onion, sliced

3 medium yellow squash, sliced

3 medium zucchini, sliced

1 (7-ounce) package sliced portobello mushrooms

1 (16-ounce) bag frozen cut okra

2 tomatoes, quartered

1 (14-ounce) can tomato sauce

Salt and black pepper, to taste

Preheat the oven to 350 degrees.

Heat the oils over medium heat in a large skillet. Add the chopped garlic and onion. Stir until the onion is clear. Layer the squash, zucchini, mushrooms, sautéed onion, okra, and tomato in a baking pan. Add the tomato sauce. Add salt and black pepper. Bake, covered, for 25 minutes. Serve over cooked rice.

For variety, serve the vegetables with cooked shrimp or diced chicken, over rice.

GWENDOLYN E. BOYD
Washington, D.C.
22nd National President
Washington, D.C., Alumnae Chapter

ROASTED WINTER VEGETABLES

MAKES 8–10 SERVINGS

I DEVELOPED THIS recipe after taking classes at a cooking school. The winter vegetables are so good this way that my grandchildren, ages seven, four, and two, love them and will eat them without complaining. If I only had known how to make these when my children were little and I couldn't get them to eat winter vegetables. . . . Better late than never.

6 cups cubed turnips, rutabaga, carrots, parsnips, sweet potatoes, onion, or beets, or a combination thereof

2 teaspoons chopped fresh rosemary

2 tablespoons extra-virgin olive oil

1 teaspoon kosher or sea salt

1 teaspoon freshly ground black pepper

Preheat the oven to 425 degrees.

Peel the vegetables and cut into ½-inch cubes. (If using beets in combination with other vegetables, keep them separate so they will not bleed onto the other vegetables.) Add the rosemary to the olive oil in a small bowl and toss with the vegetables to coat. Season with the salt and pepper.

Line the bottom of a baking sheet with parchment paper or spray with vegetable cooking spray. Spread the vegetables on to the baking sheet. Keep beets on a separate section of the sheet.

Bake for 35 to 45 minutes or until tender. Serve with beef or pork.

PEGGY BELCHER-DIXON
Inglewood, California
Inglewood Alumnae Chapter

LUCY AND ETHEL'S BAKED BEANS

MAKES 8 SERVINGS

OUR CHILDREN call us "Lucy and Ethel" because we remind them of those famous friends from the Lucille Ball television series. We met in Chicago while we were in school. Elease, from Texas, whose family owned a restaurant, inherited her mom's gift of cooking. Geneva, from Chicago, shared her family with Elease when she migrated to the city. We are still dear friends (more than fifty years together) and still act like Lucy and Ethel.

2 (16-ounce) cans red beans
2 (14½-ounce) cans tomatoes
1 green bell pepper, chopped
1 medium onion, chopped
½ cup packed dark brown sugar
½ cup catsup
½ pound bacon, cooked and crumbled (optional)

Preheat the oven to 350 degrees.

Drain the beans and tomatoes, reserving the liquid. Combine the beans, tomatoes, green pepper, and onion in a medium bowl. Mix the bean and tomato liquids in a small bowl. Add one-fourth of the liquid to the bean mixture. Stir in the brown sugar, catsup, and the crumbled bacon, if desired. Blend well; add more of the liquid as needed (don't make the mixture too soupy). Spoon the mixture into a large bean pot. Bake, covered, for 2½ hours. Uncover and continue to bake 30 minutes.

GENEVA C. BELL
ELEASE M. SMITH
Chicago, Illinois
Chicago Alumnae Chapter

DELTA OF DISTINCTION
Allison Seymour

AS CO-ANCHOR of the *FOX Morning News,* Soror Allison Seymour is a familiar presence in millions of homes in the Washington, D.C., area.

A member of Delta Sigma Theta since 1986, Soror Allison grew up in D.C. and was educated in local public schools. She graduated from Bethesda–Chevy Chase High School, received her B.A. from Hampton University, and earned a master's in mass communication from the University of South Carolina.

Having begun her journalism career as both a desk and production assistant at the Washington bureau of ABC News, she got her first on-air job in Utica, New York, in 1993 as a noon anchor, reporter, and assignment editor before moving on to become the main anchor at WBNG-TV in Binghamton, and finally returning "home" to Washington in 1999.

Waldorf Salad (page 42)

Chicken Breasts à l'Orange (page 75)

*String Beans
with Potatoes* (page 142)

Ice Box Rolls (page 176)

Five-Flavor Pound Cake (page 204)

THIS MENU is elegant but still light enough to serve for a midday meal.

TO PREPARE:

❧ Make the rolls and the cake a day ahead.

❧ The salad, beans, and chicken are all quick and easy. If the beans and potatoes are cut in advance, all three of these dishes can be completed in under an hour.

DELTA SIGMA THETA FOUNDERS' DAY LUNCHEON

Founders' Day is a formal and highly acclaimed event celebrated at a luncheon to which only members of the sorority are invited, or at one where nonmembers are also invited. The luncheon is generally held in the months as close to the actual founding date—January 13, 1913—as possible. Deltas usually dress in red, white, or black. If the program, which usually includes a speaker, is closed, it may be followed by a reception that is open to the public.

For most formal luncheons, expect to see a well-set table with an appropriate, if understated, floral centerpiece. The service itself can be formal, with platters passed by a server, preplated and served individually, or family style, with guests passing platters along the table. Whichever style you choose, do be sure that each dish is presented and garnished attractively to show your guests how much thought has gone into the preparation of their meal.

TWENTY-FIVE YEARS AGO, when Soror Carolyn Wilder was just beginning her tenure as a professor specializing in early-childhood development at West Los Angeles Junior College, she was attracted to Delta Sigma Theta because of the Head Start program sponsored by the Los Angeles Alumnae Chapter. Impressed by the center's facilities and knowledgeable staff, she felt in her heart that an organization that would provide such necessary and quality service to the children of the community was one to which she wanted to belong.

Since that time, Soror Wilder has herself founded three private schools—a preschool, a kindergarten, and an elementary school—that provide a high standard of education for minority students. What makes the Delta so important in her life, she says, is "the constant focus on scholarship, service, education, and community involvement. Delta women are versatile, sincere, and creative. If I had to give the organization a grade, it would be an A+."

OLD-FASHIONED FRIED OKRA

MAKES 4 SERVINGS

MY GRANDMOTHER taught me how to prepare this dish, which was served any day of the week. Most women during my grandmother's time did not work outside the home, and they prepared all their foods from scratch. They did not depend on many of the "instant" convenience foods we have today.

½ tablespoon vegetable oil
4 slices salt pork or fatback
1 pound okra, cut up
½ teaspoon salt, or to taste
½ teaspoon black pepper

Heat the vegetable oil in a heavy skillet. Place salt pork or fatback neatly in skillet. Fry on medium heat, turning occasionally until crisp. Remove from skillet and discard. Place okra, salt, and pepper in the skillet (you may pour some of the grease out, if desired). Fry okra until tender. If it begins to stick, add 1 tablespoon of water.

GLORIA H. ALEXANDER
Columbus, Georgia
Columbus Alumnae Chapter

STRING BEANS WITH POTATOES

MAKES 6 SERVINGS

1½ cups water
¼ cup chopped onion
2 tablespoons chicken bouillon
2 teaspoons sugar
½ teaspoon garlic powder
Dash of crushed red pepper
1½ pounds fresh green beans, cut into 1-inch pieces
1 pound small red potatoes, cut into quarters
2 tablespoons butter or margarine
2 tablespoons chopped fresh parsley (optional)

Combine the water, onion, bouillon, sugar, garlic powder, and crushed red pepper in a medium saucepan; bring to a boil. Add the green beans and potatoes; bring to a boil. Reduce heat to simmer; cover and cook until the green beans and potatoes are tender when tested with a fork, about 15 minutes. Stir in the butter and sprinkle with parsley, if desired.

ALFREDIA BOYD
Columbia, South Carolina
Chair, National Nominating Committee
Columbia, South Carolina, Alumnae Chapter

String Beans with Potatoes

MARINATED ASPARAGUS

MAKES 8–10 SERVINGS

HERE IS a nice addition to a buffet, or a good side for heavier meat dishes.

2 pounds fresh asparagus

6 tablespoons olive oil

2 tablespoons red wine vinegar

2 cloves garlic, chopped

Lemon pepper seasoning, to taste

Black pepper, to taste

Garlic powder, to taste

Onion powder, to taste

Salt, to taste

½ bunch green onions, chopped

Diced red bell pepper or roasted red pepper
    for color

Blanch the asparagus in salted water in a small saucepan. Asparagus should remain crisp. Pour off the water and rinse with cold water. Pat dry with a paper towel. Place in a shallow bowl.

Whisk together the olive oil, vinegar, garlic, and spices in a small bowl. Add the green onions to the asparagus and pour the olive oil mixture over top. Toss gently. Garnish with diced red bell pepper or roasted red pepper.

Marinate in the refrigerator overnight, mixing occasionally. Serve at room temperature.

COOK'S TIP | *You may substitute fresh snapped green beans for the asparagus.*

OLA HILL
Upper Marlboro, Maryland
Prince George's County Alumnae Chapter

FRIED COLLARD GREENS

MAKES 3–4 SERVINGS

MY GRANDMOTHER taught me how to prepare this dish around 1953.

1 tablespoon vegetable oil

4–6 slices salt pork, fatback, or thick-sliced bacon

1 bunch collard greens, washed, drained well, and
    finely cut up.

1 tablespoon sugar

½ teaspoon baking soda

1 teaspoon salt, or to taste

Heat the vegetable oil in a heavy skillet. Place salt pork or fatback neatly in the skillet. Fry on medium heat, turning occasionally until crisp. Remove from skillet and drain on paper towel. Dice and set aside. Add the greens to the hot grease. (Do not add water.) Cook, stirring constantly, for approximately 5 to 8 minutes. Add the salt pork, sugar, baking soda, and salt. Cook over low heat 20 minutes or until the greens are tender, stirring constantly.

GLORIA H. ALEXANDER
Columbus, Georgia
Columbus Alumnae Chapter

VIRGINIA'S STEAMED CABBAGE POT

MAKES 15 SERVINGS

MY SISTER was considered the best cook among our siblings; however, since she was a member of the AKA sorority and I was Delta, we competed to produce the best dishes. This is one of her most delicious pots.

1 bunch collard greens, thoroughly washed

2–3 carrots, cut into long slices

½ green bell pepper, sliced

2 heads green cabbage, chopped

1 (16-ounce) package gumbo mix

Seasoned salt, to taste

Spicy seasoning blend, to taste

Black pepper, to taste

Garlic salt, to taste

1 teaspoon sugar

Cook the greens, covered in water, in a large stockpot for 30 minutes. Add the carrots, bell pepper, and chopped cabbage. Stir in the gumbo mix. Steam over low heat. Season with the seasoned salt and the remaining 4 ingredients. To serve, top with corned beef or pastrami with corn bread on the side.

YVONNE S. WILSON
Kansas City, Missouri
Greater Kansas City Alumnae Chapter

SKILLET GREENS WITH BALSAMIC VINEGAR

MAKES 6 SERVINGS

2 pounds collard greens, washed and drained

2 cups water

2 tablespoons bacon drippings

1 small onion, thinly sliced

2 cloves garlic, minced

½ teaspoon crushed red pepper

¼ cup sugar

2–3 tablespoons balsamic vinegar

Remove and discard the woody stems from the greens. Stack the collard leaves a few at a time and roll up from bottom to top of leaf. Cut crosswise into ¼-inch-wide strips. Bring the water to a boil in a Dutch oven or large saucepan. Add the greens; cook, covered, over medium heat, stirring often until tender, about 10 to 12 minutes. Drain well.

Heat the bacon drippings in a large skillet over medium heat. Add the onion, garlic, and crushed red pepper. Cook and stir until the onion is tender, about 5 minutes. Add the greens and sugar. Cook and stir until the greens are tender, about 10 minutes. Sprinkle balsamic vinegar over the greens and toss to coat. Serve immediately.

ALFREDIA BOYD
Columbia, South Carolina
Chair, National Nominating Committee
Columbia, South Carolina, Alumnae Chapter

BROCCOLI CASSEROLE

MAKES 4 SERVINGS

AS A COLLEGE STUDENT, I thought dorm food was awful and couldn't wait to have my own apartment. This is one of the first recipes my mom gave me upon my liberation from dorm food.

2 pounds fresh broccoli florets, without stems
2 tablespoons margarine
½ teaspoon garlic powder, or to taste
¼ teaspoon seasoned salt, or to taste
¼ teaspoon black pepper, or to taste
½ cup sour cream
½ cup bread crumbs
½ cup shredded Cheddar cheese

Bring water to a boil under steaming rack in a large saucepan. Place the fresh broccoli florets in the rack. Cover the pan. Cook over medium heat 10 minutes or until the broccoli is tender when tested with a fork.

Drain and rinse the broccoli.

Remove the steaming rack and return the broccoli to the saucepan. Add the margarine; stir until coated.

Add the garlic powder, seasoned salt, and black pepper, stirring gently.

Preheat the oven to 350 degrees. Grease a 9-by-9-inch baking dish.

Place the broccoli in the prepared dish. Add the sour cream over the top in dollops. Pour bread crumbs over top. Sprinkle Cheddar cheese over everything, spreading evenly.

Bake 20 minutes or until golden brown.

CHANDRA GILL
Champaign, Illinois
Champaign-Urbana Alumnae Chapter

CORN CASSEROLE

MAKES 8–10 SERVINGS

THIS EASY, inexpensive dish is great for potluck dinners.

1 (8½-ounce) box Jiffy corn bread/corn muffin mix
1 cup sour cream
1 (14¾-ounce) can cream-style corn
1 (15½-ounce) can whole-kernel corn, drained
½ cup butter or margarine, softened
2 large eggs, beaten

Preheat the oven to 350 degrees. Mix all the ingredients in a large bowl. Spoon into a greased 9-by-9-inch baking dish and bake 1½ hours or until firm. Serve with meat and a green vegetable.

IRENE LEE WELLINGTON
Vacaville, California
Member-at-Large

STUFFED BABY EGGPLANT

MAKES 8 SERVINGS

8 (6-ounce) baby eggplants, halved lengthwise

1 tablespoon minced garlic

1 yellow bell pepper, seeded and chopped

4 ripe plum tomatoes, chopped

1 (5-ounce) bag baby spinach

2 tablespoons freshly grated lemon peel

½ teaspoon salt

2 teaspoons freshly squeezed lemon juice

3 tablespoons grated Parmesan cheese

Preheat the oven to 425 degrees. Lightly coat two large-rimmed baking sheets with nonstick cooking spray.

Scoop out eggplant flesh with a spoon and reserve, leaving ¾-inch-thick shell. Place shells, cut side up, on prepared baking sheets. Lightly coat shells with nonstick spray. Bake 20 minutes or until almost tender. Turn shells cut side down; bake 10 to 15 minutes until very tender.

While shells bake, chop the eggplant flesh (you should have about 3 to 4 cups). Lightly coat a large nonstick skillet with nonstick spray. Heat to medium. Add the garlic and chopped eggplant; stir over medium heat 3 minutes. Add pepper; stir 6 minutes or until crisp-tender. Add tomatoes; stir 2 minutes until vegetables are tender. Add spinach in two batches; cover and cook 1 minute, until just wilted but still bright green. Remove the skillet from the heat; stir in the lemon peel and ¼ teaspoon of the salt.

Stuffed Baby Eggplant

Remove the sheet with the eggplant shells from the oven. Turn shells over; sprinkle with remaining ¼ teaspoon salt and the lemon juice. Fill with vegetable mixture.

Sprinkle the eggplant with the cheese. Heat in batches in the microwave on High until hot.

ANGELA GRANT
Hawthorne, California
Rolling Hills–Palos Verdes Alumnae Chapter

EASY FRIED CORN

MAKES 8 SERVINGS

3 (15-ounce) cans whole-kernel corn, drained
½ cup milk
Salt and black pepper, to taste
¼ teaspoon brown or granulated sugar
1 tablespoon cornstarch
¼ cup vegetable oil or bacon drippings

Place the corn in a large bowl. Add the milk, salt, pepper, sugar, and cornstarch; mix well with an immersion blender or in a food processor by pulsating several times. Do not mix to liquid stage. Heat the oil in a skillet over medium heat. Pour in the corn mixture. Cook for 20 minutes, stirring often so corn does not burn.

MERLE ALLEN FRANKLIN
Atlanta, Georgia
Atlanta Suburban Alumnae Chapter

Easy Fried Corn

ELOISE'S FAVORITE CORN PUDDING

MAKES 4–6 SERVINGS

2 (16-ounce) cans cream-style corn

1 (16-ounce) can whole-kernel corn, drained

½ teaspoon salt

½ cup milk

3 large eggs, beaten

1 tablespoon all-purpose flour

3 tablespoons sugar

½ cup butter

Preheat the oven to 350 degrees.

Combine the cream-style and whole-kernel corns in a mixing bowl. Add the salt, milk, and eggs. Combine the flour and sugar and add to the corn mixture.

Place butter in a 2-quart glass casserole dish and melt in the oven. Add the corn mixture. Stir well and place dish on a baking pan to catch any runover. Bake about 1 hour. If pudding seems to be cooking too fast on the bottom, place a shallow pan of water under it.

ELOISE J. CABRERA-WHITE
Tampa, Florida
Tampa Alumnae Chapter

MIRIAN'S CORN PUDDING

MAKES 4–6 SERVINGS

THIS IS THE corn pudding recipe passed as a legacy from a legacy. Our extended family enjoyed this at every family gathering and holiday. I'm sure the faded, stained recipe card will someday find a home in my daughter's recipe box. Hope it finds a happy home in yours.

3 large eggs, beaten

2 cups milk

2 tablespoons sugar

½ teaspoon salt

1 (15-ounce) can cream-style corn

1 tablespoon butter, melted

1 tablespoon chopped onion

Preheat the oven to 325 degrees. Grease a 9-by-9-inch baking pan.

Combine all the ingredients in a large bowl; mix well. Pour into the prepared baking pan. Bake 1 to 1½ hours. The pudding is done when it pulls away from the side of the pan and when it is set in the middle.

MICHELLE ALEXANDER-CALLOWAY
Columbia, Maryland
Columbia, Maryland, Alumnae Chapter

ELAINE AND SHEILA'S CORN PUDDING

MAKES 8-10 SERVINGS

SOROR ELAINE BOURNE HEATH, who attended elementary school with my husband, Frank Shears, in Washington, D.C., gave me this recipe. It has become a family tradition, served at every holiday meal. When I invite guests to dinner, they all ask if I'm making the corn pudding.

2 tablespoons all-purpose flour

½ cup water

2 (15-ounce) cans whole-kernel corn, drained

2 (15-ounce) cans cream-style corn

1 (12-ounce) can evaporated milk

3 large eggs, beaten

1 teaspoon vanilla extract

½ cup sugar, or more to taste

Preheat the oven to 350 degrees.

Combine the flour and water in a 2½-quart baking dish. Stir in all the remaining ingredients. Set baking dish in a pan of water. Bake for 2 hours or until the top begins to brown and the pudding gets firm.

SHEILA DEAN SHEARS
Silver Spring, Maryland
Co-Chair, Information and Communications
Washington, D.C., Alumnae Chapter

SQUASH CASSEROLE

MAKES 6-9 SERVINGS

2 pounds yellow squash, peeled and cut into chunks

1 medium onion, diced

1 teaspoon salt

1 teaspoon black pepper

1 (10¾-ounce) can cream of mushroom soup

1 cup sour cream

1 carrot, grated

½ cup margarine

1 (8-ounce) bag herb-seasoned stuffing

2 cups shredded sharp Cheddar cheese

Preheat the oven to 350 degrees.

Place the squash in a medium saucepan with the onion; cover with water and boil until soft. Season with salt and black pepper. Mash the squash and strain out any excess water. Combine the squash with the soup, sour cream, and carrot in a medium bowl.

Melt the margarine in a medium saucepan and stir in stuffing. Stir with a fork until thoroughly mixed. Add half the stuffing to the squash mixture. Add half the cheese, mixing well. Spray a 9-by-9-inch baking dish with vegetable cooking spray and place squash in the dish. Top with the remaining cheese and stuffing. Bake for 40 minutes.

BLANCHE LAVENDER
Atlanta, Georgia
Atlanta Alumnae Chapter

MAMA'S CORN BREAD DRESSING

MAKES 6–8 SERVINGS

AS CHILDREN, my siblings and I often helped Mother prepare the dressing for Thanksgiving dinner. Each one of us took part. Some would chop the onion or green pepper or celery; one would crumble the corn bread. Our mother would cut the turkey parts. I will always remember sitting around the kitchen table happily chopping and cutting with the anticipation of consuming the dressing once we sat down to our dinner.

2 (8½-ounce) boxes Jiffy corn bread/corn muffin mix
2 large eggs
1 cup milk
3 tablespoons poultry seasoning
3 tablespoons chopped fresh sage
2 stalks celery, chopped
1 medium onion, chopped
¼ green bell pepper, chopped
Turkey or chicken neck, giblet, liver, or heart, boiled and chopped, juices reserved (optional)

Preheat the oven to 400 degrees.

Combine the corn bread mix with the eggs, milk, poultry seasoning, and sage in a large bowl. Spread mixture evenly in a 9-by-9-inch greased baking dish and bake for 20 to 30 minutes or until golden brown. Cool and then crumble into a large bowl.

Reduce oven temperature to 350 degrees. Add the celery, onion, bell pepper, and turkey parts, if desired, to the corn bread. Add enough juice from the turkey parts to moisten. (If not using the parts, use chicken stock to moisten.) Spoon into a greased 9-by-9-inch baking pan. Spread over entire pan and pat down evenly. Bake, uncovered, for 45 to 60 minutes.

SANDI KENNER
Washington, D.C.
Washington, D.C., Alumnae Chapter

SYLVIA'S STUFFING

MAKES 12–16 SERVINGS

MY FAMILY traveled from Charlotte, North Carolina, to Washington, D.C., to share Thanksgiving 1995 dinner with Soror Laura Fleet. She and I had been colleagues when we taught together in the School of Communication at Howard University. Never had I tasted stuffing like this, which was so delicious. Soror Fleet shared this recipe, which had been passed down from a repertoire of recipes that belonged to her mother, Mrs. Sylvia Washington. Once you taste this spectacular treat, you'll understand clearly why I always include it on my holiday menu.

Mama's Corn Bread Dressing

1 cup chopped celery
1 cup chopped onion
¼ cup butter
1 pound bacon, cooked and crumbled
1 pound sausage
3 slices ham, chopped
2 (8-ounce) bags tiny shrimp, cooked (cooking water reserved)
Salt and red pepper, to taste
1 loaf toasted Roman Meal bread, chopped
8 pats butter

Preheat the oven to 350 degrees.

Sauté the celery and the onion in the butter in a medium skillet. Combine the bacon, sausage, ham, and shrimp with the celery and onion. Sprinkle with salt and red pepper.

Layer the mixture with the bread in a 13-by-9-inch baking dish. Moisten with the water that the shrimp was cooked in, and put pats of butter on top. Bake for 30 to 45 minutes.

ROSEMARY JACKSON
Charlotte, North Carolina
Charlotte Alumnae Chapter

NITA'S SOUTHERN-STYLE CORN BREAD DRESSING

MAKES 16–20 SERVINGS

THIS RECIPE is from my late sister-in-law, Mrs. Manetha "Nita" Boykins.

Turkey parts (giblets and neck)
2 stalks celery, cut into 1-inch pieces
1 green bell pepper, cut into 1-inch pieces
1 onion, cut into 1-inch pieces
Salt and black pepper, to taste
Poultry seasoning, to taste
3 (8½-ounce) boxes Jiffy corn bread/corn muffin mix
2 cups finely chopped celery
½ cup finely chopped green bell pepper
1 cup finely chopped onion
2 hard-boiled eggs, finely chopped
2 (14-ounce) cans chicken broth
Pinch of dried sage
Pinch of dried thyme

Boil the turkey parts in 2 cups of water in a large stockpot, along with the 1-inch pieces of celery, green pepper, and onion. Add the salt, pepper, and poultry seasoning. Simmer for 15 to 20 minutes.

Remove the turkey parts from the water, cool, and chop finely.

Prepare the corn bread mix according to the package directions. Cool and crumble or cube it and transfer to a large mixing bowl.

Sauté the chopped celery, green pepper, and onion in a medium skillet for 5 to 10 minutes. Fold into the corn bread mixture. Add the turkey parts and chopped egg; mix well. Add the chicken broth. Season the mixture to taste with salt, pepper, poultry seasoning, sage, and thyme; mix well.

Place the dressing in a greased pan or dish and refrigerate overnight.

Preheat the oven to 350 degrees. Bake the dressing for 1 hour. Broil the top for a few minutes to brown.

PHOEBE BOYKINS DIXON
Washington, D.C.
Co-Chair, Housing and Properties
Federal City Alumnae Chapter

PEEZIE'S NEW ORLEANS OYSTER DRESSING

MAKES 10 SERVINGS

I GREW UP in New Orleans and had a mother who was a tremendous cook, but she would never share any of her secrets. When I moved to New Jersey and found myself homesick for my mother's cooking, I worked hard to duplicate her dishes. On her first Christmas visit to my home, I prepared dinner with my variations. Her comment was, "Li'l girl, you can cook, yeh." That was the best compliment her youngest daughter could ever receive.

¾ pound ground beef

Salt and black pepper, to taste

1 medium onion, finely chopped

1½ stalks celery, finely chopped

3 green onions, finely chopped

½ green bell pepper, finely chopped

2 tablespoons parsley flakes

2½ dozen raw oysters

1 (8-ounce) bag stuffing mix

3 large eggs, lightly beaten

½ teaspoon cayenne pepper

Bread crumbs

Preheat the oven to 350 degrees.

In a large skillet, brown the beef; season to taste with salt and black pepper. Add the chopped onion, celery, green onions, bell pepper, and parsley flakes. Pour the mixture into a large Dutch oven or large bowl for mixing. Drain the oysters and discard juice. Purée the oysters in a blender; add to the ground-beef mixture. Stir in the stuffing mix. Add the eggs, mixing well. Add cayenne pepper and additional salt and pepper; mix well.

Spoon the mixture into a lightly greased 9-by-12-inch baking dish. Sprinkle the top with bread crumbs. Bake for 30 minutes.

PEOLA SMITH
Neptune, New Jersey
Monmouth County Alumnae Chapter

DELTA OF DISTINCTION
Natasha J. Stewart

BOTH A LEGACY and an initiator, Soror Natasha Stewart is the granddaughter of Soror Altamese Childs Jenkins, charter member and first president of the West Palm Beach, Florida, Alumnae Chapter of Delta Sigma Theta, and the daughter of Soror Norma Jenkins Stewart, of the Washington, D.C., Alumnae Chapter, who served as co-chair of our ninetieth anniversary celebration. Soror Natasha herself joined the sorority at Virginia State University's Alpha Eta Chapter in the spring of 1994.

A promotions director for WPGC Radio in the Washington, D.C., metropolitan area, she has, both personally and professionally, designed programs for inner-city neighborhoods that benefit adolescents and teens. Among the programs she has initiated are workshops and seminars on the job interview process, career choice, and HIV/AIDS prevention and intervention. She has also organized block parties and musical events for inner-city neighborhoods.

Soror Stewart says that she joined Delta not only because of her family history but also because of the outstanding community services she's observed Deltas performing during her teen and college years. She wants to continue that tradition and is proud to be among a group of women who, collectively and continually, impact people's live in such positive ways.

SHRIMP DRESSING

MAKES 6 SERVINGS

1 cup chopped onion

½ cup chopped celery

½ cup chopped green bell pepper

2 cloves garlic, chopped

½ cup margarine

1 (10¾-ounce) can cream of mushroom soup

1 (10¾-ounce) can Cheddar cheese soup

1 pound shrimp, peeled and deveined

1 teaspoon hot sauce

¼ cup chopped fresh parsley

1 teaspoon Creole seasoning

2 cups cooked rice

Preheat the oven to 450 degrees.

Sauté the onion, celery, bell pepper, and garlic in the margarine in a large skillet. Add the soups and simmer 10 minutes. Add the shrimp, hot sauce, parsley, and Creole seasoning. Simmer 30 minutes. Stir in the cooked rice.

Spoon the mixture into a greased baking dish. Bake, covered, 45 minutes.

ALFREDIA BOYD
Columbia, South Carolina
Chair, National Nominating Committee
Columbia, South Carolina, Alumnae Chapter

MACARONI AND CHEESE

MAKES 8 SERVINGS

NO HOLIDAY MEAL was complete for our family without macaroni and cheese. Often people would go back for seconds just for this dish.

8 ounces elbow macaroni

½ cup butter

2 tablespoons all-purpose flour

2 cups evaporated milk

1 (10¾-ounce) can Cheddar cheese soup

½ cup each of shredded Cheddar, mozzarella, Colby, and American cheeses

½ cup sour cream

Salt and black pepper, to taste

Preheat the oven to 350 degrees.

Cook the macaroni according to package directions; drain and set aside.

In a large saucepan, melt half the butter; stir in the flour. Gradually add the evaporated milk, stirring constantly. As the mixture begins to thicken, add the soup and half of each of the shredded cheeses. Stir in the sour cream. Add salt and black pepper.

Place half the macaroni on the bottom of a large greased baking dish. Sprinkle with half the remaining cheeses; then pour on half the cheese sauce. Add the remaining macaroni, dot with the remaining butter, top with the remaining cheese sauce, and sprinkle with the remaining shredded cheeses.

Bake 30 minutes or until lightly browned on top.

Carol E. Ware
Westerville, Ohio
Columbus Alumnae Chapter

Mom's Mac
and Cheese

MAKES 8–10 SERVINGS

THIS IS one of my mom's signature dishes. My family makes it for all family gatherings.

1 (16-ounce) box elbow macaroni, shells, or penne
  pasta
6 tablespoons butter or margarine
4 tablespoons all-purpose flour
5 cups milk
2½ cups shredded extra-sharp Cheddar cheese
¼ teaspoon salt
⅛ teaspoon garlic powder
1–2 cups shredded sharp Cheddar cheese
½ cup Italian bread crumbs

Cook the macaroni al dente, according to package directions; drain, rinse with cold water, and drain again thoroughly.

Preheat the oven to 350 degrees. Grease a 13-by-8-inch baking dish. Add the macaroni.

In a large skillet, melt the butter over low heat; add the flour and whisk until creamy. Slowly add 1 cup of the milk and whisk slowly until blended. Add the remaining milk, 1 cup at a time, whisking after each addition. Increase the heat and let mixture thicken, whisking occasionally to prevent sticking.

Once sauce begins to thicken, slowly add the extra-sharp cheese, salt, and garlic powder; whisk occasionally. When cheese has melted, remove skillet from the heat and pour over the macaroni in the prepared baking dish. Mix until the macaroni is covered. Top with the sharp cheese. Sprinkle with the bread crumbs. Bake 15 to 20 minutes. Place under broiler for 1 minute, if needed, to brown top of casserole.

Yvonne Garner
Washington, D.C.
Federal City Alumnae Chapter

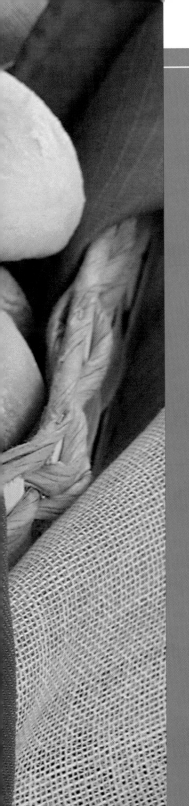

8

BREADS

AND

BREAKFAST

FOODS

SHAPED BY OUR PURPOSE

Stacy Nicole Smith

Stacy Nicole Smith sometimes believes that becoming a Delta was actually imprinted on her DNA. "For as long as I can remember," she says, "all the women who have played a significant role in my life have been members of Delta Sigma Theta. My attendance at Florida A&M was predicated on two givens: securing a B.S. degree in psychology and becoming a member of Beta Alpha Chapter of Delta."

For as long as she can remember, her mother, aunts, cousins, teachers, and neighbors always seemed to be attending meetings or participating in Delta community projects. Founders' Day, Jabberwocks, Social Action Luncheons, Step Shows, Arts and Letters Commission, and National Convention were familiar events throughout her life, and oftentimes she wondered, as she put it, "What it was that so many dynamic women had found so attractive about Delta, why it was such an important part of their life, and whether I would have the strength and fortitude to stand beside them and 'measure up,' so to speak.

"Being a Delta has shaped me in so many ways that it's hard to separate the standards and goals I've set for myself from those of the organization. As a psychologist, one of my main concerns is finding ways to make the theories I learned in school work in a 'real life' setting. I want to assist African-Americans and other minorities in dealing with the mental health issues that impact their lives on a daily basis. And I now understand that what has made Delta so attractive for women is the fact that our focus is on what we can do collectively and individually to make the world better for others. Our Delta membership puts us in contact with groups of like-minded women who are on the same path.

"Holidays at home were always special. As the youngest child, I was the one who woke everyone up to rush downstairs and tear open all of our presents on Christmas morning. My mom always opened hers first because she was then required to go to the kitchen and make her famous Simple Monkey Bread (see recipe page 174). Monkey bread is so much a part of our family's tradition that I'm torn between learning to make it and not wanting to because it might not taste as good as hers.

"Later in the day I'd help her prepare some of the other traditional dishes we always served to family and friends—turkey, ham, Swiss green beans, mac and cheese, rolls, sweet potatoes, stuffing, cranberry sauce, and always lots of desserts. Three hours after the meal we were usually still sitting and talking at the table. Christmas food is certainly important, but the thing I remember most is the time of sharing and exchanging family stories and experiences."

Seafood Nachos (page 7)

*Chicken and Broccoli
Casserole* (page 88)

Buttered Noodles

Dinner Rolls (page 171)

7-Up Cake with Icing (page 208)

ANNIVERSARIES ARE NOT just for weddings. They occur for any number of reasons, but whatever you're celebrating, the dishes on this menu will make it a festive and memorable occasion.

TO PREPARE:

❧ Make the cake a day in advance and store it airtight at room temperature.

❧ On the afternoon of the celebration, combine the seafood mixture for the nachos and store it in the refrigerator. Cook and shred the chicken, cook the broccoli, and layer them in their baking dish. Cover and refrigerate.

❧ Start the rolls late in the afternoon so that the dough will have time to rise.

❧ Just before your guests are due, take the chicken out of the fridge to come to room temperature and get the nachos into the oven. Sauté the onion and garlic for the casserole, combine the sauce, and pour it over the chicken and broccoli. When the nachos come out, turn down the heat and put in the casserole. Put up the water for the noodles. When the casserole has finished cooking, cover it with foil to keep warm while you bake the rolls.

A DELTA CELEBRATION

Deltas always remember the year they were initiated into the sorority. Those who were initiated at the same time are called "line sisters," and many of them get together each year to celebrate their initiation anniversary.

Like any get-together of old friends, this is a time to bring one another up to date with what's going on in our lives as well as to share memories, funny stories, and photographs. Wherever it takes place, an Initiation Anniversary Celebration is always decorated with Delta paraphernalia, colors, and symbols. If there's a cake, like the one on this menu, it might be decorated with a candle for each year of membership.

Whatever anniversary you're celebrating, be it a reunion of classmates, bunkmates from camp, or even a holiday tour group, to name just a few of the many possibilities, be sure to gather your own memorabilia and decorate the room and the table in a way that is appropriately symbolic.

BELLHOUSE HOT ROLLS

MAKES 12–15 ROLLS

2 (0.25-ounce) packets active dry yeast (not quick-rise yeast)

1 tablespoon plus ½ cup sugar

1 cup scalded milk

1 cup butter or margarine

1 teaspoon salt (optional)

3 large eggs, at room temperature, beaten

4 cups sifted all-purpose flour

Combine the yeast and the 1 tablespoon sugar in a small bowl; let stand.

Combine the scalded milk, remaining ½ cup sugar, ½ cup of the butter, and the salt, if desired, in a large bowl. When slightly cooled, add the eggs and stir well. Add the yeast mixture and stir well.

Gradually add the sifted flour until all the ingredients are well mixed. (Dough consistency should be moist.) Lightly flour the top of the dough. Cover with a cloth and allow the dough to rise for about 1½ hours or until doubled in size.

Melt the remaining ½ cup butter in a small saucepan; cool slightly.

Remove part of the dough. Roll out on floured wax paper. Cut with a round cutter; then brush individual rolls with the melted butter.

Fold each piece in half and place on greased baking sheet. Repeat the procedure until all the dough is rolled, cut out, buttered, and placed on the baking sheet. Cover dough with a cloth and let rise again until doubled in size.

Preheat the oven to 400 degrees.

Bake rolls for 15 to 20 minutes. Serve hot.

GENEVA C. BELL
Chicago, Illinois
Chicago Alumnae Chapter

PERFECTLY EASY DINNER ROLLS

MAKES 2 DOZEN

IF YOU HAVE a family like mine that enjoys food made from scratch, they'll love these rolls. I have had people ask me to make them for Thanksgiving, Christmas, or even when they just had a hankering for them. Folks believe that I spend a lot of time making these, but I don't. When the recipe said "perfectly easy," it meant it. So here's to good eats!

1 cup warm water or milk (105 to 115 degrees)

2 (0.25-ounce) packets active dry yeast

½ cup melted butter

½ cup sugar

3 large eggs

1 teaspoon salt

4½ cups all-purpose flour

Additional melted butter (optional)

Combine the warm water or milk and yeast in a large bowl. Let the mixture stand until the yeast is foamy, about 5 minutes. Stir in the butter, sugar, eggs, and salt. Beat in the flour, 1 cup at a time, until the dough is too stiff to mix (you may not need all the flour). Cover and refrigerate dough for 2 hours or up to 4 days.

Grease a 13-by-9-inch baking sheet. Turn the chilled dough out onto a lightly floured board. Divide the dough into 24 equal pieces. Roll each piece into a smooth round ball; place in even rows on the prepared baking sheet. Cover and let dough balls rise until doubled in volume, about 1 hour.

Preheat the oven to 375 degrees. Bake rolls for 15 to 20 minutes, or until they are golden brown. Brush warm rolls with melted butter, if desired. Break rolls apart to serve.

VICKI L. MORGAN
Pontiac, Michigan
Member-at-Large

DINNER ROLLS

MAKES 12 ROLLS

THIS RECIPE comes from my mother, Soror Barbara Anderson. She says the key is having the patience to let the dough rise fully each time.

2 cups milk
½ cup margarine
½ cup sugar
2 teaspoons salt
1 (0.25-ounce) packet active dry yeast
¼ cup lukewarm water
6 cups all-purpose flour
2 large eggs
Melted margarine or butter

Scald the milk (don't let it boil) in a large saucepan. Remove from the heat and add the ½ cup of margarine, the sugar, and salt. Stir and cool to lukewarm. Pour into a large bowl. Dissolve the yeast in the ¼ cup lukewarm water. Add to the milk mixture. Stir in 3 cups of the flour and blend vigorously until consistency is like cake batter but stringy (an electric mixer can be used).

Place a plate over the bowl and let mixture sit for about ½ hour in a warm place out of draft. It will become puffy. Stir it down. Beat in the eggs and the remaining 3 cups flour. Cover again and let rise until it doubles in bulk and collapses on touch.

Preheat the oven to 425 degrees.

Flour a board and roll the dough with a rolling pin; then use a round cookie cutter to cut rolls into circles. Add a little melted butter to muffin tins; fold each circle over to shape rolls. Place in muffin tins. Let rise again until doubled in bulk. Bake for 10 minutes.

ROSANNE ANDERSON SMITH
Knoxville, Tennessee
Oak Ridge Alumnae Chapter

Homemade Biscuits, Peaches Style

MAKES 4–6 SERVINGS

When I was a teenager, we lived next door to a family with eight or nine children. The mother made biscuits that melted not only in your mouth but also in your hand. When my mother wasn't looking, I would work out a deal with the oldest girl to trade my well-balanced meal for a plate of her mom's biscuits and Louisiana syrup with butter mixed in it. Many years later, I was invited to my future husband's home for dinner. After tasting his mother's biscuits, I knew I was going to marry that boy . . . and his mother! Now I don't have to trade away my food; she taught me how to make my own delicious biscuits.

2 cups all-purpose flour

1 tablespoon baking powder

1 teaspoon salt

1 teaspoon sugar

$^1/_3$ cup plus 1 tablespoon vegetable shortening

1 cup buttermilk

1 cup melted bacon fat

Homemade Biscuits, Peaches Style

Sift all the dry ingredients a couple of times in a large bowl. Using your hands, mix the shortening with the dry ingredients until crumbly (don't worry about a few large pieces). Add the buttermilk, a little at a time, mixing with a fork until the mixture is moist. Flour a work surface and your hands. Knead the dough 10 times (no more). Pat the dough into a 9- to 9½-inch round. Use a biscuit or cookie cutter to cut the biscuits.

Completely saturate each biscuit with the bacon fat. Place the biscuits very close together around the outside of a 9-inch cake pan (or a 9-inch cast-iron skillet). Take the last scraps and mold into a big biscuit, saturate, and place in the center. This is the hoe-cake.

Place the biscuits in a cold oven. Set to 425 degrees. Watch closely after 10 minutes. When biscuits start to brown, turn the oven to broil but do not move them. Watch until the biscuits are a desired brownness; then remove them from the oven. Wrap in a big clean towel to keep them warm and moist until served.

Do not cook biscuits until everything else is prepared. Serve piping hot.

VASA "PEACHES" SELLERS
Golden, Colorado
Denver Alumnae Chapter

AFTER GRADUATING from Oberlin College in 1884, honorary soror Mary Church taught at a Black secondary school in Washington, D.C., and at Wilberforce College in Ohio before traveling and studying for two years in Europe. Upon her return, she met and married Robert Heberton Terrell, an attorney who later became the first Black municipal court judge in Washington.

An active member of the National American Woman Suffrage Association, she was particularly concerned about ensuring that the organization continued to fight for Black women's suffrage. She was a co-founder of the Federation of Afro-American Women and in 1896 became the first president of the newly formed National Association of Colored Women. When she was invited to speak at the Berlin International Congress of Women in 1904, she was the only Black woman in attendance and, determined to make a good impression, created a sensation by delivering her speech in German, French, and English.

In 1909 she joined with Mary White Ovington to form the National Association for the Advancement of Colored People and as recently as the early 1950s was actively involved in the struggle to desegregate public eating places in Washington, D.C. Her autobiography, *A Colored Woman in a White World,* was published in 1940. She died in Annapolis, Maryland, at the age of ninety, in 1954.

POTATO MONKEY BREAD

MAKES 12–15 SERVINGS

2 medium potatoes, scrubbed
½ cup vegetable shortening
¼ cup butter
½ cup sugar
1 teaspoon salt
2 large eggs
1 (0.25-ounce) packet quick-rise dry yeast
½ cup potato water
6 cups all-purpose flour, sifted twice
¾ cup lukewarm milk
Melted butter

Place the potatoes in a medium saucepan; cover with water and boil until soft; drain, reserving ½ cup of the potato water. Cool, peel, and mash the potatoes to make 1 cup.

Cream the vegetable shortening and the butter together in a large bowl until thoroughly mixed. Add the sugar and salt, creaming until well blended. Add the 1 cup mashed potatoes and mix well. Add the eggs, mixing well.

Dissolve the yeast in the ½ cup warm potato water. Blend with the potato mixture, along with 1 cup flour (use wooden spoons rather than an electric mixer at this point).

Add the remaining 5 cups flour, 1 cup at a time, alternating with the warm milk.

Knead the dough until smooth. Place in a lightly greased mixing bowl. Cover with a clean towel. Let rise until light and doubled in bulk.

Preheat the oven to 400 degrees.

Divide the dough in half and roll on a lightly floured bread board to about ¼ inch thick. Cut with a diamond, crescent, or round biscuit cutter. Dip each piece in melted butter. Lay pieces in a 12-cup aluminum tube pan with a large center opening until pan is half full. Bake for 30 minutes.

BEULAH R. STAMPS
Chicago, Illinois
Chicago Alumnae Chapter

SIMPLE MONKEY BREAD

MAKES 8–10 SERVINGS

THIS IS A Christmas-morning tradition that my family has observed for more than twenty-five years. It is our custom to have the youngest child wake everyone up. We go to the tree and open our presents, then I go to the kitchen and begin to prepare the traditional monkey bread.

1½ cups chopped pecans
1½ cups sugar
4 teaspoons ground cinnamon, or more to taste
3 (10-count) cans buttermilk biscuits
½ cup butter, melted

Preheat the oven to 350 degrees. Grease a 12-cup Bundt pan.

Place the chopped pecans in the bottom of the prepared pan.

Mix the sugar and cinnamon together in a medium bowl. Quarter the biscuits with scissors and roll them in the sugar/cinnamon mixture. Layer the coated biscuit quarters evenly in the pan. Combine the melted butter and the remaining sugar/cinnamon mixture. Pour the mixture over the layered biscuits.

Bake for 35 to 40 minutes. Remove from the oven and invert the baked bread on a platter so that the pecans are on top.

BEVERLY EVANS SMITH
Marietta, Georgia
Chair, Long-Range Planning Committee
Marietta-Roswell Alumnae Chapter

MAMA'S MONKEY BREAD

MAKES 6–8 SERVINGS

MY SIBLINGS and I enjoyed Mama's bread from childhood. We now make it for friends and relatives to share around the table.

2 (0.25-ounce) packets active dry yeast
¼ cup warm water
1 cup butter
1 cup milk
2 large eggs
½ cup sugar
½ teaspoon salt
3 cups all-purpose flour
Melted butter

Dissolve the yeast in the warm water. Heat the butter and milk together in a saucepan until lukewarm. Set aside to cool.

Cream the eggs and sugar in a large bowl. Add the cooled milk mixture. Add the salt and 1½ cups of the flour. Stir in the dissolved yeast. Let the mixture rise for 30 minutes.

Knead in the remaining 1½ cups flour. Cover bowl with a damp cloth, and refrigerate until the dough doubles in bulk.

Remove the dough from the refrigerator. Use enough extra flour for easy handling and knead the dough well, about 10 minutes. Roll out and cut with a biscuit cutter. Dip each piece in melted butter. Place in a buttered Bundt pan until half full. Cover pan with a damp cloth and let dough rise again.

Preheat the oven to 325 degrees.

Bake for 30 minutes, then raise the temperature to 350 degrees and bake for an additional 15 minutes. Eat hot, with food or by itself. Just pull the individual rolls off the bread and enjoy!

MERLE ALLEN FRANKLIN
Atlanta, Georgia
Atlanta Suburban Alumnae Chapter

ICE BOX ROLLS

MAKES 3 DOZEN ROLLS

THIS RECIPE was given to our mother, Clara Gipson, to prepare for a special dinner party in 1946. The rolls have been served at every special family occasion ever since.

2 cups hot water

½ cup sugar

½ cup butter

3 or 4 drops yellow food coloring

1 (0.25-ounce) packet active dry yeast

½ cup lukewarm water

1 teaspoon salt

2 teaspoons baking powder

6–7 cups all-purpose flour

Pour the hot water over the sugar and butter in a large bowl; stir until well blended. Add yellow food coloring and cool.

Dissolve the dry yeast in the lukewarm water; mix well and add the salt and baking powder. Add the sugar/butter mixture. Mix in 6 cups of flour; add more if necessary to make a stiff dough.

Let rise; then flour hands well and shape dough into golf-ball-size rolls.

Preheat the oven to 350 degrees.

Bake rolls on a greased baking sheet until an even brown, about 15 to 20 minutes. (Rolls may also be baked in greased muffin tins.)

LINDA GIPSON HITCHENS
PAMELA C. GIPSON
Alexandria, Virginia
Northern Virginia Alumnae Chapter

FESTIVALS

MAKES 8

ON SUNDAYS, my Jamaican mother would make special dishes from her country of birth. When my sister was about three years old, she asked Mother what she was making. When she told her Festivals, my sister ran around the house singing, "We're gonna have Festivals." My father played a Bob Marley record and started to dance with us and our mother. The Festivals almost burned, but it was a memorable family day.

Ice Box Rolls

1½ cups all-purpose flour
Pinch of ground allspice
½ teaspoon salt
¾ teaspoon baking powder
3 tablespoons cornmeal
2½ tablespoons brown sugar
¼ teaspoon rose water
½ teaspoon vanilla extract
¾ cup water
3 tablespoons all-purpose flour mixed with
   1 tablespoon cornmeal
Oil for frying

Sift the first 4 ingredients into a large bowl. Add the cornmeal and brown sugar. Add the rose water and vanilla to the water in a small bowl. Add the water mixture to the dry ingredients, binding to form a soft dough. Knead lightly. Cover and let rise for 30 minutes.

Divide the dough into eight portions. With your hands well floured, knead each portion lightly and then pull to form a 6-by-1½-inch length that's about ⅛ inch thick. Dip each festival into the flour/cornmeal mixture.

Heat the oil and fry the festivals in a large skillet until golden brown. Pierce with a fork while turning. Serve hot.

COOK'S TIP | *Toss in sifted powdered sugar for a sweeter taste.*

TRACIE J. WARD
Chicago, Illinois
Chicago Alumnae Chapter

TEA FOR MORE THAN TWO

(DELTEEN TEA)

Jean's Scones   (page 182)

Butter and Assorted Jams

Old-Fashioned Tea Cakes   (page 261)

Sand Tarts   (page 263)

Carolyn's Cream Cheese Squares   (page 258)

Red Velvet Cake   (page 210)

Long-Stemmed Strawberries

Assorted Teas and Coffee

Some may prefer coffee but, served with these sweet treats, this late-afternoon repast is still "tea." In these over-scheduled times, such an elegant break from the daily tasks of life is a pleasure we all should experience at least once in a while.

TO PREPARE:

- Just when you begin preparing most of these dainty baked goods is really a matter of choice. All but the scones can be made at least a day in advance and either refrigerated (the cream cheese squares) or stored airtight at room temperature.

- Give yourself and your guests a real treat by baking the scones at the last minute and serving them still warm, with plenty of butter and jam.

A DELTEEN TEA

Deltas hold teas for teens as part of the Delteen program to introduce young women to the fine art of social etiquette. The young ladies are exposed to social situations in which they are expected to "dress up," engage in polite conversation, and, in general, "be charming and personable." We sometimes ask the teens to wear a hat, a corsage, or gloves in order to emphasize the fact that this is, indeed, a special—and memorable—occasion. We also sometimes ask members to bring special tea services or cups and saucers to provide a topic of conversation that can also serve as a teaching tool.

Whatever the occasion for your tea, taking photos to put in a memory book or to send to the guests is always a way to keep the memory alive. Make it an elegant afternoon by setting your table with a lace or damask cloth, getting out the "good" flatware and your best china, and polishing up your silver trays. A beautiful floral arrangement might reflect the season or the theme of the event. The centerpiece will also reflect the thought and care you've put into preparing the food and the proper ambience.

Cinnamon Rolls

MAKES 30–36 ROLLS

THIS IS a variation on Ice Box Rolls, page 176.

2 cups hot water

2½ cups sugar

½ cup butter

2 or 3 drops yellow food coloring

1 (0.25-ounce) packet active dry yeast

½ cup lukewarm water

1 teaspoon salt

2 teaspoons baking powder

6–7 cups all-purpose flour

½ cup melted butter

4 tablespoons ground cinnamon

1 cup chopped nuts, optional

Icing (see following recipe)

Pour hot water over ½ cup of the sugar and butter in a large bowl; stir well. Add yellow food coloring and cool.

Dissolve the yeast in the lukewam water; mix well and add the salt and baking powder. Add the sugar/butter mixture. Mix in 6 cups of flour; add more if necessary to make a stiff dough.

Let rise, then roll dough out to ½ inch thick on a floured board. Brush with the melted butter. Mix the cinnamon and remaining 2 cups of sugar in a medium bowl. Sprinkle over the butter. Sprinkle with chopped nuts, if desired.

With floured hands, roll up the dough from the long side. Cut into rolls. Let rise again on a greased baking sheet or in greased cake pans.

Preheat the oven to 350 degrees.

Bake the rolls for 25 to 30 minutes or until golden brown.

After the rolls have cooled, frost with Icing.

ICING

1 (16-ounce) box powdered sugar, sifted

½ cup margarine, softened

½ teaspoon salt

1 teaspoon vanilla extract

Combine all the icing ingredients in a small bowl. Mix well.

LINDA GIPSON HITCHENS
PAMELA C. GIPSON
Alexandria, Virginia
Northern Virginia Alumnae Chapter

Christmas Morning Sticky Buns

MAKES ABOUT 15 ROLLS

I'VE ALWAYS enjoyed baking and began to prepare this recipe when I was ten years old. It's now become part of our family's Christmas tradition, and I still make them each Christmas morning.

3–4 cups all-purpose flour

⅓ cup plus 2 tablespoons granulated sugar

1 teaspoon salt

2 (0.25-ounce) packets quick-rise dry yeast

1 cup very warm milk

⅓ cup plus 3 tablespoons butter or margarine, softened

1 large egg

1 cup packed plus 2 tablespoons light brown sugar

½ cup butter or margarine

¼ cup dark corn syrup

1 cup pecan halves

1 teaspoon ground cinnamon

Combine 2 cups of the flour, ⅓ cup of the granulated sugar, the salt, and the yeast in a large bowl. Add the warm milk, ⅓ cup of the softened butter, and the egg. Beat the mixture on low speed for 1 minute, scraping the sides of the bowl frequently. Beat on medium speed for 1 minute longer, again scraping the sides of the bowl, then stir in enough of the remaining flour (usually ¾ to 1 cup) to form a dough that's easy to handle.

Turn the dough onto a lightly floured surface and knead for 5 minutes, until smooth and elastic. Place in a greased bowl and turn greased side up. Cover and set aside to rise in a warm place until doubled in bulk, about 1½ hours.

Combine 1 cup of the brown sugar and the ½ cup of butter in a medium saucepan and bring to a boil over medium-low heat, stirring continuously. Remove from the heat, stir in the corn syrup, and pour into an ungreased 13-by-9-inch baking pan. Sprinkle with the pecan halves.

Punch down the dough, turn it out onto a floured surface, and flatten it with a rolling pin into a 15-by-10-inch rectangle. Spread the dough with the remaining 3 tablespoons of softened butter. In a small bowl, combine the remaining 2 tablespoons of granulated sugar, the remaining 2 tablespoons of brown sugar, and the cinnamon. Sprinkle the mixture evenly over the butter. Roll up the dough tightly, beginning on a long side, and pinch the edges to seal the roll. Stretch and shape the roll until it's even along its length. Cut into 15 (1-inch) slices and place them, slightly apart, in the pan with the corn syrup mixture. Set the pan aside and let the rolls rise in a warm place for about 30 minutes or until doubled in bulk.

While the rolls are rising, preheat the oven to 350 degrees.

Bake the rolls for 30 to 35 minutes, until golden brown. Immediately invert the pan onto a heatproof tray or plate and let the caramel drizzle over the rolls.

COOK'S TIP | *If you like, you can also add a couple of tablespoons of chopped pecans to the cinnamon-and-sugar mixture before sprinkling it on the dough.*

KEYANA MITCHELL
Decatur, Georgia
Member-at-Large

JEAN'S SCONES

MAKES 12 SCONES

THESE SCONES are soft, moist, and chewy; they don't get hard and are even good cold.

2 cups all-purpose flour
1 cup whole-wheat flour
¾ cup packed brown sugar
2 tablespoons baking powder
½ teaspoon baking soda
¾ cup cold butter, cut into pieces
1 cup buttermilk
½ cup mixed blueberries, raisins, nuts, and diced, steamed apples (optional)

Preheat the oven to 400 degrees.

Mix the flours, brown sugar, baking powder, and baking soda in a large bowl. Cut in the butter until the mixture resembles coarse crumbs.

Jean's Scones

Stir in the buttermilk until a soft dough forms. Add the fruit mixture, if desired. Turn onto a floured board and knead gently until no longer sticky.

Divide dough in half; gently roll out each half to ½-inch thickness. Or cut each half into a 10-inch circle, ½ inch thick.

Place on a greased baking sheet. Bake 15 minutes or until golden brown.

VALERIE FLEMING GOINGS
Long Beach, California
Rolling Hills–Palos Verdes Alumnae Chapter

COFFEE CAKE

MAKES 12–16 SERVINGS

MY MOTHER, Loretta Woods, got this recipe from a co-worker in the 1970s, long before Betty Crocker and Duncan Hines began putting instant pudding in boxed cake mixes.

1 (18.25-ounce) package yellow cake mix
1 (3.4-ounce) box instant vanilla pudding mix
4 large eggs
¾ cup water
¾ cup cooking oil
1 teaspoon vanilla extract
1 teaspoon butter-flavored extract
¼ cup sugar
1 teaspoon ground cinnamon
¼ cup ground pecans
Glaze (see following recipe)

Preheat the oven to 350 degrees.

Combine the cake mix and the next 6 ingredients in a large bowl; beat 8 minutes. Pour half the batter into a 12-cup tube pan. Combine the sugar, cinnamon, and pecans in a small bowl. Add half the nut mixture to the batter in the pan, and swirl it in with a knife. Add the rest of the batter and sprinkle the remaining nut mixture over the top.

Bake 50 to 55 minutes or until a toothpick inserted in the center comes out clean. Remove from the oven. Cool slightly, then remove from the pan. Pour the Glaze over the cake while it's still warm. Serve warm or cooled.

GLAZE
½ cup sifted powdered sugar
1 teaspoon butter-flavored extract
Milk

Combine the sugar and flavoring. Gradually add enough milk to make a thin mixture.

JARITA MOORE
Schaumburg, Illinois
Schaumburg–Hoffman Estates Alumnae Chapter

SWEET POTATO BREAD

MAKES 8 SERVINGS

DURING THE FALL when I was a little girl, my grandmother kept crates full of sweet potatoes in her house. We made them in various ways, such as fried, stewed, baked, and in pies. However, this was my favorite.

1 tablespoon reduced-fat margarine
1 tablespoon sugar
1 cup boiled, mashed sweet potatoes
1½ cups all-purpose flour
1 teaspoon ground cinnamon
1 teaspoon grated nutmeg
1 teaspoon baking soda
2 teaspoons vanilla extract
3 large egg whites

Preheat oven to 350 degrees.

Beat the margarine, sugar, and mashed sweet potatoes together in a medium bowl until light and fluffy. Add the flour, cinnamon, nutmeg, baking soda, and vanilla. Stir in the egg whites and mix well. Pour the batter into an 8-by-4-inch nonstick loaf pan. Let set 10 minutes in a warm place (about 85 degrees). Bake 50 to 60 minutes or until the top is brown and the center is firm. Remove from pan to cool on a wire rack. Serve warm with sweet butter or honey.

COOK'S TIP | *If desired, a deeper shade of orange can be obtained by adding ½ teaspoon of orange food coloring to the batter before baking.*

GLORIA FREEMAN BENNETT
Roseboro, North Carolina
Fort Bragg Area Alumnae Chapter

BANANA BREAD

MAKES 1 LOAF

I BEGAN baking this bread about twenty years ago to help raise money for my church youth group, and it has been a popular item at bake sales ever since. After I pledged the alumnae chapter in Okaloosa County in 1992, I began taking my banana bread to share with sorors after step practice or informal meetings.

In 1997, our Panama City Alumnae Chapter hosted the State Cluster Meeting for Florida and the Bahamas. Another Soror, Lori Robinson, and I baked four hundred small loaves of banana bread to place in souvenir bags as sorors checked in for the meeting. The bread was a welcome treat to our weary, jet-lagged sorors.

Since that time, my bread recipe has appeared at sorority meetings for refreshment and been given as a gift to new sorors in the area.

1 cup butter or margarine, softened

1 cup sugar

2 eggs, lightly beaten

3 ripe bananas, mashed

2 cups all-purpose flour

1 teaspoon baking soda

¼ teaspoon salt

½ cup nuts and / or chocolate chips (optional)

Preheat the oven to 325 degrees.

In a large bowl, cream the margarine and sugar. Add the eggs and mashed bananas; stir only enough to blend. Add the flour, baking soda, and salt. Do not overstir. Add nuts or chocolate chips, if desired. Pour into a lightly greased, lightly floured 9-by-5-inch loaf pan. Bake for 60 to 70 minutes or until a tooth-pick inserted comes out clean. Cool for 10 minutes; turn out of pan onto a rack to cool completely.

CHARLOTTE Y. MARSHALL
Lynn Haven, Florida
Panama City Alumnae Chapter

ZUCCHINI BREAD

MAKES 2 LOAVES (24 SLICES)

ONE OF MY favorite childhood memories is Grandma Amy mixing up this bread while making sure that I did not see the inclusion of the secret ingredient, zucchini. She knew I never would have eaten it if I had known that dark green veggie was included. Imagine my delight when I tricked my nephew the same way. His positive reaction confirmed that I had hit the mark in re-creating my grandma's wonderful bread.

3 cups all-purpose flour

¼ teaspoon baking powder

1 teaspoon baking soda

1 teaspoon salt

3 teaspoons ground cinnamon

½ teaspoon freshly grated nutmeg

3 large eggs

1½ cups sugar

2 cups grated zucchini

2 teaspoons vanilla extract

1 teaspoon butter-flavored extract

1 cup golden raisins

1 cup chopped walnuts

½ cup vegetable oil

½ cup water

Preheat the oven to 350 degrees. Lightly spray or grease two 9-by-5-inch loaf pans.

In a large bowl, sift together the flour, baking powder, baking soda, salt, cinnamon, and nutmeg; set aside.

In another large bowl, beat the eggs. Add the sugar, zucchini, vanilla and butter-flavored extracts, the raisins, walnuts, oil, and water; mix well.

Add the flour mixture to the egg mixture and mix until just moistened.

Pour half the batter into each loaf pan. Bake for 1 hour.

Let cool on wire racks for 30 minutes; remove from pans and cool completely.

KIMBERLY POWELL
Centreville, Virginia
Fairfax County Alumnae Chapter

BLUEBERRY-ORANGE BREAD

MAKES 1 LOAF

2 cups all-purpose flour

1 teaspoon baking powder

½ teaspoon salt

¼ teaspoon baking soda

¼ cup boiling water

2 tablespoons butter, cut into pieces

1 large egg, slightly beaten

1 cup sugar

½ cup orange juice

1 cup fresh blueberries

Preheat the oven to 350 degrees. Grease the bottom and ½ inch up sides of an 8-by-4-inch loaf pan; set aside.

In a large bowl, combine the flour, baking powder, salt, and baking soda. Make a well in the center of the flour mixture; set aside. In a small bowl, stir together the boiling water and butter until the butter has melted.

In a medium bowl, combine the egg, sugar, and orange juice. Stir in the butter mixture. Then add the egg mixture to the flour mixture, stirring just until moistened. Fold in the blueberries. Spoon the batter into the prepared pan.

Bake for about 1 hour or until a wooden toothpick inserted near center comes out clean. Cool in the pan on a wire rack for 10 minutes. Remove the loaf from the pan. Cool completely on wire rack. Wrap in foil and store overnight for easier slicing.

GLORIA LEE
Palos Verdes Estate, California
Rolling Hills–Palos Verdes Alumnae Chapter

SISTER VEE'S GINGERBREAD WAFFLES

MAKES 8–10 SERVINGS

ON ONE of Morgan State University's choir tours, we stopped for breakfast somewhere in Illinois, where I was introduced to gingerbread pancakes for the first time. I adapted that recipe for waffles. ⎯

2 cups all-purpose flour

2 tablespoons sugar

1 tablespoon baking powder

1 cup apple butter

1¼ cups 2% milk

¼ teaspoon salt

½ teaspoon ground cinnamon

½ teaspoon ground ginger

½ teaspoon ground nutmeg

6 tablespoons vegetable oil

2 large eggs

Combine all the ingredients in a large bowl until well blended and smooth. Let the batter sit 5 minutes. Preheat the waffle maker. Choose a lighter setting because the batter is thicker than for plain waffles. Pour the batter onto the grid, spreading evenly. Cook according to waffle-maker directions.

COOK'S TIP | *This recipe works for Belgian waffles and nonstick waffle irons as well.*

VALERIE A. FOSTER
Washington, D.C.
Member, National Commission on Arts and Letters
Washington, D.C., Alumnae Chapter

CORNY CORA LEE CAKES

MAKES 10–12 SMALL SERVINGS

THIS RECIPE is named for my mother, Cora Lee, who used to make my sister and me pancakes for breakfast. My mom used to tell corny jokes, and one day, as a joke, she decided to put cream-style corn in the pancakes. Much to her surprise, they were a hit. Thirty-two years later I carry on the tradition. The name may be corny, but the pancakes are no joke.

1 cup self-rising flour

1 large egg

2 tablespoons vegetable shortening, melted

⅓ cup milk

1 teaspoon vanilla extract

1 (8½-ounce) can cream-style corn

Blend together the flour, egg, shortening, milk, and vanilla in a large bowl. Add the cream-style corn a little at a time, beating after each addition until the batter is as thin or as thick as you desire. Place heaping tablespoonfuls on a hot griddle or skillet. Turn when bubbles appear and edges begin to dry.

DANYELL P. SMITH
Owings Mills, Maryland
Baltimore County Alumnae Chapter

BREAKFAST SAUSAGE CASSEROLE

MAKES 10–12 SERVINGS

½ cup butter

1 pound ground beef, turkey, or pork breakfast
sausage

6–8 slices white bread (day-old is best), cut
into cubes

1 tablespoon each of dried dill, basil, and thyme

¾ cup shredded Cheddar cheese

6 large eggs

2 cups milk

Preheat the oven to 350 degrees.

Melt the butter in a small saucepan. Pour into a
13-by-9-inch baking pan.

Brown the sausage in a medium skillet, breaking up
the large pieces; drain and set aside.

In the baking pan, layer half the bread, herbs, and
cheese (layer will be thin and sparse). Layer the remaining bread, herbs, and cheese. Sprinkle with
the cooked sausage over top.

Combine the eggs and milk in a small bowl. Beat
well with a fork. Pour over the ingredients in the
baking pan. Bake for 30 minutes or until set.

TANYA W. WATSON
Akron, Ohio
Akron Alumnae Chapter

DELTA OF DISTINCTION
Osceola McCarthy Adams

A CO-FOUNDER of
Delta Sigma Theta
Sorority, Inc., Osceola
McCarthy Adams
received her under-
graduate degree from
Howard University,
where she was a mem-
ber of the Howard
Players and studied under the first African-
American Rhodes Scholar, Alain Locke, as
well as the renowned mathematician Kelly
Miller. She then went on to earn a master's
degree in drama from New York University.

Ms. McCarthy made her Broadway debut in
1934, appearing in Elmer Rice's *Between Two
Worlds,* and went on to enjoy a long and successful acting career on stage and television
that lasted well into the 1960s. In addition,
she was a pioneering director who fought re-
lentlessly to end racial barriers. In the 1940s
she worked with the American Negro Theatre,
directing plays and teaching Harry Belafonte,
Sidney Poitier, and Ossie Davis, among others. From 1946 to 1956 she held the position
of resident director at the Putnam County
Playhouse in Mahopac, New York.

Soror McCarthy was married to Dr. Numa
P. G. Adams, the first dean of the Howard
University Medical School, and together they
had one son. She died in 1983 at the age of
ninety-three.

Breakfast Sausage Casserole (page 187)

Country Breakfast Pie (page 190)

Homemade Biscuits,
Peaches Style (page 172)

Butter and Jam

Coffee Cake (page 182)

THIS HEARTY BREAKFAST fare will keep everyone pleasantly satisfied throughout the day. Invite a group of friends on a mid-Sunday morning and enjoy one another's company throughout the afternoon.

TO PREPARE:

- Make the coffee cake the night before and try not to eat it right away.

- First thing in the morning, prepare the pie and get it baking.

- When the pie goes into the oven, set up the casserole to go in thirty minutes later.

- While the pie and casserole are baking, prepare the biscuit dough. As soon as they come out, put in the biscuits, turn up the heat, and watch until they're done. It doesn't take long.

BREAKFAST WITH A SONG AND A PRAYER

A prayer breakfast is a time for people to seek a spiritual connection to the mission of our organization and to consider where they believe their own contributions might lie. There is generally a spiritual speaker present to deliver a sermon or engage in a dialogue during which each member is given the opportunity to speak from her heart. Music and the singing of traditional Delta songs are also very much a part of this event.

A leisurely breakfast on a day free from other obligations, whether or not it involves a spiritual component, can be a time to relax and reflect, and sharing that meal with close friends and loved ones can help us to reconnect with all the loving relationships we might take for granted as we go about our weekly business.

BREAKFAST CASSEROLE

MAKES 4–6 SERVINGS

1 pound hot or mild pork sausage

¼–½ cup small noodles

¼–½ cup sharp Cheddar cheese

1 (10¾-ounce) can cream of chicken soup

1 (2-ounce) jar pimientos, drained

½ cup milk

Black pepper, to taste

3 tablespoons chopped green bell pepper

Buttered bread crumbs

Preheat the oven to 350 degrees.

Fry the sausage in a medium skillet and drain. Boil the noodles for 4 to 6 minutes; drain. Mix all the ingredients, except the bread crumbs, together in a large bowl. Pour into a 2-quart baking dish. Sprinkle with bread crumbs. Bake for 25 minutes.

DANETTE CARR
Oklahoma City, Oklahoma
Oklahoma City Alumnae Chapter

COUNTRY BREAKFAST PIE

MAKES 20 SERVINGS

2½ cups cooked ground turkey, drained

1 cup cooked crumbled turkey bacon

1 cup cooked diced ham

1½ cups uncooked hash browns

1 cup shredded Cheddar cheese

1 cup shredded Swiss cheese

5 eggs, lightly beaten

4–4½ cups evaporated skimmed milk

½ cup chopped green bell pepper

½ cup chopped red bell pepper

3 tablespoons chopped onion

2 teaspoons ground black pepper

4 (9-inch) unbaked deep-dish pie shells

Preheat the oven to 350 degrees.

Combine the turkey, turkey bacon, ham, hash browns, and cheeses in a large mixing bowl. Mix the eggs and milk together in a medium bowl; beat well. Add the peppers, onion, and black pepper; mix well. Pour about 2 cups of the meat mixture into each pie shell; then pour 1 cup of the milk mixture over the meat in the pie shells. Add more milk to each for a moister pie. Bake for 1 hour.

DEBBIE W. TIJANI
Upper Marlboro, Maryland
Potomac Valley Alumnae Chapter

QUICHE LAVITA

MAKES 8 SERVINGS

AS A CHILD, I'd watch Mama cook for our family of eight, not including extra relatives or anyone Daddy, the preacher man, brought home. Mama's cooking is legendary—cooking without a recipe in sight. She loaned me a cookbook as I began my trek toward legendary (or at least honorable mention) cooking status. Twenty years later it remains on loan. One day I ran across a Quiche Lorraine recipe and tried it. The problem was I hated making piecrust. In the late '80s Mama hipped me to piecrust sticks, which made it easier, but then I discovered refrigerated crusts, my friends for life. The spices for this quiche were carefully selected for their distinctive yet complementary nature. Caution: Real men do actually like this quiche.

1 (9-inch) refrigerated pie shell

1½ cups torn spinach, washed

Crumbled cooked bacon, to taste

Grated cheese of your choice, to taste

Chopped onion, to taste

¾ teaspoon seasoned salt

4 large eggs

2 cups whipping cream

¼ teaspoon garlic powder

½ teaspoon dried parsley flakes

½ teaspoon sugar

¼–½ teaspoon cayenne pepper

Preheat the oven to 425 degrees.

Lightly coat a pie plate with cooking spray. Unfold the slightly chilled pastry, place in the baking dish, and crimp the edges. Line the pastry with the spinach. Layer the bacon, cheese, and onion; sprinkle with the seasoned salt. Beat the eggs slightly in a medium bowl; beat in the cream and the remaining ingredients. Pour into the pan. Bake 15 minutes.

Reduce the oven temperature to 300 degrees and bake 30 minutes longer. Place aluminum foil around the edges and tented over the top, if necessary, during the last 10 to 12 minutes of baking. Remove from the oven, and let stand 10 minutes before cutting. Serve in wedges.

LAVITA ALSTON EMERSON
Seattle, Washington
Seattle Alumnae Chapter

BREAKFAST AT MIDNIGHT

(A RED-AND-WHITE MIDNIGHT BREAKFAST)

Garden Vegetable Quiche   (page 195)

Sausage and Potatoes   (page 194)

Mama's Monkey Bread   (page 175)

Blueberry-Orange Bread   (page 185)

Butter and Assorted Jams

WHAT MORE SATISFYING way to end a celebratory evening than with breakfast at midnight? This savory buffet will send guests home to bed prepared for very sweet dreams.

TO PREPARE:

❧ Make the Blueberry-Orange Bread the day before and wrap it in foil as the recipe directs.

❧ On the day of the event, make the quiche and store it in the refrigerator to be reheated before serving. Make the monkey bread and leave it in the pan to be reheated before serving. Have all the ingredients for the Sausage and Potatoes chopped and ready so that you can cook the dish quickly at the last minute.

A RED-AND-WHITE MIDNIGHT BREAKFAST

Dancing is the main activity at a Delta midnight breakfast, which may or may not be a black-tie event. We hold these breakfasts for various purposes, one of which might be to raise money for scholarships. There is generally a short formal program before the real festivities—dining and dancing—begin, and the room is always decorated to reflect the purpose of the evening. We might, for example, send the invitations to a scholarship fund-raiser in the form of a report card and repeat that same theme, as on the programs and other printed materials.

A midnight gathering is almost always the culmination of a celebratory evening, so why not take a tip from us and plan your own breakfast, Delta style. Whatever the theme or purpose of the evening, make it the theme of your after-party as well. The dishes on this menu are all meant to be partially or completely prepared in advance and set out on a buffet so that guests can help themselves and even go back for more.

Even when people are formally dressed, informality tends to take over as the clock strikes midnight. Buffet service will help to get everyone mingling as they step up to the table and fill their plates with traditional midnight breakfast fare.

SAUSAGE QUICHE

MAKES 4–6 SERVINGS

JUST IMAGINE a lazy Sunday morning . . . you can smell the sausage cooking and can't wait until all of the ingredients have been added and the quiche baked. In just a few minutes you have a complete breakfast. Just add fresh juice, fruit, and coffee or tea.

1 pound sausage, ground or cut into bite-size pieces
1 (9-inch) deep-dish pie shell
6–7 large eggs, lightly beaten
1 cup milk
About ½ cup shredded Cheddar cheese

Preheat the oven to 350 degrees.

Brown the sausage in a medium nonstick skillet; drain well and layer in the bottom of the pie shell. Whisk together the eggs and the milk in a medium bowl. Pour over the sausage. Top with shredded cheese.

Bake for approximately 40 to 60 minutes or until the egg mixture sets. Let stand for 5 minutes before serving.

PAULETTE C. WALKER
Valrico, Florida
Southern Regional Director
Tampa Alumnae Chapter

SAUSAGE AND POTATOES

MAKES 4 SERVINGS

SERVE HOT with breakfast bread and jam.

1 pound ground sausage meat
1 pound bacon, cut into 1-inch pieces
2½ cups diced small potatoes
1 cup chopped onion
1 cup chopped green onion with tops
1 cup chopped red bell pepper
1 cup chopped green bell pepper
Dash of salt and white pepper
6 large eggs, slightly beaten

Brown the sausage, bacon, and potatoes over high heat in a skillet; stir until done. Drain well and return the mixture to the pan. Add onion and peppers to the meat and potatoes; add salt and white pepper. Cook, stirring, for 3 minutes. Add the eggs, cooking and stirring until no longer runny.

HELEN J. NEWTON FOBI
Rolling Hills, California
Rolling Hills–Palos Verdes Alumnae Chapter

GARDEN VEGETABLE QUICHE

MAKES 6 SERVINGS

5 large eggs

2½ cups low-fat milk

⅓ cup baking mix (such as Bisquick)

1 (10-ounce) package frozen chopped spinach,
    thawed

½ onion, chopped

1 carrot, sliced

2 stalks celery, sliced

½ teaspoon salt

½ teaspoon white pepper

4 ounces sharp Cheddar cheese, shredded

4 ounces Swiss cheese, shredded

6 slices bacon, cooked and crumbled (optional)

¼ cup chopped fresh parsley

¼ cup grated Parmesan cheese

Preheat the oven to 375 degrees.

Whip the eggs and milk together in a blender. Whip in the baking mix. Microwave the spinach, onion, carrot, and celery 2 minutes or until crisp-tender; drain well. Combine the vegetables, salt, pepper, and batter in a large bowl. Stir in the Cheddar cheese, Swiss cheese, and bacon, if desired. Spoon into a greased 13-by-9-inch baking dish. Sprinkle with the parsley and the Parmesan cheese. Bake 20 to 30 minutes. Let cool 10 minutes before slicing and serving.

REGINA D. COOK
Columbia, Maryland
Columbia Alumnae Chapter

9

DESSERTS

Keeping the Connection

Dorothy I. Height
Shares a Memory

Soror Dorothy I. Height, the tenth national president (1947–1956) of Delta Sigma Theta Sorority, Inc., and chair and president emerita of the National Council of Negro Women, is a woman who knows how to enter a room. It was a cold December evening as she paused in the doorway of our national headquarters at 1707 New Hampshire Avenue, NW, Washington, D.C., wearing a beautifully cut red tweed suit beneath an elegant black mink coat, her face framed by a deep-ruby-red felt hat. Her posture was perfectly erect and proper, but her eyes twinkled with pleasure. After pausing for a moment to get her bearings amid the cameras, lights, cables, and sound equipment that seemed to have taken over the room, she moved with graceful purpose toward the handful of women who had gathered to eat a light repast before being interviewed on camera for a documentary in celebration of our ninetieth anniversary.

The film *90 Years Young: Delta Sigma Theta* would commemorate the sorority's history, but it would also serve to document the many ways in which we Black women are connected to our past and to one another by the cultural values and traditions we pass from one generation to the next. Not only women like Soror Height, whose accomplishments in the public arena have touched millions of lives, but every mother, grandmother, aunt, or mentor among us, has been responsible in some way for passing down a life lesson or womanly secret that then became a thread in the ever-evolving tapestry of Black women's history.

Throughout the meal that evening Soror Height kept her fellow diners enthralled, telling tales of her involvement with Delta Sigma Theta and what it had meant to her life. The sense of pride was audible in her voice as she spoke of the time, in August 1951, when she took the Executive Board on a tour of the United Nations, where they met members of the Department of Information and the Political and Economic Committee on the Rights of Women. And it was with equal pride that she remarked upon our having been given our NGO (Non-Government Organization) Special Consultative status with the UN in March of 2003. "How far we have come," she said then, "since the day I was installed as the tenth national president in the basement of a Baptist church."

Although she was quick to add that it had been a wonderful ceremony and one that would always hold a special place in her heart, she also said that she knew even then that Delta Sigma Theta would have to progress beyond a church basement and change the way we conducted our business if we were to make a significant difference in the world. The promise she made to herself in that moment was to dedicate her administration to putting in place a structure strong enough to support the powerful organization she knew Delta could and would become. "I knew," she said, "that we had to find ways to make Delta stand out on a daily basis. We had to take a hard look at ourselves and see how we could implement a stronger and better program, one that would allow us to work together, play together, and develop a unified vision for our organization."

One of her first initiatives was to appoint our first executive director, Soror Patricia Roberts Harris, in February of 1953. The next item on her agenda was to find a permanent home for our national headquarters. The consensus among the membership was that it should be located in Washington, D.C., which was, then as now, the hub of national legislative activity. A fund-raising campaign was instituted to finance the purchase of a suitable building, and Soror Height encouraged donations with an open letter in *The Delta Newsletter*. "Once in a lifetime you have the opportunity to be an angel for your sorority," she wrote. "It [the contribution] expresses your desire to join your sorors to pioneer in Delta's greatest venture. It does what only love can do—it exemplifies the true spirit of the Delta woman."

At dinner that night, Soror Height told the story of the day she went with Soror Patricia Roberts Harris and Soror Dorothy Penman Harrison, who was Delta's treasurer at the time, to complete the purchase of that first building at 1814 M Street, NW. "It was a Sunday, and the realtor seemed a bit skeptical of dealing with three Black women. In retrospect, I realize that, given how segregated the city was back then, it was probably his first experience of doing business with any Black person at all, much less three women. Nevertheless, he was most polite, and we looked around and decided the space would be suitable, so we asked him the price. He was still looking dubious, but he quoted the asking price and the amount that would be required for a down payment. When Soror Harrison asked if a check would be acceptable, he seemed to need a moment to comprehend the question before he was able to respond that, of course, a check would be just fine. 'Good,' Soror Harrison said without a moment's hesitation. 'We'll have it delivered to your office in the morning.' And with that business taken care of, the three of us walked off, leaving a very puzzled realtor standing in the doorway."

We were all still smiling at the significance of that small triumph as dessert was put before us while cameras and microphones were being set up. Taking a delicate forkful of her small sweet tart square, Soror Height looked up and said, "You know, I remember a story Soror Mary McLeod Bethune used to tell us about the time a dessert helped her out of a real financial difficulty. She always did enjoy both cooking and dining, and she used to say that it was while she was cooking that she came up with the solutions to some of her most difficult problems. It was as if keeping her hands busy mixing or peeling or chopping freed her mind to come up with the answers she needed. The particular time I'm thinking of, though, the answer turned out to be right there in the kitchen with her. Maybe she was peeling a sweet potato, maybe not, but she was thinking about schemes for raising money to finance her school, Bethune-Cookman College, when she came up with the idea of baking sweet potato pies with her students and selling them to help raise the funds she needed." Then she paused before adding, with a little smile, "I'm sure you know the story, and, as you also surely know, her fund-raising plan, simple as it was, proved to be a success."

As Soror Height pointed out, that story is certainly familiar to many Black women concerned with education; in fact, it's almost taken on the power of a myth. But hearing it told by someone who had actually known and worked with Soror Bethune was a forceful reminder of the many generations of Black women who have come up with ingenious plans, many of them involving the cooking and selling of food, to keep their dreams for their families and loved ones alive. The kitchen, in fact, is not only the place where we've found the means to support ourselves; it's also the place where we have traditionally shared support among ourselves—passing along not only recipes for special dishes but also recipes for survival and strategies for success. Before she left the table to go on camera, Soror Height graciously offered to put Soror Bethune's pie to work one more time by sending us the recipe, which you'll find on page 233.

Soror Height, by her very presence, reminds us of the sense of dignity that has kept us focused and forceful in even the most troublesome times. She is the living embodiment of our reasons for respecting the past while at the same time we forge an even better tomorrow. But she is also much more than a symbol; she is a woman very much like the rest of us, and when she spoke that evening about her friend and mentor, we heard the warmth in her voice and were able to conjure up the image of a time that was not only simpler but also more difficult than ours for Black women.

On that special evening, Soror Height provided those of us who were lucky enough to share her table with many worthwhile lessons, both spoken and unspoken. She demonstrated the value of remaining connected with and true to our cultural heritage. She showed us, without having to say a word, the importance of maintaining a standard of elegance and decorum. And she certainly proved the worth of being able to "entertain" by telling a good story.

PERFECT POUND CAKE

MAKES 15–18 SERVINGS

I RECEIVED this recipe from one of my girlfriends after tasting it at a social gathering. I made it for Homecoming at my grandmother's church, and everyone kept telling me how good it was. My grandmother, who hardly ever eats sweets, asked me to wrap two pieces for her to take home!

1½ cups butter or margarine

3 cups sugar

5 large eggs

1 cup lukewarm milk

2 teaspoons vanilla extract

1 teaspoon lemon extract

3 cups sifted all-purpose flour

Preheat the oven to 325 degrees. Grease and flour a 12-cup tube pan or two 9-by-5-inch loaf pans.

Cream the butter and sugar thoroughly in a large bowl with an electric mixer. Add the eggs, one at a time, beating well after each addition.

Mix the milk and the extracts in a small bowl. Fold the flour into the creamed mixture, alternately with the milk mixture. Pour into the prepared pan and bake 1 hour to 1 hour 20 minutes or until the cake tests done when a toothpick is inserted in the middle. Remove from the oven and cool on a wire rack. Remove from the pan when cool.

CAROLYN C. JOHNSON
Warsaw, Virginia
Williamsburg Alumnae Chapter

SOUR CREAM POUND CAKE

MAKES 15–18 SERVINGS

1 cup butter

3 cups sugar

6 large eggs

3 cups all-purpose flour

¼ teaspoon baking soda

Pinch of salt

1 cup sour cream

1 teaspoon vanilla extract

1 teaspoon lemon extract or rum extract

Preheat the oven to 325 degrees. Generously grease and flour a 12-cup tube pan.

Cream the butter and sugar together in a large bowl until light and fluffy. Add the eggs, one at a time, and blend after each addition. After the eggs have been added, beat again until light and fluffy. Sift together the flour, baking soda, and salt. Add the flour mixture to the butter and egg mixture, beating constantly. Blend in the sour cream, adding the vanilla and lemon extracts, one at a time.

Turn the batter into the prepared pan. Bake 70 to 80 minutes or until a toothpick inserted in the center comes out clean. Cool 5 minutes before removing from pan.

COOK'S TIP | *Add a glaze of sifted powdered sugar, milk, and vanilla, if desired.*

EMMA B. KING
Durham, North Carolina
Durham Alumnae Chapter

CHOCOLATE–SOUR CREAM POUND CAKE

MAKES 15–18 SERVINGS

1 cup butter, softened
2 cups granulated sugar
1 cup firmly packed brown sugar
6 large eggs
2½ cups all-purpose flour
¼ teaspoon baking soda
½ cup unsweetened cocoa powder
1 (8-ounce) container sour cream
2 teaspoons vanilla extract
Sifted powdered sugar (optional)

Preheat the oven to 325 degrees. Grease and flour a 12-cup Bundt pan.

Beat the butter with an electric mixer at medium speed about 2 minutes or until soft and creamy. Gradually add the sugars, beating on medium speed 5 to 7 minutes. Add the eggs, one at a time, beating just until the yellow disappears. Combine the flour, baking soda, and cocoa; add to the creamed mixture alternately with the sour cream, beginning and ending with the flour mixture. Stir in the vanilla.

Pour the batter into the prepared pan. Bake 1 hour and 20 minutes or until a toothpick inserted in the center comes out clean. Cool in the pan on a wire rack 10 to 15 minutes. Remove from the pan and cool completely. Sprinkle with the sifted powdered sugar, if desired.

NANCY PITTMAN
Chicago, Illinois
Chicago Alumnae Chapter

DELTA OF DISTINCTION
Soror Mary McLeod Bethune

THE FIFTEENTH of seventeen children born to former slaves in 1875, honorary Delta Mary McLeod Bethune was a founder and the first president of the National Council of Negro Women.

Unable to receive any formal education until the age of eleven when a school finally opened five miles from her home, Soror Bethune saw education as being key to improving the lives of Blacks. In 1904, with virtually no money, she founded the Daytona Educational and Industrial Training School for girls in Daytona Beach, Florida. The original student body, consisting of five small girls and her own four-year-old son, used boxes for chairs and packing crates for desks. The story of how she baked and sold sweet potato pies to keep the school going is now the stuff of legend. Nevertheless, by 1923 her school had become Bethune-Cookman College, with six hundred students, thirty-two faculty members, and an $800,000 campus free of debt.

Recognized as a pioneering leader and innovator within her own time, Soror Bethune served four presidents—Coolidge, Hoover, Roosevelt, and Truman—in appointed or advisory positions.

CHOCOLATE POUND CAKE

MAKES 16 SERVINGS

I RECEIVED this recipe from a co-worker. One time I made it for a bridal shower I hosted. I forgot to put the shortening in and everyone still commented on how good it was.

1 cup butter or margarine
½ cup vegetable shortening
3 cups sugar
3 cups all-purpose flour
½ cup unsweetened cocoa powder
1 teaspoon vanilla extract
1¼ cups milk
¼ teaspoon salt
5 large eggs
Dream Whip Icing (see following recipe)

Preheat the oven to 325 degrees. Grease and flour a 12-cup tube pan.

Beat the butter, shortening, and sugar in a large bowl. Add the flour, cocoa, vanilla, milk, salt, and eggs. Pour into the prepared pan. Bake for 1½ hours. Remove from the pan before the cake completely cools. Cool completely and add icing just before serving.

DREAM WHIP ICING

1 (1.3-ounce) package Dream Whip
1 (3.4-ounce) box instant chocolate pudding mix
1½ cups milk
1 teaspoon vanilla extract

Mix ingredients for icing until blended well. Beat until stiff peaks form. Refrigerate until ready to use.

CAROLYN C. JOHNSON
Warsaw, Virginia
Williamsburg Alumnae Chapter

FIVE-FLAVOR POUND CAKE

MAKES 16 SERVINGS

½ pound butter, at room temperature
½ cup vegetable shortening
3 cups sugar
5 large eggs, well beaten
3 cups all-purpose flour
½ teaspoon baking powder
1 cup milk
1 teaspoon rum extract
1 teaspoon butter-flavored extract
1 teaspoon coconut extract
1 teaspoon lemon extract
1 teaspoon vanilla extract
Glaze (see following recipe)

Preheat the oven to 325 degrees. Grease and flour a 10-inch tube pan.

Cream the butter, shortening, and sugar until light and fluffy (at least 10 minutes). Add the eggs. Combine the flour and baking power. Add to the creamed mixture, alternating with the milk. Mix in the extracts, one at a time. Spoon into the prepared tube pan and bake 1 hour and 20 minutes or until a toothpick inserted in the center comes out clean. Remove from the oven. Pour glaze over hot cake. Leave cake in the pan to cool.

GLAZE

1 cup sugar

½ cup water

½ teaspoon each of coconut, lemon, rum, butter-flavored, almond, and vanilla extracts

Combine the ingredients in a heavy saucepan. Bring to boil. Stir constantly until the sugar has melted.

RITA L. SIMPKINS-SMITH
Chicago, Illinois
Chicago Alumnae Chapter

Five-Flavor Pound Cake

MISS VERNON MUNDY'S POUND CAKE

MAKES 15–18 SERVINGS

VERNON MUNDY, a cook for the Atlanta Board of Education until retirement, loved to cook. She passed away in 2001 at age eighty-three.

2 cups butter

3 cups sugar

8 large eggs

½ cup milk

4 cups all-purpose flour

1 tablespoon lemon extract

Lemon Glaze (see recipe below)

Preheat the oven to 325 degrees. Grease and flour a 10-inch tube pan.

Cream the butter and sugar in a large bowl until the mixture is light and fluffy. Add the eggs, one at a time, beating for 1 minute after each addition. Add the milk. Add the flour. Stir in the lemon extract.

Pour the batter into the prepared pan. Bake for 1 hour; increase the temperature to 350 degrees for the last 10 minutes. Remove from the oven. Let cool in pan for 10 minutes. Invert onto plate and drizzle glaze over top of cake.

LEMON GLAZE

½ cup sifted powdered sugar

Juice of 1 lemon

1 tablespoon melted butter

Mix all the ingredients in a small bowl.

MERLE ALLEN FRANKLIN
Atlanta, Georgia
Atlanta Suburban Alumnae Chapter

LEMON-THYME POUND CAKE

MAKES 12–16 SERVINGS

THIS CAKE takes some time to prepare, but the taste makes it all worthwhile.

2¾ cups all-purpose flour

2 tablespoons chopped fresh thyme

½ teaspoon baking soda

½ teaspoon cinnamon

½ teaspoon salt

6 eggs, separated

1 cup unsalted butter, softened

2 cups sugar

1 teaspoon lemon extract

1 cup plain low-fat yogurt

¼ cup lemon juice

2 teaspoons lemon zest

1 teaspoon vanilla extract

Glaze (see following recipe)

Preheat the oven to 350 degrees. Grease and flour a 10-inch Bundt pan.

Combine the flour, chopped thyme, baking soda, cinnamon, and salt.

Beat the egg whites until stiff peaks form; set aside.

In a large bowl, beat the butter, sugar, and lemon extract until fluffy. Add the egg yolks, one at a time. Combine the yogurt, lemon juice, lemon zest, and vanilla in a small bowl. With an electric mixer at low speed, beat the flour mixture into the butter mixture alternately with the yogurt mixture, beginning and ending with flour.

Fold in the egg whites; mix well. Pour the batter into the prepared Bundt pan.

Bake 55 minutes. Remove cake from pan and cool. Brush with Glaze.

GLAZE

½ cup lemon juice
½ cup sugar
1 tablespoon chopped fresh thyme

In a small saucepan, combine all the ingredients. Over medium-high heat, stir until the sugar has dissolved. Boil, without stirring, about 10 minutes or until syrupy. Strain and let cool 5 minutes.

MARION T. WHITE
Inglewood, California
Rolling Hills–Palos Verdes Alumnae Chapter

DELTA OF DISTINCTION
Nannie Helen Burroughs

BORN IN ORANGE, Virginia, in 1883, honorary soror Nannie Burroughs was taken to Washington, D.C., at an early age by her widowed mother, who hoped to give her the advantage of a better education. She graduated from high school with honors in 1896.

When the District of Columbia Board of Education denied her a teaching position, she moved to Philadelphia where she became associate editor of *The Christian Banner*, a Baptist newspaper. Always proud and self-sufficient, she held a variety of jobs and started two organizations for helping African-American women before opening her own school, the National Trade and Professional School for Women and Girls, in Washington. The school, which opened its doors in 1909, was established with the support of the National Baptist Convention under the motto "We specialize in the wholly impossible." Her curriculum stressed the practical and professional skills that would help students to become both self-sufficient wage earners and expert homemakers.

Soror Nannie Helen Burroughs died in 1961, and in 1964 the school she had founded was renamed the Nannie Burroughs School in her honor. In 1975, in recognition of "her courage and wisdom in espousing education for black women against the consensus of society," Mayor Walter E. Washington proclaimed May 10 Nannie Helen Burroughs Day in the District of Columbia.

7-UP POUND CAKE

MAKES 12 SERVINGS

1½ cups butter

3 cups sugar

5 large eggs

3 cups all-purpose flour

¾ cup 7-Up

2 teaspoons lemon extract

Preheat the oven to 325 degrees. Grease and flour a 12-cup Bundt pan; set aside.

Beat the butter at medium speed in a large bowl until soft and creamy. Gradually add the sugar, beating at medium for 5 to 7 minutes.

Add the eggs, one at a time, beating just until the yellow disappears. Gradually add the flour, mixing until well blended. Stir in the 7-Up and lemon extract.

Pour the batter into the prepared pan and bake for 1 hour and 20 minutes or until a toothpick inserted in the center comes out clean. Cool in the pan on a wire rack for 10 to 15 minutes; remove from the pan and cool completely.

Serve with ice cream, strawberries, and whipped topping, if desired.

NANCY PITTMAN
Chicago, Illinois
Chicago Alumnae Chapter

MARY TRICE
Grand Rapids, Michigan
Grand Rapids Alumnae Chapter

7-UP CAKE WITH ICING

MAKES 10–12 SERVINGS

MY LATE MOTHER, Mae D. Williams, handed down this twenty-three-year-old recipe to me. It was first used as a fund-raiser at my church for the Helping Hand Auxiliary.

1½ cups butter

½ cup vegetable oil

3 cups sugar

5 large eggs

3 cups cake flour

1 cup 7-Up, at room temperature

1 teaspoon vanilla extract

1 teaspoon butternut extract

1 teaspoon lemon extract

Icing (see following recipe)

Preheat the oven to 350 degrees. Grease and flour a 12-cup Bundt pan.

Cream the butter and oil in a large mixing bowl. Add the sugar, 1 cup at a time, beating well after each addition. Add the eggs, one at a time, mixing well after each addition. Add the remaining ingredients and mix until the batter is smooth and creamy. Pour into the prepared Bundt pan and bake for 1½ hours. Cool before icing.

ICING

1 cup sifted powdered sugar

1 tablespoon unsweetened cocoa powder

¼ cup butter

⅓ cup condensed milk

1 teaspoon almond, coconut, or vanilla extract

Chopped pecans or almonds (optional)

Chocolate syrup (optional)

Combine the sugar, cocoa, butter, milk, and extract in a medium bowl. Spread over cooled cake. Sprinkle the nuts over the top of the cake and the sides, if you like. Place cake on a round platter and drizzle with chocolate, if desired.

Gussie J. Glapion
New Orleans, Louisiana
New Orleans Alumnae Chapter

Coca-Cola Cake

MAKES 16–20 SERVINGS

Don't make the frosting ahead of time—you need to pour it over the cake while it's still warm.

1 cup Coca-Cola

½ cup buttermilk

1 cup butter, softened

1¾ cups sugar

2 large eggs, separated

2 teaspoons vanilla extract

2 cups all-purpose flour

¼ cup unsweetened cocoa powder

1 teaspoon baking soda

1 cup miniature marshmallows

Coca-Cola Frosting (see following recipe)

¾ cup chopped pecans, toasted (optional)

Preheat the oven to 350 degrees. Grease and flour a 13-by-9-inch baking pan.

In a medium bowl combine the Cola-Cola and buttermilk; set aside.

Beat the butter with an electric mixer at low speed in a large bowl until creamy. Gradually add the sugar; beat until blended. Add one egg yolk at a time. Add the vanilla; beat at low speed until blended.

In a medium bowl, whip the egg whites until stiff peaks form; set aside.

Combine the flour, cocoa, and baking soda in a medium bowl. Add to the butter mixture alternately with the buttermilk mixture, beginning and ending with the flour mixture. Fold in the egg whites. Beat at low speed just until blended.

Stir in the marshmallows.

Pour the batter into the prepared baking pan. Bake 30 minutes. Remove from oven and cool 10 minutes. Pour Coca-Cola Frosting over warm cake; garnish with toasted pecans, if desired. Cool 10 minutes before cutting.

Coca-Cola Frosting

½ cup butter

⅓ cup Coca-Cola

3 tablespoons unsweetened cocoa powder

1 (16-ounce) box powdered sugar, sifted

1 tablespoon vanilla extract

In the top of a double boiler, bring the butter, Coca-Cola, and cocoa to a boil, stirring until the butter melts. Remove from heat; whisk in the sugar and vanilla. Cook 5 minutes.

Helen J. Newton Fobi
Rolling Hills, California
Rolling Hills–Palos Verdes Alumnae Chapter

RED VELVET CAKE

MAKES 8–10 SERVINGS

ITS CRIMSON layers and cream frosting make this a Delta dessert favorite.

2½ cups all-purpose flour

1½ cups sugar

1 teaspoon baking soda

1 tablespoon unsweetened cocoa powder

1 cup buttermilk

1½ cups vegetable oil

1 teaspoon distilled white vinegar

2 large eggs

1 small bottle (1 fluid ounce) red food coloring

Cream Cheese Frosting (see recipe below)

Preheat the oven to 350 degrees. Grease and flour two 9-inch round cake pans.

Sift together the dry ingredients. Make a well in the center, pour in the liquid ingredients, and stir until well incorporated. Divide the batter equally between the prepared pans and rap the pans on the counter to remove any air bubbles. Bake for 25 minutes or until a toothpick inserted in the center comes out clean. Cool the layers in their pans for 10 to 15 minutes, then turn out onto a rack and cool completely before frosting.

CREAM CHEESE FROSTING

½ cup butter, softened

1 (8-ounce) package cream cheese, softened

1 (16-ounce) box powdered sugar

1 tablespoon granulated sugar

1 tablespoon vanilla extract

Red Velvet Cake

With an electric mixer, cream the butter and cream cheese together until light and fluffy. Beat in the sugars until the mixture is smooth and creamy. Stir in the vanilla.

Fill and frost the layers once they have cooled completely.

GWENDOLYN E. BOYD
Washington, D.C.
22nd National President
Washington, D.C., Alumnae Chapter

CHOCOLATE CAKE À LA HICKS

MAKES 8–10 SERVINGS

FOR MY BIRTHDAY one year, I received this cake, complete with plate, server, and the recipe, from Mr. and Mrs. John Hicks.

2 cups all-purpose flour

1⅓ cups sugar

⅓ cup vegetable shortening

3 teaspoons baking powder

1 teaspoon salt

2 cups milk

2 large eggs

1 teaspoon vanilla extract

Chocolate Frosting (see following recipe)

Preheat the oven to 350 degrees. Grease and flour two 9-inch round cake pans; set aside.

Combine the flour, sugar, shortening, baking powder, salt, and milk in a large bowl; beat with an electric mixer at medium speed for 2 minutes or 200 strokes by hand. Add the eggs and vanilla extract and beat an additional 2 minutes at medium speed or another 200 strokes by hand. Divide the batter equally between the prepared cake pans. Bake for 30 to 35 minutes or until a toothpick inserted in the center comes out clean. Cool in the pans on a rack for 10 to 15 minutes before removing layers. Cool completely, then frost.

Chocolate Cake à la Hicks

CHOCOLATE FROSTING

6 tablespoons butter or margarine

½ cup unsweetened cocoa powder

2⅔ cups sifted powdered sugar

4 tablespoons milk

1 teaspoon vanilla extract

Cream the butter in a small mixing bowl with an electric mixer until softened. Add the cocoa and blend well. Gradually add the sifted powdered sugar, alternating with the milk and the vanilla. Beat until the frosting reaches a spreading consistency. Immediately spread frosting between and around cake layers.

KATHY E. TANNER
Washington, D.C.
Federal City Alumnae Chapter

CHOCOLATE PEPPERMINT CAKE

MAKES 15–18 SERVINGS

2 cups sifted cake flour
1 teaspoon baking soda
½ teaspoon salt
⅓ cup vegetable shortening
1¼ cups sugar
1 large egg, unbeaten
3 (1-ounce) squares unsweetened chocolate, melted
1 teaspoon vanilla extract
½ cup sour cream
¾ cup milk
Peppermint Glaze (see following recipe)
Chocolate flakes

Preheat the oven to 350 degrees. Grease two 9-inch round cake pans.

Sift the flour, baking soda, and salt together in a large bowl; set aside. Cream the shortening with the sugar in a large bowl until fluffy. Add the egg and beat thoroughly. Add the chocolate and the vanilla; blend well. Add about one-fourth of the flour mixture and beat well. Add the sour cream and beat thoroughly.

Add the remaining flour mixture and the milk alternately in small amounts, beating well after each addition. Pour into the prepared cake pans and bake for 30 minutes.

Remove cake from the oven; cool for 10 minutes in the pans. Remove from the pans and cool completely.

Spread Peppermint Glaze between layers and over cake. Decorate with a border of chocolate flakes.

PEPPERMINT GLAZE

¼ cup crushed peppermint-stick candy
½ cup milk
1 (16-ounce) box powdered sugar, sifted

Heat the candy and the milk in the top of a double boiler over hot water until the candy melts. Add sifted powdered sugar until the frosting is thick enough to spread.

Edna Lee Long-Green
Washington, D.C.
Co-Chair, National Commission on Arts and Letters
Washington, D.C., Alumnae Chapter

MOCHA HALO CUPCAKES

MAKES 16 SERVINGS

Tasty and easy to make, these are a great choice for when you're asked to "bring something" to a meeting or a group activity. My mother, Edna Thomas Lee, gave me the recipe.

1½ cups sifted cake flour

½ cup unsweetened cocoa powder

2 teaspoons baking powder

½ teaspoon baking soda

¼ teaspoon salt

½ cup vegetable shortening

1 cup sugar

1 large egg

2 large egg yolks

½ cup cold strong coffee

½ cup buttermilk

Fluffy White Icing (see following recipe)

1 (1-ounce) square semisweet chocolate

1 teaspoon butter

Preheat the oven to 350 degrees.

Sift the flour, cocoa, baking powder, baking soda, and salt together three times. Cream the shortening with the sugar in a large bowl until fluffy. Combine the egg and egg yolks; beat well and add to the creamed mixture. Combine the coffee and buttermilk in a small bowl.

Add the sifted dry ingredients and the coffee mixture alternately in small amounts to the creamed mixture, beating well after each addition. Pour into greased cupcake pans. Bake for 20 minutes.

Remove from the oven and cool on wire racks. When cool, frost with Fluffy White Icing.

Melt the chocolate square in the top of a double boiler. Stir in the 1 teaspoon butter. Drizzle a band of chocolate around the top of each cupcake using either a teaspoon or a pastry brush.

FLUFFY WHITE ICING

¾ cup sugar

¼ cup water

⅛ teaspoon cream of tartar

1 teaspoon corn syrup

2 large egg whites, stiffly beaten

1 tablespoon vanilla extract

Combine the first 4 ingredients in a saucepan. Slowly bring to a boil and cook, without stirring, until a small amount dropped from the tip of a spoon spins a long thread. Pour the syrup slowly onto stiffly beaten egg whites, beating constantly. Beat until cool and thick enough to spread; add the vanilla.

EDNA LEE LONG-GREEN
Washington, D.C.
Co-Chair, National Commission on Arts and Letters
Washington, D.C., Alumnae Chapter

RUM CAKE

1 cup chopped pecans
1 (18.25-ounce) package yellow cake mix
1 (3.4-ounce) box instant vanilla pudding mix
½ cup water
½ cup rum
½ cup vegetable oil
4 large eggs
Topping (see recipe below)

Preheat the oven to 325 degrees. Grease and flour a 12-cup Bundt pan. Line the pan with the pecans.

Combine all the remaining ingredients except the Topping in a large bowl; beat with an electric mixer at medium speed for 2 minutes.

Pour the batter into the prepared pan and bake for 45 to 60 minutes or until a toothpick inserted in the center comes out clean. Remove from the oven and pour the topping over the hot cake. Spoon excess over top until most of it is absorbed.

TOPPING
½ cup butter
½ cup sugar
¼ cup rum

Combine all the ingredients in a small saucepan. Heat to a boil.

GWENDOLYN E. BOYD
Washington, D.C.
22nd National President
Washington, D.C., Alumnae Chapter

CARROT CAKE

2½ cups all-purpose flour
1½ teaspoons baking powder
½ teaspoon baking soda
½ teaspoon salt
1 teaspoon ground cinnamon
1 teaspoon ground cloves
1 teaspoon grated nutmeg
1 cup salad oil
2 cups sugar
4 tablespoons hot water
4 large eggs, separated
1½ cups grated carrots
1 cup chopped walnuts
Cream Cheese Icing (see following recipe)

Preheat the oven to 350 degrees. Grease and flour a 9-inch tube pan.

Sift together the flour and other dry ingredients and set aside. Beat together the oil, sugar, and water. Add the egg yolks, one at a time, beating well after each addition. Beat the flour mixture into the oil mixture. Add the carrots and nuts. Beat the egg whites until stiff peaks form; then fold them into the cake mixture. Spoon the batter into the prepared pan. Bake for 60 to 70 minutes or until a toothpick inserted in the center comes out clean. Cool the cake on a wire rack. Remove from pan when cool. Spread Cream Cheese Icing on cooled cake.

CREAM CHEESE ICING

1 (8-ounce) package cream cheese, softened

1 cup sifted powdered sugar

½ cup butter or margarine, softened

½ teaspoon vanilla extract

Combine all the ingredients in a small bowl. Beat with an electric mixer at medium speed until creamy, smooth, and spreadable.

ALTHEADA L. JOHNSON
Brooklyn, New York
North Manhattan Alumnae Chapter

CARROT NUT CAKE
WITH PINEAPPLE

MAKES 18–20 SERVINGS

THE TARTNESS of the icing gives this cake its unique flavor.

2 cups sugar

1¼ cups corn oil

4 large eggs

3 cups grated carrots (about 4 medium carrots)

3 cups sifted all-purpose flour

1–2 teaspoons ground cinnamon

1 teaspoon baking soda

½ teaspoon baking powder

Dash of salt

1 cup chopped nuts of your choice

1 (8-ounce) can crushed pineapple, undrained

1 tablespoon vanilla extract

Cream Cheese Icing (see following recipe)

Preheat the oven to 350 degrees. Grease and flour a 12-cup tube pan.

Combine the sugar and the oil in a large bowl, mixing well. Add the eggs, one at a time, beating well after each addition. Stir in the carrots.

In another large bowl, sift together the flour and next 4 ingredients. Then stir into the liquid mixture.

Add the nuts, pineapple, and vanilla, mixing well. Pour into the prepared pan. Bake for about 1 hour or until a toothpick inserted in the center comes out clean. Remove from the oven and cool on a wire rack. Remove from the pan and spread with Cream Cheese Icing.

CREAM CHEESE ICING

1 (3-ounce) package cream cheese, softened

1 tablespoon butter, softened

1 cup sifted powdered sugar

2–3 tablespoons lemon juice

1 tablespoon vanilla extract

Stir the first 4 ingredients together in a small bowl until creamy. Stir in the vanilla extract.

BLANCHE LAVENDER
Atlanta, Georgia
Atlanta Alumnae Chapter

Modern Marble Cake

MAKES 9 SERVINGS

THIS WAS PASSED down from my Big Mama Katie to my mother, Edna Thomas Lee, to me, and now to all of you. Enjoy it!

1¾ cups sifted cake flour

2 teaspoons baking powder

½ teaspoon salt

½ cup vegetable shortening

1 cup sugar

2 eggs, beaten

½ cup plus 2 tablespoons milk

1 teaspoon vanilla extract

1 (1-ounce) square unsweetened chocolate

Preheat the oven to 350 degrees. Grease an 8-by-8-inch baking pan.

Sift the flour, baking powder, and salt together into a large bowl; set aside.

Cream the shortening with the sugar in a large bowl until fluffy. Add the beaten eggs. Add the sifted dry ingredients and ½ cup of the milk alternately in small amounts to the creamed mixture, beating well after each addition. Add the vanilla. Divide the batter in half.

Melt the chocolate in top of a double boiler. Stir in the remaining 2 tablespoons milk. Add to one-half of the batter; blend well. Drop the batter by tablespoons into the prepared baking pan, alternat-ing white and chocolate batters. Bake for 50 to 60 minutes.

Frost with your favorite icing.

EDNA LEE LONG-GREEN
Washington, D.C.
Co-Chair, National Commission on Arts and Letters
Washington, D.C., Alumnae Chapter

Sister Vee's Apple Cake

MAKES 12–16 SERVINGS

2 cups all-purpose flour

1 cup whole-wheat flour

2¾ cups granulated sugar

3 teaspoons baking powder

1 teaspoon salt

1 cup vegetable oil

⅓ cup orange juice

4 large eggs

1 teaspoon vanilla extract

1 cup chopped pecans

1 teaspoon cinnamon

1–3 Granny Smith apples, peeled and sliced

¼ cup packed dark brown sugar

Preheat the oven to 350 degrees. Grease and flour a 9-inch tube pan.

Combine the flours, 2½ cups of the granulated sugar, the baking powder, and the salt in a large bowl. Add the vegetable oil, orange juice, eggs, and vanilla; mix well. Stir in the pecans.

Mix the remaining ¼ cup sugar and the cinnamon in a medium bowl. Add the apples, stirring to coat.

Alternate layers of batter and coated apples in the prepared tube pan, starting with batter and ending with apples. Sprinkle the top layer of apples with the brown sugar. Bake for 1½ hours. Cool and remove from the pan.

VALERIE A. FOSTER
Washington, D.C.
Member, National Commission on Arts and Letters
Washington, D.C., Alumnae Chapter

SUPREME LEMON-FILLING CAKE

MAKES 12 SERVINGS

FOR MANY YEARS I made this for my church club, Circle Ruth, to serve at our June and December socials. Everyone always wanted a piece, so it was sliced very thin to go as far as possible.

1 (18.25-ounce) package moist deluxe golden
   butter cake
1½ cups granulated sugar
3 tablespoons cornstarch
3 tablespoons all-purpose flour
Dash of salt
1½ cups water
2 large eggs
2 tablespoons butter
⅓ cup lemon juice
1 teaspoon grated lemon rind
Sifted powdered sugar

Bake the cake in two 9-inch cake pans, according to the package directions; set aside.

Combine the sugar, cornstarch, and flour with a dash of salt in the top of a double boiler. Gradually stir in the water. Cook, stirring frequently, over medium heat until thick. Remove from the heat. Beat the eggs in a small bowl. Stir 1 cup of the hot mixture into the eggs. Return the hot egg mixture to the double boiler. Cook, stirring constantly, for 2 minutes. Remove from the heat and add the butter, lemon juice, and lemon rind. Set aside to cool.

Cut each cake layer in half horizontally while still on the cooling racks, to make 4 layers. Have a large cake plate next to cakes on rack. Transfer the top half layer to the cake plate. Handle with care to keep layers from breaking. Cover the first half layer with filling. Place another half layer on top and cover with filling. Repeat for the remaining layers. Leave top of cake plain until ready to serve; then cover with sifted powdered sugar.

DOROTHY P. HARRISON
Chicago, Illinois
Past National President (1956–1958)
Chicago Alumnae Chapter

Old-Fashioned Vegetable Soup   **(page 52)**

Smothered Chicken   **(page 76)**

White Rice

Old-Fashioned Fried Okra   **(page 142)**

Sister Vee's Apple Cake   **(page 216)**

WHEN THE WEATHER turns warm, it's time to warm your heart and tummy with good friends grouped around the dinner table. All the dishes on this menu are designed to make everyone feel right at home.

TO PREPARE:

❧ The soup can be made a day in advance and reheated before serving.

❧ Make the cake early in the day and store it, covered, at room temperature.

❧ A couple of hours before dinner, brown the chicken and have it ready to go into the oven.

❧ Cook the rice and okra while the chicken is baking.

INSTALLING LOCAL OFFICERS

Each spring, when local officers from the previous year leave office and new officers are installed, there is a dinner to both celebrate and implement the changing of the guard. Seating is important as outgoing and incoming officers intermingle and plan for a smooth transition.

Although our dinner is a time to "do business" as we share our meal, it is also a time for people to get to know one another better and, perhaps, in different ways. Your own dinner party might serve the same purpose. Use it as an opportunity to introduce one group of friends to another. Plan your seating so that "strangers" will have a chance to chat and get to know one another. There's nothing like good, honest food served in an intimate and cozy atmosphere to create warm feelings of friendship.

Apple Caramel Cake

MAKES 12–16 SERVINGS

I TOOK THIS cake to our 2002 Rush party and served it while it was still warm. It was a big hit, and the recipe is now frequently requested by other sorors in my chapter.

1½ cups vegetable oil
1½ cups granulated sugar
½ cup packed brown sugar
3 large eggs
3 cups all-purpose flour
2 teaspoons ground cinnamon
½ teaspoon grated nutmeg
1 teaspoon baking soda
½ teaspoon salt
2 teaspoons vanilla extract
3½ cups peeled, diced apples (about 3 medium apples)
1 cup finely chopped walnuts (optional)
Icing (see following recipe)
Chopped walnuts (optional)

Preheat the oven to 325 degrees. Grease and flour a 10-inch Bundt pan.

Combine the oil and sugars in a large mixing bowl. Add the eggs, one at a time, beating well after each addition. Combine all the dry ingredients in a small bowl and add to batter slowly, mixing well. Add the vanilla, apples, and walnuts, if desired, to the mixture. Pour mixture into the prepared pan.

Bake for 1½ hours or until a toothpick inserted in the center comes out clean. Cool on a wire rack for 10 minutes before removing from the pan and then let the cake cool completely. Drizzle Icing over the cooled cake. Sprinkle with walnuts, if desired.

ICING

½ cup packed light brown sugar
⅓ cup light cream
¼ cup butter or margarine
Dash of salt
¼ teaspoon vanilla extract
1 cup sifted powdered sugar

Slowly heat the brown sugar, cream, butter, salt, and vanilla in a saucepan, stirring until the sugar has dissolved. Let cool to room temperature, then beat in sifted powdered sugar to desired consistency.

RENÉE TUCKER
Loveland, Ohio
Cincinnati Queen City Alumnae Chapter

Holmes Cake

MAKES 12–15 SERVINGS

1 (18.25-ounce) package butter cake mix
1 cup butter
4 large eggs
1 teaspoon vanilla extract
1 cup orange juice
1 (11-ounce) can mandarin oranges, drained
Topping (see following recipe)

Preheat the oven to 350 degrees. Grease and flour a 13-by-9-inch baking pan.

Combine the cake mix with the butter, eggs, vanilla, and orange juice in a large bowl. Add the oranges. Pour into the prepared baking pan. Bake according to directions for the cake mix. Remove cake from the oven; cool. Add Topping.

TOPPING

1 (20-ounce) can crushed pineapple
1 (3.4-ounce) box instant vanilla pudding mix
1 teaspoon vanilla extract
½ cup sifted powdered sugar
½ (8-ounce) container or more frozen whipped
    topping, thawed

Drain the pineapple; mix the juice with the pudding and the vanilla. Add the sifted powdered sugar and the whipped topping. Fold in the pineapple. Top the cake. Refrigerate until serving time.

Anita Holmes
Oklahoma City, Oklahoma
Oklahoma City Alumnae Chapter

DUMP CAKE

MAKES 10–12 SERVINGS

THIS IS a quick-and-easy recipe my mother, an excellent baker, gave me many years ago. I love to entertain, especially at cookouts, but baking is not my strong point. This cake, however, is foolproof and tasty.

1 (20-ounce) can sliced peaches in heavy syrup
1 (16-ounce) can apple pie filling
1 (18.25-ounce) package butter cake mix
¾–1 cup margarine or butter
Ground cinnamon, to taste

Preheat the oven to 350 degrees. Grease a 12-by-8-inch baking pan.

Mix the peaches and pie filling in a large bowl. Dump into the prepared baking pan. Spread the cake mix on top of the fruit mixture. Put pats of the margarine on top of cake mix. Sprinkle the cinnamon on top of the margarine.

Bake for 50 to 60 minutes or until a toothpick inserted in the center comes out clean. Serve warm, topped with vanilla ice cream if desired.

Marcia L. Fudge
Warrensville Heights, Ohio
Past National President (1996–2000)
Greater Cleveland Alumnae Chapter

PINEAPPLE POKE CAKE

MAKES 10–12 SERVINGS

1 (18.25-ounce) package yellow cake mix
1 (20-ounce) can crushed pineapple, undrained
1 (8-ounce) package cream cheese, softened
1 (3.4-ounce) box instant vanilla pudding mix
1 cup cold milk
1 (8-ounce) container frozen whipped topping, thawed
1 cup pecan pieces

Bake the cake in a 13-by-9-inch baking pan according to package directions.

Remove the cake from the oven. Punch large holes in top of cake with the handle of a wooden spoon. Spoon the pineapple and juice evenly over the cake. Combine the cream cheese, pudding mix, and milk in a medium bowl; beat until thick enough to spread over the pineapple. Spread the whipped topping over the cream cheese mixture. Top with pecans. Store in the refrigerator.

MARY HAMMOND
Oklahoma City, Oklahoma
Chair, National Nominating Committee
Oklahoma City Alumnae Chapter

CHOCOLATE NEVER-FAIL ICING

MAKES ENOUGH FOR 2 LAYERS

1 (16-ounce) box powdered sugar, sifted
1 cup unsweetened cocoa powder
1 tablespoon soft butter or margarine
½ cup cold coffee

Sift together the sugar and cocoa in a medium bowl. Add the butter and cream thoroughly, adding coffee while mixing for a smoother icing.

ALFREDIA BOYD
Columbia, South Carolina
Columbia, South Carolina, Alumnae Chapter

SHOOFLY GINGERBREAD

MAKES 12–16 SERVINGS

2 cups sifted all-purpose flour
2 teaspoons baking powder
¼ teaspoon baking soda
¼ teaspoon salt
1½ teaspoons ground ginger
1 teaspoon ground cinnamon
⅓ cup vegetable shortening
½ cup sugar
1 large egg, well beaten
⅔ cup light-colored molasses
¾ cup buttermilk

Preheat the oven to 350 degrees. Grease an 8-by-8-inch baking pan.

Sift together the flour, baking powder, baking soda, salt, ginger, and cinnamon into a medium bowl.

Cream the shortening in a large bowl. Add the sugar gradually, creaming until light and fluffy. Add the egg; beat thoroughly. Add the molasses.

Stir in the dry ingredients alternately with the buttermilk; blend well after each addition.

Pour into the prepared baking pan. Bake 40 to 50 minutes or until a toothpick inserted in the center comes out clean. Serve with whipped cream or ice cream.

MERLE ALLEN FRANKLIN
Atlanta, Georgia
Atlanta Suburban Alumnae Chapter

CHARLOTTE'S CHEESECAKE

MAKES 8–10 SERVINGS

ALTHOUGH CHEESECAKE is far from an original recipe, the love and soul my mother uses to make this delightful treat is felt in every bite. Everyone, from her former co-workers (she's retired) to family and close friends, has been touched by Charlotte's creamy dream. So much so that people put their orders in before the holiday season even rears its head. Maybe I'll help her start her own business . . . Charlotte's Cheesecakes. I like how that sounds.

For now, though, I'm just glad that she was gracious enough to share her recipe. It has definitely done my heart and ego good. It's about the only thing I can cook!

3 large eggs, well beaten
1 cup sugar
2 teaspoons vanilla extract
2 (8-ounce) packages cream cheese, softened
¼ teaspoon salt
¼ teaspoon almond extract
1 (24-ounce) container sour cream
2 (9-inch) prepared graham cracker piecrusts

Preheat the oven to 375 degrees.

Combine the eggs and the next 5 ingredients in a large bowl; beat until smooth. Blend in the sour cream. Pour into the piecrusts.

Bake 35 minutes or until just set. Cool, then chill in the refrigerator 4 to 5 hours. The filling will be soft. Serve with your own choice of topping.

JENNIFER R. SMITH
Detroit, Michigan
Delta Iota Chapter

APPLE CHEESECAKE

MAKES 12–16 SERVINGS

SEVERAL YEARS ago, as the holidays approached, I began to think of different ways to make extra "shopping money." Baking was the obvious choice. For this creation, I've combined my two favorite ingredients—apples and cheese.

2 (8-ounce) packages cream cheese, softened
3 large eggs
1 (14-ounce) can sweetened condensed milk
¼ cup lemon juice
2 (8-inch) prepared graham cracker piecrusts
1 (16-ounce) container sour cream
2 (21-ounce) cans premium apple topping
Ground cinnamon, to taste

Preheat the oven to 350 degrees.

Combine the cream cheese and the eggs in a large bowl. Add the condensed milk, mixing until smooth. Add the lemon juice; mix well. Pour the mixture into the prepared piecrusts.

Bake for 50 to 60 minutes or until the center is somewhat firm.

Top each cake with sour cream and bake for 2 minutes. Remove cakes from the oven and cool. Add apple topping to each cake and sprinkle with cinnamon. Serve chilled or at room temperature.

TREVA J. SPENCER-DUPREE
Teaneck, New Jersey
Delta Zeta Chapter

TAFFY APPLE CHEESECAKE

MAKES 8–12 SERVINGS

2 baking apples, peeled, cored, and thinly sliced
¼ cup caramel sauce
2 (8-ounce) packages cream cheese, softened
⅔ cup sugar
1 tablespoon plus 1 teaspoon all-purpose flour
1 teaspoon vanilla extract
2 large eggs
2 tablespoons plus 2 teaspoons milk
1 (9-inch) prepared graham cracker piecrust

Preheat the oven to 375 degrees.

Combine the apples and the caramel sauce in a small saucepan on medium heat. Cook, stirring constantly, until the apples are tender, about 10 minutes. Remove from the heat and set aside.

Combine the cream cheese, sugar, flour, and vanilla in a large bowl. Beat with an electric mixer at medium speed until well combined. Add the eggs, beating until well mixed. Stir in the milk. With a slotted spoon, remove two-thirds of the apples from the saucepan and stir into the cream cheese mixture.

Pour the mixture into the prepared piecrust. Drizzle 1 tablespoon of the caramel sauce over the top. Swirl with a knife.

Bake for 35 to 40 minutes or until the center appears nearly set when shaken gently.

Cool in the pan for 45 minutes. Spread 1 teaspoon caramel sauce over the cheesecake. Using a slotted spoon, place the remaining apples on top of the cheesecake to decorate. Cover and chill at least 4 hours before serving.

DYANI SEXTON
Chicago, Illinois
Chicago Alumnae Chapter

GERMAN CHOCOLATE CHEESECAKE

MAKES 15 SERVINGS

IN 1988 OR 1989, when my present pastor was ordained as a priest at our church, someone made this cake for the celebration, and I fell in love with it after the first bite. After that, I didn't have it again for several years, until a fellow member of my investment club gave me the recipe. This is one recipe I hope never to lose.

1 (18.25-ounce) package German chocolate cake mix
2 (8-ounce) packages cream cheese
4 large eggs
1½ cups sugar
Frosting (see following recipe)

Preheat the oven to 325 degrees. Grease a 13-by-9-inch baking pan.

Prepare the cake mix according to package directions. Do not bake. Pour half the batter into the prepared pan.

Whip the cream cheese, eggs, and sugar in a medium bowl. Pour over the batter in the pan. Add the rest of the cake batter.

Bake 50 minutes. Cool completely and add frosting.

FROSTING

1 cup evaporated milk
1 cup sugar
½ cup butter or margarine, softened
1 tablespoon vanilla extract
1 cup flaked coconut
1 cup chopped nuts

Combine all the ingredients in a medium saucepan. Cook over medium heat, stirring constantly, until thickened. Cool and spread over cooled cake. Keep refrigerated.

SONDRA L. SMITH
St. Louis, Missouri
St. Louis Alumnae Chapter

Ricotta, Lighter-Textured Cheesecake

MAKES 12 SERVINGS

10 graham crackers

½ cup packed dark brown sugar

4 tablespoons unsalted butter, melted

1 (15-ounce) container whole-milk ricotta cheese

2 (8-ounce) packages cream cheese

1½ cups sugar

4 large eggs

3 tablespoons cornstarch

3 tablespoons all-purpose flour

1 teaspoon vanilla extract

2 cups sour cream

Place the graham crackers in a plastic bag; crush into fine crumbs with a rolling pin. Combine the crumbs and the brown sugar in a small bowl. Stir in the butter; mix well. Press crumb mixture into the bottom and about 1 inch up the sides of a greased 9-inch springform pan. Refrigerate for at least 20 minutes.

Preheat the oven to 325 degrees.

Beat the ricotta in a bowl with an electric mixer until fluffy, about 2 minutes. Add the cream cheese and sugar; beat until fluffy and smooth. Add the eggs, one at a time, beating until well blended. Stir in the cornstarch, flour, and vanilla until well combined. Beat in the sour cream until just blended. Pour into the crust.

Bake on a baking sheet for 1 hour 25 minutes or until golden and just set. Cool completely on a wire rack. Refrigerate for at least 8 hours.

Serve plain or topped with a favorite sauce.

Eugenia B. Hardaway
Chicago, Illinois
Chicago Alumnae Chapter

Sweet Potato Cheesecake

MAKES 16 SERVINGS

Sonya Jones of Atlanta has brought sweet potatoes and cheesecake to a new level.

1 medium sweet potato

1 loaf pound cake (about 20 thin slices)

3 (8-ounce) packages cream cheese, softened

1 cup sugar

3 large eggs

1 cup heavy cream

1 teaspoon lemon extract

2 teaspoons vanilla extract

2 teaspoons grated nutmeg

Whipped cream (optional)

Boil the sweet potato until tender. Cool, peel, and mash the sweet potato; set aside.

Preheat the oven to 350 degrees. Line two 9-inch pie pans with thin slices of pound cake. Firmly press into the bottom of the pans; set aside.

Beat the cream cheese in a large bowl until fluffy. Gradually add the sugar, mixing well. Add the eggs, one at a time, beating well after each addition. Pour in the cream, mixing well. Add the potato; mix well. Stir in the extracts and the nutmeg. Divide the batter equally between the two prepared pans.

Bake for 45 to 60 minutes, until the center is almost set. Remove from the oven; cool for 1 hour. Refrigerate until ready to serve. Garnish with whipped cream, if desired.

JEAN MCCRAY ASHE
Atlanta, Georgia
East Point/College Park Alumnae Chapter

SWEET POTATO (OR PUMPKIN) NUT ROLL

MAKES 8–10 SERVINGS

¾ cup all-purpose flour
1 teaspoon baking powder
2 teaspoons ground cinnamon
1 teaspoon ground ginger
½ teaspoon grated nutmeg
½ teaspoon salt
3 large eggs
1 cup sugar
⅔ cup puréed sweet potato or pumpkin
1 teaspoon lemon juice
Filling (see recipe below)
Sifted powdered sugar for garnish

Preheat the oven to 375 degrees. Grease and flour a 15-by-10-inch baking pan.

Combine the flour and the next 5 ingredients together in a large bowl; set aside.

Beat the eggs in a medium bowl for 5 minutes; gradually add the sugar. Add the sweet potato and the lemon juice; mix well. Fold into the dry ingredients. Spoon into the prepared pan or onto a baking sheet that has 1-inch sides. Bake for 15 minutes.

Turn the cake out onto a clean, dry dish towel sprinkled with sifted powdered sugar. Roll the cake and towel together from the short end, and cool in the refrigerator.

Make the Filling. When the cake is cool, unroll and spread with Filling. Reroll without the towel. Sprinkle with sifted powdered sugar before serving.

FILLING

2 (3-ounce) packages cream cheese, softened
4 tablespoons butter
½ teaspoon vanilla extract
1 cup sifted powdered sugar
1 cup chopped walnuts

Cream the cream cheese, butter, and vanilla in a medium bowl. Add the sugar and nuts; mix well.

TANYA WATSON
Akron, Ohio
Akron Alumnae Chapter

DELTA OF DISTINCTION
Ruby Dee

AN ALUMNA of Hunter College, Soror Ruby Dee first came to national attention in 1950 with her performance in *The Jackie Robinson Story.* In 1965 she became the first African-American woman to play leading roles at the American Shakespeare Festival in New York City.

She won an Obie Award for playing the title role in Athol Fugard's *Boesman and Lena,* a Drama Desk Award for her performance in *Wedding Band,* an Ace Award for Eugene O'Neill's *Long Day's Journey into Night,* in which she appeared as Mary Tyrone, and an Emmy for *Decoration Day.*

She and her husband, Ossie Davis, met in 1946 when they were both appearing on Broadway in *Jeb.* Married two years later, they made their film debuts together in *No Way Out* and have since starred together on Broadway in Lorraine Hansberry's acclaimed *A Raisin in the Sun.*

Close friends of the Reverend Martin Luther King, Jr., the couple served as masters of ceremonies for the historic 1963 March on Washington. Celebrated as "national treasures," they received a National Medal of Arts in 1995 and in 2000 were presented with the Lifetime Achievement Award of the Screen Actors Guild, its highest honor.

PIECRUST

MAKES 1 9-INCH CRUST

1 cup all-purpose flour
½ teaspoon salt
½ cup vegetable shortening
2–3 tablespoons cold water

In a medium bowl lightly stir together flour and salt with a fork. Use a pastry blender or two knives used scissor-fashion to cut in shortening until mixture resembles coarse crumbs. Sprinkle in cold water, 1 tablespoon at a time, mixing lightly with a fork after each addition until pastry holds together. Shape pastry into a ball.

On a lightly floured surface with a lightly floured rolling pin, roll ball into a 1-inch-thick circle, 2 inches larger all around than the 9-inch pie plate. Roll half the circle onto a rolling pin; transfer pastry to pie plate and unroll, easing into bottom and side of plate. With scissors or a sharp knife, trim the pastry edges, leaving 1-inch overhang all around the pie plate rim. Fold overhang under; pinch a high edge; make a decorative edge. Fill and bake pie as recipe directs.

COOK'S TIP | *For a baked piecrust, prepare as above. With a fork, prick the bottom and sides of crust in many places to prevent puffing during baking. Bake at 425 degrees for 15 minutes or until golden. Cool and fill as directed.*

ELLA PATTERSON
Oklahoma City, Oklahoma
Oklahoma City Alumnae Chapter

NO-SUGAR
PEAR PIE

MAKES 6 SERVINGS

A FAVORITE DESSERT for diabetics or those just cutting back on sugar.

2–3 cups sliced fresh pears
2 (9-inch) unbaked pie shells
15 (1-gram) packets sugar substitute
1 teaspoon grated nutmeg
1 teaspoon ground allspice
⅓ cup melted butter
⅓ cup white wine

Preheat the oven to 300 degrees.

Place the sliced pears in 1 pie shell. Sprinkle the pears with the sugar substitute, the spices, and the butter. Add the wine, and cover with the second shell. Punch or cut holes in the top crust. Bake for 50 minutes.

Serve with ice cream, if desired.

BARBARA RANDALL CLARK
Orangeburg, South Carolina
Orangeburg Alumnae Chapter

UNCLE ROY'S
LIGHT PECAN PIE

MAKES 6–8 SERVINGS

¼ cup butter or margarine
1½ cups light corn syrup
½ cup sugar
¼ teaspoon salt
3 large eggs
½ teaspoon vanilla extract
1 cup pecans
1 (9-inch) frozen deep-dish pie shell, thawed

Preheat the oven to 400 degrees.

Combine the butter, corn syrup, sugar, and salt in a small saucepan; bring to a boil, stirring constantly until the sugar has dissolved. Let cool.

Combine the eggs and vanilla in a medium bowl; add the cooled syrup. Drop the pecans into the cooled mixture. Stir once so that both sides of the pecans are coated. Pour the mixture into the pie shell and place on a cookie sheet.

Bake the pie for 10 minutes. Reduce the oven temperature to 375 degrees and bake for another 30 minutes or until the pie is firm in the center. Remove from the oven and cool on a wire rack.

CHERYL J. DOBBINS
Washington, D.C.
Federal City Alumnae Chapter

Grandma's Southern Pecan Pie (Inspired by Laura Miller)

MAKES 6–8 SERVINGS

WHEN I WAS twelve years old, I used to visit the neighborhood grocery store daily and buy an individual pecan pie. At first, my grandmother would just sit there and watch me eat it. Then one day she said, "Grandma is going to teach you how to make a real pie." Needless to say, I took her up on her offer. I still love pecan pie, and I love baking this one so much that it's become a staple at Sunday dinners, family reunions, birthdays, and holidays. It's the first thing I served to my in-laws, and it's a favorite with family and friends.

3 large eggs
1 cup light corn syrup
1 cup sugar
½ tablespoon melted butter
1 teaspoon vanilla extract
¼ teaspoon salt
1 cup pecan halves
1 (9-inch) unbaked deep-dish pie shell

Preheat the oven to 400 degrees.

Beat the eggs lightly in a medium bowl. Add the corn syrup, sugar, melted butter, vanilla, and salt; mix thoroughly. Stir in the pecans and pour into the pie shell.

Bake for 10 minutes; reduce the oven temperature to 350 degrees and bake for 30 to 35 minutes until a toothpick inserted into the center comes out clean.

THELMA JAMES DAY
Los Angeles, California
Regional Director, Far West
Inglewood Alumnae Chapter

Yolanda's Key Lime Pie

MAKES 6–8 SERVINGS

1 (14-ounce) can sweetened condensed milk
½ cup Key (Mexican) lime juice
2 large eggs, separated
1 (9-inch) prepared graham cracker piecrust
¼ teaspoon cream of tartar
¼ cup sugar

Preheat the oven to 425 degrees.

Blend the condensed milk with the lime juice and egg yolks in a bowl. Pour into the graham cracker crust. Beat the egg whites and cream of tartar in a bowl until foamy. Add the sugar gradually and beat until stiff peaks form. Spread over the filling to edge of crust.

Set the pie on a cookie sheet. Bake for about 10 minutes or until brown.

YOLANDA A. LIGGINS
Tampa, Florida
Tampa Alumnae Chapter

ARLENE HANTON YOUNG
Southfield, Michigan
Chair, National Heritage and Archives
Southfield Alumnae Chapter

MOLASSES PIE

MAKES 6 SERVINGS

THIS RECIPE, which originated in Germantown, Tennessee, has sustained my African-American family for three generations at various dinners and celebrations.

1 cup dark-colored molasses

2 tablespoons lemon juice

½ teaspoon grated lemon rind

3 large eggs, separated, at room temperature

¼ cup sugar

1 tablespoon all-purpose flour

¼ teaspoon grated nutmeg

¼ teaspoon ground cinnamon

2 tablespoons melted butter

⅛ teaspoon salt

1½ cups pecans or peanuts (optional)

1 (8-inch) unbaked pie shell

Preheat the oven to 350 degrees.

Mix the molasses with the lemon juice and rind in a small bowl. Beat the egg yolks with the sugar in a medium bowl, and gradually beat in the flour, nutmeg, cinnamon, butter, and salt. While beating, slowly add the molasses mixture. Beat the egg whites in a large bowl until stiff peaks form. Fold the molasses mixture into the egg whites.

Place pecans in bottom of piecrust, if desired. Spoon the molasses mixture into the pie crust. Bake for 10 minutes; then reduce the oven temperature to 325 degrees; Bake 25 to 35 minutes longer or until the center is set. Cool slightly on a wire rack before serving.

CARNIECE BROWN-WHITE
Denver, Colorado
Denver Alumnae Chapter

FRUIT PIE

MAKES 6–8 SERVINGS

1 (21-ounce) can cherry pie filling

2 bananas, sliced

1 (8-ounce) can crushed sweetened pineapple, drained

1 package chopped nuts of your choice

1 (9-inch) prepared graham cracker piecrust

1 (8-ounce) container frozen whipped topping, thawed

Mix the first 4 ingredients and pour into the piecrust. Top with the whipped topping, and refrigerate for 2 hours.

COOK'S TIP | *Add 1 tablespoon sugar to the first 4 ingredients to reduce tartness, if desired.*

BLANCHE LAVENDER
Atlanta, Georgia
Atlanta Alumnae Chapter

Deep-Dish Apple Crumb Pie

MAKES 6–8 SERVINGS

½ cup sugar

3 tablespoons all-purpose flour

1 teaspoon ground cinnamon

⅛ teaspoon salt

6 cups peeled and thinly sliced baking apples
   (about 4 medium apples)

1 (9-inch) unbaked deep-dish pie shell

Crumb Topping (see recipe below)

Preheat the oven to 375 degrees.

Combine the sugar, flour, cinnamon, and salt in a large mixing bowl.

Add the apples, tossing gently until completely coated. Place the apple mixture in the pie shell. Sprinkle the Crumb Topping over the apples.

Cover the pie edge with foil to protect it from burning. Bake for 25 minutes; remove foil. Bake an additional 25 to 30 minutes. Cool before serving.

CRUMB TOPPING

½ cup packed brown sugar

¼ cup all-purpose flour

¼ cup quick-cooking oats

¼ cup butter

Combine the brown sugar, flour, and oats in a small bowl. Cut in the butter until the topping becomes like coarse crumbs.

Deep-Dish Apple Crumb Pie

COOK'S TIP | *If you like lots of crumbs, just double the ingredients for the topping.*

Renée McCarthy Buckman
Bowie, Maryland
Prince George's County Alumnae Chapter

Crustless English Apple Pie

MAKES 8 SERVINGS

½ cup butter or margarine, softened

½ cup packed brown sugar

1 cup all-purpose flour

2 teaspoons ground cinnamon

3 tablespoons water

½–¾ cup coarsely chopped pecans

4 medium cooking apples, peeled and sliced
   (about 6 cups)

½ cup sugar

Heavy cream, ice cream, or half-and-half (optional)

Preheat the oven to 375 degrees. Grease a 9-inch pie plate.

In a medium-size bowl, beat the butter and brown sugar with a wooden spoon or an electric mixer until fluffy and pale in color. Stir in the flour a little at a time, 1 teaspoon of the cinnamon, and the water until the mixture is smooth and thick. Stir in the pecans.

Mound the apples in the prepared pie plate. Mix the granulated sugar with the remaining teaspoon of cinnamon. Sprinkle over the apples. Spoon the pecan topping over the apples in dollops. Bake on the lowest rack for 45 minutes or until the apples are tender when pierced with a fork.

Serve in bowls, with heavy cream, ice cream, or half-and-half, if desired.

CRYSTAL R. BROWN
Oak Park, Illinois
Glen Ellyn Area Alumnae Chapter

PEACH CRISP PIE

MAKES 6 SERVINGS

WARM DESSERTS . . . warm hearts. This dessert is great throughout the year. Serve it hot with ice cream for dessert or for breakfast with tea or coffee.

2 (16-ounce) cans sliced peaches, lightly drained, or
   6 medium peaches, peeled and sliced
1 (9-inch) unbaked deep-dish pie shell
⅓ cup all-purpose flour
⅓ cup packed light brown sugar
2 tablespoons granulated sugar (optional)
⅓ cup old-fashioned oats
1 tablespoon grated nutmeg
1 tablespoon ground cinnamon
¼ cup butter or margarine, melted

Preheat the oven to 350 degrees.

Pour the peaches (with juice) into the pie shell. Combine the flour, sugars, oats, nutmeg, and cinnamon in a small bowl. Stir in the melted butter. The mixture will thicken. Pour over the peaches. Make sure the mixture covers the peaches.

Bake for 30 minutes. Serve warm with ice cream for dessert or with coffee as a breakfast dish.

FELICIA U. EVANS
Lumberton, North Carolina
Alpha Rho, Shaw University Chapter

CHERRY PIE

THE CINNAMON and nutmeg in this recipe give the pie an exotic dimension.

1 cup sugar

2 tablespoons all-purpose flour

1 teaspoon ground cinnamon

½ teaspoon grated nutmeg

Dash of salt

2 (4.5-ounce) cans pitted cherries, drained, and
⅔ cup juice reserved

1 teaspoon lemon extract

2 (9-inch) unbaked deep-dish pie shells

1 tablespoon butter

Preheat the oven to 425 degrees.

Combine the sugar, flour, cinnamon, nutmeg, and salt in a medium bowl. Heat the ⅔ cup cherry juice in a medium saucepan. Slowly stir in the dry ingredients, stirring constantly over low heat, until the mixture thickens. Stir in the lemon extract.

Pour the cherries into one of the pie shells. Pour the warm cherry juice mixture over the cherries. Dot with the butter. Use the second pie shell to cover the pie or cut it into strips for a lattice top. Bake for 30 to 35 minutes.

COOK'S TIP | *Serve topped with vanilla ice cream, if desired.*

LENORA PARRISH
Fairfield, California
Solano Valley Alumnae Chapter

FLUFFY STRAWBERRY PIE

MAKES 12 SERVINGS

1 (14-ounce) can condensed fat-free milk

¼ cup lemon juice

2 cups frozen sweetened sliced strawberries, thawed and drained

1 (12-ounce) container frozen whipped topping, thawed

½ cup frozen strawberry daiquiri mix, thawed

2 (8-ounce) prepared graham cracker piecrusts

In a medium bowl, combine the milk with the lemon juice. Add the strawberries, whipped topping, and daiquiri mix; mix well. Pour into the graham cracker crusts. Refrigerate for 3 hours or until firm.

COOK'S TIP | *The filling could be served in parfait glasses with the berries and crushed nuts on top.*

DEBBIE W. TIJANI
Upper Marlboro, Maryland
Potomac Valley Alumnae Chapter

BERRY TARTLETS

MAKES 8 SERVINGS

FOR EASIER PREPARATION, purchase the tartlet shells from your local market.

¾ cup unsalted butter, softened

¾ cup sifted powdered sugar

1½ cups all-purpose flour

1½ cups heavy cream

1½ tablespoons granulated sugar

¾ teaspoon vanilla extract

½ teaspoon lemon extract

8 tablespoons fruit preserves, any flavor

2 pints assorted fresh berries or frozen berries, thawed

Beat the butter and sifted powdered sugar in a small bowl with an electric mixer at low speed. Gradually stir in the flour until the dough begins to come together.

Divide the dough into eight balls. Press evenly into eight tartlet pans. Refrigerate for 30 minutes or overnight.

Preheat the oven to 350 degrees.

Bake the tartlet shells on a baking sheet until golden brown. Cool on wire racks, then tap on the bottom of each pan to remove the crusts. Set aside.

Whip the heavy cream until soft peaks form. Add the granulated sugar; fold in the vanilla and lemon extracts. Continue whipping until stiff peaks form. Spread the bottom of each tartlet with 1 tablespoon of preserves. Spread the whipped cream to the top of each crust and arrange fruit on top.

TAMMARA BROWN
New Orleans, Louisiana
Nu Mu Citywide Chapter—Tulane—New Orleans

DELTA OF DISTINCTION
Lesli Foster
Broadcast Journalist

ONE OF THE MOST influential newscasters in the Washington, D.C., area, Soror Lesli Foster was initiated into the Alpha Chapter of Delta Sigma Theta in 1996.

Born and raised in Detroit, she originally aspired to a career as a dancer until a series of knee injuries derailed that ambition. She received her degree in broadcast journalism from Howard University's School of Communications. She began her career as a reporter for WEYI, the NBC affiliate in Flint, Michigan, and moved on from there to Baltimore, where she covered the crime beat for WBAL-TV. In January 2001 she joined the 9NEWS team in Washington as the five and six A.M. and noontime newscaster.

Soror Lesli says that her interest in journalism grew out of her passion for gathering information and her love of telling "the whole story." She now anchors the weekend morning newscasts and reports for the weekday morning news three days a week. Life is hectic, she says, but the daily challenges make her job all the more exciting.

SOUTHERN SWEET POTATO PONE

MAKES 18–24 SERVINGS

THIS MISSISSIPPI RECIPE has been in my family for more than fifty years. We've enjoyed it on many occasions, especially at Christmastime and during the winter months. During the winter, Mother used to bake the potato pone for us to eat as a late snack while we sat around the fireplace telling stories and jokes or playing games. My father would usually have three times as much as the kids. He even poured brandy on top of his pone. The highlight of the evening was seeing which child would eat the leftover batter from the mixing bowl and the large spoon.

3 large sweet potatoes, peeled and quartered

½ cup butter or margarine

2 large eggs, slightly beaten

½ pint whipping cream

2 teaspoons vanilla extract

2 tablespoons brown sugar

½ teaspoon ground cinnamon

½ teaspoon ground allspice

½ teaspoon ground cloves

Dash of grated nutmeg

½ cup golden raisins (optional)

½ cup flaked coconut (optional)

1 cup chopped pecans or walnuts

1 teaspoon lemon zest

½ cup all-purpose flour

1 tablespoon baking powder

Topping (see following recipe)

TOPPING

1 cup whole pecans or walnuts

1 cup marshmallows

½ cup butter or margarine, melted

Boil the sweet potatoes until tender, approximately 30 minutes. Drain and mash the potatoes.

Preheat the oven to 350 degrees.

Lightly grease a 13-by-9-inch baking dish. In a heavy saucepan melt the butter over low heat; cook until brown, about 5 minutes. Stir the butter and the remaining ingredients, except topping, into the mashed sweet potatoes, blending well. Spread the mixture evenly in the preapared dish; set aside.

To prepare the topping, place the pecans or walnuts and marshmallows on top of the potatoes. Pour the melted butter evenly over the topping. Bake for 30 minutes or until golden brown. Serve hot or cold.

ESSIE M. JEFFRIES
Los Angeles, California
Member, National Commission on Arts and Letters
Los Angeles Alumnae Chapter

PEACH COBBLER WITH A FLAIR

MAKES 4–6 SERVINGS

AS A HOME ECONOMICS teacher for more than thirty years, I shared many recipes with my students, and on Fridays the students would bring their own recipes. One young lady shared the recipe for this wonderful peach cobbler. Later that year, I made it for a teachers' meeting, and one of the administrators fell in love with it. After he retired, he managed the parking lot closest to Ohio State stadium. Needless to say, a peach cobbler for him and his attendants helped "the beautiful teacher with the great peach cobbler" find a free space. Moral: Always give a child a chance to shine—you never know how or when that child's sun will shine back on you.

¼ cup butter
1 cup all-purpose flour
½ teaspoon grated nutmeg
¼ teaspoon ground cinnamon
1 teaspoon baking powder
1 cup sugar
1 cup milk
½ teaspoon vanilla extract
¼ teaspoon almond extract
1 (29-ounce) can sliced peaches, undrained

Preheat the oven to 350 degrees. Melt the butter in a 12-by-8-inch glass baking dish; set aside.

Sift the flour, nutmeg, cinnamon, and baking powder in a large bowl. Add the sugar. Combine the milk and vanilla and almond extracts in a small bowl. Stir into the dry ingredients and mix well. Pour the ingredients evenly over the melted butter. Do not stir. Spread the canned peaches with their juice on top of the batter. Do not stir.

Bake 45 minutes or until brown.

MAYME SWANSON
Columbus, Ohio
Columbus Alumnae Chapter

COBB'S PEACH COBBLER

MAKES 4–6 SERVINGS

½ cup all-purpose flour
Pinch of salt
¾ cup sugar
½ teaspoon baking powder
½ cup milk
3 tablespoons butter or margarine
2 cups sliced canned or fresh peaches with syrup

Preheat the oven to 350 degrees.

Mix the flour, salt, ¼ cup of the sugar, the baking powder, and milk in a medium bowl.

Melt the butter in a large ovenproof skillet. Pour the flour mixture over the melted butter. Add the peaches and syrup; top with the remaining ½ cup sugar.

Bake 30 to 35 minutes.

GLORIA COBB FLOURNOY
Dubberly, Louisiana
Minden Alumnae Chapter

QUICK PEACH COBBLER

MAKES 16–18 SERVINGS

FOR THE PERSON who has a sweet tooth but doesn't like cooking.

2 (29-ounce) cans sliced peaches in heavy syrup
1 cup butter, cut into pieces
2 (9-ounce) packages Jiffy yellow cake mix
1 tablespoon ground cinnamon (optional)

Preheat the oven to 350 degrees. Grease a 13-by-9-inch glass baking dish.

Pour the peaches and their juice into the dish and dot with the butter. Pour the cake mix evenly over the top. Sprinkle with cinnamon, if desired.

Bake 50 minutes or until the juices rise up through the cake mix and a crust forms.

Serve with vanilla ice cream, if desired.

ALMETTA J. JONES
(MOTHER OF
PAMELA L. PATCH)
Chicago, Illinois
Chicago Alumnae Chapter

CARAMEL-COATED YAM FLAN

MAKES 10–12 SERVINGS

AN AFRICAN-AMERICAN–Caribbean staple, the yam, or sweet potato, makes this wonderful dessert.

2¼ cups granulated sugar
2 cups water
4 cups heavy cream
1 vanilla bean or 1 teaspoon vanilla extract
2 cinnamon sticks
1 pound yams, baked, peeled, and puréed
¾ cup packed brown sugar
1 tablespoon ground cinnamon
1½ teaspoons ground allspice
1½ teaspoons ground cloves
6 large eggs
6 large egg yolks
2 tablespoons rum
2 tablespoons Kahlúa

Combine 2 cups of the sugar and 1¼ cups of the water in a heavy saucepan. Cook on medium heat, without stirring, until the sugar melts and turns a dark amber, swirling occasionally (be careful because caramel burns quickly). Pour about 1 cup into an 11-by-7-inch baking dish to cover the bottom and sides. Let cool. Add the remaining ¾ cup water to the remaining caramel. Carefully boil until the caramel has dissolved and mixture is smooth. Refrigerate.

For the flan, place the cream, vanilla, and cinnamon sticks in a saucepan over medium heat. Bring to a boil. Remove from the heat and cool about 1 hour. Strain into a large bowl.

Preheat the oven to 325 degrees.

Add the remaining ingredients to the cream and whisk until smooth. Strain into a baking dish. Put the dish into a baking pan and add an inch or so of water to the pan. Bake about 1¼ hours. Remove and place in a cool water bath. Cover with plastic and chill. Serve with reheated caramel.

SONYA E. CHILES
Silver Spring, Maryland
Potomac Valley Alumnae Chapter

DIRT CAKE

MAKES 8–10 SERVINGS

THIS unusual party cake us made in a flowerpot. If you like, you can decorate the top with silk or real flowers that are removed just before serving. (Add gummy worms throughout the layering for a fun surprise.)

1 (8-ounce) package cream cheese, softened
1 cup sifted powdered sugar
1 (3.4-ounce) box instant vanilla pudding mix
1½ cups milk
1 (8-ounce) container frozen whipped topping,
    thawed
1 (1-pound) package chocolate cream-filled cookies,
    crushed in a blender or food processor

Combine the cream cheese and powdered sugar in a large bowl until creamy. Blend in the pudding mix and the milk. Fold in the whipped topping.

Begin by layering some of the cookie crumbs in a clean medium-size flowerpot. Add a layer of the cream cheese mixture, then more cookie crumbs. Continue layering until all ingredients are used, ending with cookie crumbs.

JACQUELINE JACKSON HOWARD
Washington, D.C.
Federal City Alumnae Chapter

Hiding in plain sight: Dirt Cake made in a flowerpot.

FRUITY POUND CAKE COMPOTE

MAKES 8–10 SERVINGS

2 (8-ounce) packages cream cheese, softened
4 teaspoons vanilla extract
1 (8-ounce) can sweetened condensed milk
½ cup lemon juice
2 loaves pound cake of choice (banana, plain, lemon, or nut)
1 (20-ounce) can crushed pineapple, drained
1 (20-ounce) can cherry pie filling
1 (20-ounce) can sliced peaches, drained
2 cups chopped toasted walnuts, pecans, or almonds

Combine the cream cheese and the next 3 ingredients in a medium bowl. Mix well with an electric mixer; set aside at room temperature.

Cut the pound cake into thin slices. Place one layer of slices in a 3-quart, deep glass dish. Spread with a layer each of pineapple, cherry pie filling, and peach slices, then sprinkle with nuts. Spread with a a layer of cream cheese filling.

Repeat with three additional layers, ending with cream cheese and a sprinkle of nuts.

Chill for at least 4 hours or overnight. Serve chilled.

CIESTA L. CATO
Anchorage, Alaska
Alaska Alumnae Chapter

CRIMSON RASPBERRY AND CREAM BLOSSOMS

MAKES 12 SERVINGS

AS A DELTA hostess, I have often been challenged to create a red-and-white dessert. Sometimes, red velvet cake is just too much. Here's one that's light, tasty, and crimson and cream.

3 (10-ounce) packages frozen raspberries, thawed
¼ cup butter, melted
8 sheets phyllo dough (Cover with plastic wrap, then a damp towel to keep from drying out.)
1 (8-ounce) package cream cheese, softened
½ cup cottage cheese
1 large egg
½ cup plus 3 tablespoons sugar
4 teaspoons lemon juice
4 teaspoons vanilla extract
Fresh raspberries and sliced kiwi for garnish

Preheat the oven to 350 degrees. Grease 12 (2½-inch) muffin cups. Drain the raspberries, reserving the syrup.

Brush melted butter onto 1 phyllo sheet. Cover with a second phyllo sheet; brush with butter. Repeat with remaining butter and sheets of dough.

Cut the stack of phyllo dough in thirds lengthwise and then into fourths crosswise to make a total of 12 squares. Gently fit each stacked square into a prepared muffin cup.

Place the cream cheese, cottage cheese, egg, 3 tablespoons of the sugar, 1 teaspoon of the lemon juice, and the vanilla in a food processor or blender. Process until smooth. Divide the mixture evenly among the muffin cups.

Bake for 10 to 15 minutes or until lightly browned. Carefully remove from the muffin cups onto wire racks to cool.

Bring the reserved raspberry syrup to a boil in a small saucepan over medium-high heat. Cook until reduced to ¾ cup, stirring occasionally. Place the thawed raspberries in a food processor or blender. Process until smooth; press through a fine-meshed sieve or cheesecloth to remove seeds.

Combine the raspberry purée, reduced syrup, remaining ½ cup sugar, and the remaining 3 teaspoons lemon juice in a small bowl; mix well.

To serve, spoon the raspberry sauce onto dessert plates. Place a cheesecake blossom on each plate. Garnish with the fresh fruit.

LaShawn Ames-McConnell
Brooklyn, New York
Member, National Commission on Arts and Letters
Brooklyn Alumnae Chapter

Cobb's Cherry Pizza

MAKES 6–10 SERVINGS

2 (16-ounce) cans cherry pie filling
1 (18.25-ounce) package yellow cake mix
2 cups pecan halves
¾ cup cold butter or margarine

Preheat the oven to 350 degrees.

Spread the cherry pie filling evenly over the bottom of a 12-by-9-inch baking dish. Spread the yellow cake mix evenly on top of the filling. Scatter the pecans on top. Cut the butter as thinly as possible and lay side by side all over the top. Bake for 45 to 60 minutes or until golden brown.

Gloria Cobb Flournoy
Dubberly, Louisiana
Minden Alumnae Chapter

CHERRIES JUBILEE

MAKES 4 SERVINGS

A DESSERT for "oohs" and "ahhs." Men are always thrilled to be asked to light the cherries.

1 (16-ounce) can Bing cherries

1 tablespoon arrowroot or cornstarch

1 tablespoon sugar or honey

2 tablespoons finely chopped preserved ginger

1½ cups cherry brandy or ¼ cup cognac, warmed

4 scoops firm vanilla ice cream

Drain the cherries, reserving the liquid. Make a smooth paste of the arrowroot and several tablespoons of the cherry liquid. Gradually add the remainder of the liquid. Stir in the sugar.

Place a heavy skillet over medium heat. Add the mixture and heat until it thickens, stirring constantly for 3 or 4 minutes. Add the cherries and chopped ginger and reheat. Pour the warmed brandy over the cherries and ignite. When flame dies down, ladle the cherries over the ice cream; serve immediately.

COOK'S TIP | *If using cherries in light syrup, you may want to add more sugar or honey for a sweeter taste.*

BERTHA "BERT" HOPKINS BREESE
Durham, North Carolina
Durham Alumnae Chapter

STRAWBERRY DELIGHT

MAKES 12 SERVINGS

MY GREAT-AUNT served this recipe at many holiday family gatherings. As a child, I stood in the kitchen the night before the holiday and watched her prepare dinner and desserts for the big day. It was hard getting recipes from her because she never measured anything, so I observed and came up with my own recipe that tasted as good as hers.

2 (3-ounce) packages strawberry gelatin

2 cups hot water

1 quart vanilla ice cream, softened

1½ pints sour cream

1 (16-ounce) package sliced frozen strawberries, thawed, juices reserved

Combine the gelatin and hot water; stir until well mixed and cool to lukewarm. Stir in the ice cream, sour cream, and ½ cup juice from the frozen strawberries. Pour into a round gelatin mold or a 12-cup Bundt cake pan. Refrigerate for 15 minutes and then stir in the strawberries. Chill overnight.

Before serving, dip the mold pan into warm water for 2 seconds and turn upside down onto a silver platter. The mold will slide onto the plate.

ANDREA CANTY
Los Angeles, California
Century City Alumnae Chapter

Strawberry Delight

TROPICAL FRUIT DESSERT

MAKES 6–8 SERVINGS

W HEN A CO-WORKER celebrated her thirty-year anniversary, everyone brought a dish. This was my contribution, and I've made it often for celebrations since then.

1 (20-ounce) can pineapple tidbits
1 (29-ounce) can sliced peaches, drained and chopped
2 (15-ounce) cans mandarin orange slices, drained
1 (3.4-ounce) box instant French vanilla pudding mix
1 tablespoon powdered orange drink mix
1–2 large bananas

Drain and reserve the juice from the pineapple tidbits. Place all the canned fruit in a large bowl. Combine the pineapple juice with the pudding mix and orange drink mix in a medium bowl. Slice the bananas and add to the other fruit. Pour the pudding mixture over the fruit and mix well. Chill in refrigerator.

SONDRA L. SMITH
St. Louis, Missouri
St. Louis Alumnae Chapter

CHERRY FRUIT SALAD

MAKES 4–6 SERVINGS

1 (16-ounce) can crushed pineapple, drained
1 (21-ounce) can cherry pie filling
1 cup chopped walnuts
1 (14-ounce) can sweetened condensed milk
1 cup flaked coconut
1 (16-ounce) container frozen whipped topping, thawed

Combine all the ingredients in a large bowl and refrigerate overnight. Serve in clear sherbet glasses.

CAROLYN WILDER
Los Angeles, California
Los Angeles Alumnae Chapter

STRAWBERRY PRETZEL

MAKES 10–12 SERVINGS

2 cups crushed salted or unsalted pretzels
1 cup butter, melted
½ cup granulated sugar
1 cup sifted powdered sugar
1 (8-ounce) package cream cheese
1 (8-ounce) container frozen whipped topping, thawed
1 (0.6-ounce) box strawberry gelatin
2 cups boiling water
1 (20-ounce) can crushed pineapple, drained
2 (10-ounce) packages frozen strawberries, thawed

Preheat the oven to 350 degrees.

Combine the pretzels, melted butter, and granulated sugar in a small bowl. Spread in a 13-by-9-inch baking pan. Bake 5 to 7 minutes. Do not let it bubble up; cool.

Combine the sifted powdered sugar, cream cheese, and whipped topping in a medium bowl. Mix well with an electric mixer; spread over the pretzel crust once it has cooled.

Combine the gelatin and boiling water in a medium bowl; let gel slightly. Then add the drained pineapple and strawberries with their juice. Let gel slightly; then pour over the creamy layer. Refrigerate overnight.

CHERYL Y. HUDSON
Columbus, Ohio
Columbus Alumnae Chapter

BLACKBERRY DUMPLINGS

MAKES 8 SERVINGS

I DECIDED TO SHARE THIS recipe because it brought back such great memories from my childhood. My brothers, sisters, and I knew the location of every blackberry patch near our home in South Carolina. We would go down by the railroad tracks to pick the berries so our mother could make her great blackberry dumplings. And since I enjoyed eating them so much, I had to learn how to make them.

1 cup water
½ cup sugar, or more if desired
2 tablespoons cornstarch
1 tablespoon vanilla extract
1 teaspoon ground cinnamon
1 cup butter
2 cups blackberries

DUMPLINGS
1 cup all-purpose flour
2 tablespoons sugar
1½ teaspoons baking powder
¼ teaspoon salt
¼ cup cold butter or margarine, cut into pieces
1 large egg
¼ cup milk

Combine the water, sugar, cornstarch, vanilla, cinnamon, butter, and blackberries in a large saucepan. Cook over medium heat until the mixture begins to thicken, stirring frequently.

In a bowl, combine the flour, sugar, baking powder, and salt; cut in the butter until crumbly. Whisk the egg and milk in a small bowl; stir into the crumb mixture just until moistened. Divide the dough and roll into 8 balls. Drop the balls into the blackberry mixture; cook 25 to 30 minutes or until the dumplings are cooked through. Lower the heat and cook about 10 minutes longer to thicken the sauce. Serve warm or cold.

VIRGINIA R. TOOMER
New York, New York
New York Alumnae Chapter

PEACH CREAM TRIFLE

MAKES 8–10 SERVINGS

THIS IS A Sunday-evening delight, to serve with hot vanilla sauce or ice cream.

Crème Anglaise (see following recipe)
3 tablespoons granulated sugar
7 fresh ripe peaches, peeled and sliced (4 cups)
1¾ cups whipping cream
¼ cup sifted powdered sugar
1 (16-ounce) pound cake, cut into cubes
½ cup amaretto liqueur
¼ cup sliced almonds, toasted

Prepare crème anglaise; chill until ready to use.

Sprinkle the granulated sugar over the peaches; toss and let stand 20 minutes or until juicy.

Combine the whipping cream and sifted powdered sugar in a chilled mixing bowl. Beat with an electric mixer at medium speed until soft peaks form. Fold half of the whipped cream into the crème anglaise.

Place half of the cake cubes in a 3-quart trifle bowl. Sprinkle ¼ cup amaretto over the cubes. Top with half of the crème anglaise and half of the peaches. Repeat the layers.

Spread the remaining whipped cream on top of the trifle. Cover and chill 8 hours. Sprinkle with almonds before serving.

COOK'S TIP | *You can substitute 1 package instant vanilla pudding mix mixed with 1¾ cup milk for the crème anglaise; you can also substitute 1 (12-ounce) container frozen whipped topping, thawed, for the whipping cream and ½ cup orange juice for the amaretto.*

CRÈME ANGLAISE
2 cups milk
½ cup sugar
5 large egg yolks
1 teaspoon vanilla extract

Bring the milk to a simmer over medium heat in a heavy saucepan. In a medium bowl, beat the sugar and the egg yolks at high speed with electric mixer until a ribbon forms. Gradually add the hot milk to the egg yolk mixture, whisking until blended; return to the saucepan. Cook over low heat, stirring constantly, until the custard thickens and coats a spoon. Remove from the heat; pour through a wire-mesh sieve into a bowl and stir to mix. Stir in the vanilla; cover and chill.

NGWEBIFOR FOBI WALKER
Rolling Hills, California
Rolling Hills–Palos Verdes Alumnae Chapter

VINTAGE FRUIT STARTER

MAKES 2 CUPS

GREAT TO GIVE, and great to get!

¾ cup canned peaches in heavy syrup
¾ cup canned pineapple chunks in heavy syrup
6 maraschino cherries
1½ cups sugar
1 (0.25-ounce) package active or quick-rise dry yeast

Drain the peaches and cut into pieces; place fruit in a medium bowl. Drain the pineapple chunks; add to peaches. Cut the cherries in half; add to the bowl. Stir in the sugar and yeast; mix well. Place the fruit in a glass jar with a loose-fitting lid. Keep in a warm place. Stir several times the first day, then once daily for two weeks.

Every three or four weeks, add more fruit in rotation with more sugar: for example, peaches and sugar; then three or four weeks later, pineapple and sugar. Stir until the sugar dissolves. Don't put lid on tightly.

Serve the fruit on pound cake, pudding, ice cream, grapefruit halves, or yogurt.

Give 2-cup portions as gifts along with the recipe, but never let your fruit get below 2 to 3 cups.

COOK'S TIP | *Do not use fresh fruit, only canned.*

MIGNON BROWN
Las Vegas, Nevada
Las Vegas Alumnae Chapter

SASSY FRUIT 'N' SAUCE

MAKES 12 SERVINGS

2 (16-ounce) cans peaches in natural juices, drained and liquid reserved
1 (11-ounce) can mandarin orange slices, drained and liquid reserved
1 (20-ounce) can pineapple tidbits, drained and liquid reserved
Seedless grapes (as many as you like)
2 (3.4-ounce) boxes instant vanilla pudding mix
2 (10-ounce) packages frozen sliced strawberries
3 bananas, sliced
Sliced fresh strawberries

Combine and measure the liquid from the canned fruit. You should have 3 cups. If not, add water. Place the canned fruit and grapes in a large bowl.

Combine the fruit juice and the vanilla pudding mixes in a medium saucepan. Cook until thickened. Pour thickened pudding over fruit. Add the frozen strawberries. Stir until the strawberries are thawed and all ingredients are mixed well. Refrigerate for at least 8 hours.

Add the bananas and fresh strawberries just before serving. Serve by itself or over plain cake.

CYNTHIA J. RODGERS
Clinton, Maryland
Prince George's County Alumnae Chapter

LEMON PUDDING SOUFFLÉ

MAKES 8 SERVINGS

1 cup granulated sugar

¼ cup all-purpose flour

¼ teaspoon salt

4 ounces pitted prunes

3 tablespoons water

2 large egg yolks

Grated zest of 1 lemon

⅓ cup fresh lemon juice

1 cup fat-free milk

4 large egg whites

Sifted powdered sugar, mint leaves, lemon slices
   for garnish (optional)

Lemon Pudding Soufflé

Preheat the oven to 350 degrees. Spray 8 (5-ounce) custard cups with vegetable cooking spray; set aside.

Combine ¾ cup of the sugar, the flour, and the salt in a large bowl. Blend well with an electric mixer; set aside.

In food processor, blend the prunes and the water until the prunes are finely chopped. Add to the flour mixture and blend thoroughly.

Add the egg yolks, lemon zest, and lemon juice; blend thoroughly. Add the milk; blend thoroughly and set aside.

Beat the egg whites in a medium bowl until soft peaks form. Gradually beat in the remaining ¼ cup sugar until stiff peaks form. Fold the egg white mixture gently into the lemon mixture.

Divide the mixture equally among the custard cups. Set the cups in a shallow pan and add ½ inch boiling water to the pan. Place on center rack in oven and bake 45 to 50 minutes, until puffed, set, and light golden brown.

Cool 10 minutes. The soufflés will sink, but that's okay. Dust with sifted powdered sugar and garnish with mint leaves and lemon slices, if desired.

ERA JEAN DAVIS
Los Angeles, California
Rolling Hills–Palos Verdes Alumnae Chapter

LEMON BREEZE

½ cup margarine
1 cup all-purpose flour
¼ cup chopped pecans
1 cup sifted powdered sugar
1 (8-ounce) package cream cheese
1 (3.4-ounce) box instant lemon pudding mix
1½ cups whole milk
½ (8-ounce) container frozen whipped topping, thawed
Additional chopped pecans

Preheat the oven to 350 degrees. Grease an 8-by-8-inch baking pan.

Combine the margarine, flour, and pecans in a medium bowl; mix until crumbly. Press into the prepared baking pan. Bake for 20 minutes; let cool.

Combine the sifted powdered sugar and the cream cheese in a medium bowl. Mix well and spread on top of crust after it is cool.

Mix the instant pudding mix and milk in a medium bowl. Mix until thickened. Spread on top of the cream cheese mixture.

Spread the whipped topping on top of the lemon pudding. Sprinkle with extra nuts. Refrigerate for at least 3 hours or overnight before serving.

COOK'S TIP | *For a stronger lemon flavor, add ½ teaspoon lemon flavoring to the pudding mixture.*

JESSIE W. FOSTER
Baton Rouge, Louisiana
Baton Rouge Sigma Alumnae Chapter

APPLE PUDDING

THIS WAS SERVED and enjoyed at a membership intake training session.

5 medium apples
2 cups all-purpose flour
2 cups sugar
2 large eggs, beaten
4 teaspoons baking powder
6 tablespoons butter, melted
⅓ cup milk

Preheat the oven to 350 degrees. Grease a 9-by-9-inch baking dish.

Peel and slice the apples. Place the apples in the prepared baking dish, so they fill the dish halfway.

Combine the flour and the remaining ingredients in a large bowl; mix well. Pour over the apples. Bake for 50 to 60 minutes.

REGINA D. COOK
Columbia, Maryland
Columbia Alumnae Chapter

ATLANTA LEMON WHIP LUSH

MAKES 10–12 SERVINGS

½ cup margarine

1 cup all-purpose flour

¼ cup granulated sugar

1 cup chopped pecans

2 (3.4-ounce) boxes instant lemon pudding
mix

4 cups whole milk

1 (8-ounce) package cream cheese, at room
temperature

2 (8-ounce) containers frozen whipped topping,
thawed

1 cup sifted powdered sugar

¼ cup chopped, well-drained maraschino cherries

Preheat the oven to 350 degrees. Place the margarine in a 13-by-9-inch glass dish and melt in the oven for 3 minutes. Remove the dish. Mix the flour, granulated sugar, and ⅔ cup of the pecans in a small bowl; press into the melted margarine. Return to the oven and bake for 10 minutes.

Combine the instant pudding mixes with the milk, and set aside.

Combine the cream cheese, 8 ounces of the whipped topping, and the sifted powdered sugar in a medium bowl until smooth. Spread over the crust in the baking dish. Pour the instant pudding over the cream cheese layer. Spread the remaining 8 ounces whipped topping over the pudding layer.

Sprinkle with the maraschino cherries and the remaining ⅓ cup chopped pecans. Refrigerate overnight.

JEAN FLOYD
Atlanta, Georgia
Atlanta Alumnae Chapter

LEMON BARS

MAKES 24 BARS

SWEETEN UP your day with a lemon bar and milk.

2½ cups all-purpose flour

½ cup sifted powdered sugar

¾ cup butter or margarine

½ teaspoon baking powder

4 large eggs, lightly beaten

2 cups granulated sugar

½ teaspoon grated lemon rind (optional)

⅓ cup fresh lemon juice

Additional sifted powdered sugar

Preheat the oven to 350 degrees. Grease a 13-by-9-inch baking pan.

Combine 2 cups of the flour and the sifted powdered sugar in a large bowl. Cut in the butter with a pastry blender until crumbly.

Spoon the mixture into the prepared pan; press firmly and evenly into the pan. Bake for 20 to 25 minutes or until the crust is lightly browned. Set it aside to cool while you prepare the filling.

Lemon Bars

Combine the remaining ½ cup flour and the baking powder in a small bowl; set aside.

Combine the eggs, granulated sugar, lemon rind, if desired, and lemon juice; stir in the flour mixture. Pour over the baked crust. Bake for 25 minutes or until lightly browned and set. Cool on a wire rack. When completely cool, dust lightly with sifted powdered sugar; cut into bars.

NGELAH ALYSSA FOBI
New Orleans, Louisiana
Nu Mu Citywide Chapter—Tulane—New Orleans

LOUISE R. WILSON'S TWO-WAY BROWNIES

MAKES 12–16 SERVINGS

¼ cup plus 3 tablespoons butter

2 (1-ounce) squares unsweetened chocolate

1 large egg

½ cup granulated sugar

¼ cup all-purpose flour

¼ cup pecans

1 cup sifted powdered sugar

1 tablespoon heavy cream

¼ teaspoon vanilla extract

Preheat the oven to 350 degrees.

Melt ¼ cup of the butter and 1 square of the chocolate in the top of a double boiler. Pour into a large bowl; add the egg, granulated sugar, flour, and pecans; mix well. Pour into an 8-by-8-inch baking pan. Bake for 20 minutes.

While brownies are baking, make the icing: Combine 2 tablespoons of the remaining butter, the powdered sugar, cream, and vanilla in a medium bowl; mix well. Cool brownies, then spread with icing. Melt the remaining square of chocolate with the remaining tablespoon of butter. Drizzle over the brownies.

CRYSTAL R. BROWN
Oak Park, Illinois
Glen Ellyn Area Alumnae Chapter

ICE CREAM CRUNCH

MAKES 8–10 SERVINGS

THIS IS A RECIPE I received from a co-worker.

½ gallon vanilla ice cream, softened

2½ cups crisped rice cereal

1 cup chopped nuts of your choice

1 cup flaked coconut

½ cup melted butter

¾ cup brown sugar

Spoon the ice cream into a 13-by-9-inch pan; then place back in the freezer.

Preheat the oven to 300 degrees. Mix the rice cereal, nuts, coconut, and melted butter in a small bowl. Place in a pan or on a cookie sheet. Bake until golden brown, stirring every 5 minutes. Remove from the oven. Combine with the brown sugar. Remove the ice cream from the freezer and pat the crunch evenly over the entire surface. Put back in freezer until ready to serve. Let sit at room temperature for 10 minutes and then cut with a knife dipped in hot water. Use a spatula to remove the squares.

COOK'S TIP | *You can add chocolate chips to the crunch or delete the coconut.*

SONDRA L. SMITH
St. Louis, Missouri
St. Louis Alumnae Chapter

DELICIOUS GOOEY DELTA BUTTER BARS

MAKES 30 SERVINGS

THIS RECIPE is about ten years old, a treat we would enjoy at Sunday dinners.

1 (18.25-ounce) package yellow cake mix
½ cup butter, melted
1 large egg
Filling (see recipe below)

Preheat the oven to 350 degrees.

Combine the cake mix, butter, and egg in a large bowl; beat 2 minutes. Pat into the bottom of an ungreased 13-by-9-inch pan. Pour the Filling over the crust. Bake for 45 to 50 minutes (you will see a big bubble come over the cake). Remove from the oven and cool. Cut into squares.

FILLING

1 (8-ounce) package cream cheese, softened
2 large eggs
1 teaspoon vanilla extract
½ cup butter, melted
1 (16-ounce) box powdered sugar, sifted

Blend the cream cheese in a medium bowl until fluffy. Add the 2 large eggs and vanilla. Beat the butter in a small bowl for 1 minute. Add the butter to the cream cheese mixture. Add the sifted powdered sugar. Beat until incorporated. Beat for 1 more minute.

TRACY MILLER
McBee, South Carolina
Hartsville Alumnae Chapter

GOOEY SQUARES

MAKES 12–15 SERVINGS

THIS RECIPE was given to me by my mother-in-law in the 1980s. I serve it for social gatherings both at home and at work.

1 (18.25-ounce) package yellow cake mix
½ cup margarine, melted
1 cup chopped pecans
1 (16-ounce) box powdered sugar, sifted
1 (8-ounce) package cream cheese, softened
3 large eggs

Preheat the oven to 325 degrees. Grease and flour a 16-by-11-inch baking pan.

Combine the cake mix, melted margarine, and pecans in a large bowl. Mix well. Pour into the prepared pan; then press into pan.

Combine the powdered sugar, cream cheese, and eggs in a medium bowl; beat until smooth and creamy. Pour over the cake layer in the pan. Bake for 35 to 45 minutes or until brown. Cool and then cut into squares to serve.

ROSETTA MONCRIEF
Montgomery, Alabama
Montgomery Alumnae Chapter

CAROLYN'S CREAM CHEESE SQUARES

MAKES 24 SQUARES

MY AUNT AND I can't remember which one of us came up with this recipe, but we have never heard of anyone else making it. I started making the squares for potluck parties at work about ten years ago, and everyone loved them. They are also a big hit at chapter potluck parties.

2 (8-ounce) cans crescent rolls
2 (8-ounce) packages cream cheese, softened
1 cup sugar
1 teaspoon vanilla extract
3 teaspoons bottled lemon juice
1 egg white (optional)

Preheat the oven to 325 degrees.

Open 1 can of the crescent rolls and lay the dough on the bottom of an 11-by-9-inch baking dish, spreading it to the edges of the dish and smoothing the seams. Mix the cream cheese, sugar, vanilla, and lemon juice in a medium bowl until blended and

Carolyn's Cream Cheese Squares

smooth. Spread the cream cheese mixture over the dough. Unroll the second can of crescent rolls and spread it on top of the cream cheese mixture. (The crescent rolls are easier to spread if they are cooler than room temperature.)

If desired, brush the top layer of dough with the egg white to make it appear glossy. Bake 35 to 45 minutes or until the top is golden brown. Cool, cut into squares, and refrigerate.

COOK'S TIP | *The pastry cuts better when cool, but the warm squares are also tasty. You can use one-third less fat cream cheese and reduced-fat rolls, if desired.*

CAROLYN C. JOHNSON
Warsaw, Virginia
Williamsburg Alumnae Chapter

DELTA OF DISTINCTION
Patricia Roberts Harris

THE FIRST EXECUTIVE DIRECTOR of the national headquarters of Delta Sigma Theta, Soror Patricia Roberts Harris earned her law degree from George Washington University and began her academic career as a lecturer at Howard University Law School, rising to a full professorship and serving as both associate dean of students and dean of the law school.

In 1963 President Kennedy named her, along with Mildred McAfee Horton, to co-chair the National Women's Committee for Civil Rights. Her subsequent career as a public servant includes many significant "firsts." She became the first African-American woman to hold ambassadorial rank when President Johnson appointed her ambassador to Luxembourg in 1965. In 1977 she was named secretary of Housing and Urban Development by President Carter and thus became the first African-American woman ever appointed to a presidential cabinet. In 1979 she became secretary of Health, Education, and Welfare, and, a year later, the very first secretary of the newly formed department of Health and Human Services.

After serving in the Carter administration Soror Harris returned to full-time teaching as a professor of law at George Washington University and, in 1982, ran unsuccessfully for mayor of Washington, D.C. Unfortunately, she died when she was only sixty, in 1985.

PECAN PIE BARS

MAKES 2½ DOZEN

❧

1¾ cups all-purpose flour

1⅓ cups firmly packed dark brown sugar

1 cup butter or margarine

4 large eggs

1 cup dark corn syrup

1 teaspoon vanilla extract

⅛ teaspoon salt

1¼ cups chopped pecans

Preheat the oven to 350 degrees.

Grease a 13-by-9-inch baking dish. Combine the flour and ⅓ cup of the brown sugar in a medium bowl; cut in ¾ cup of the butter with a pastry blender until crumbly. Press the mixture evenly into the prepared pan. Bake 15 to 17 minutes.

Melt the remaining ¼ cup butter; cool slightly. Combine the melted butter with the remaining 1 cup brown sugar, the eggs, corn syrup, vanilla, and salt, stirring well. Stir in the pecans.

Pour the filling over the prepared crust. Bake 35 minutes or until set. Cool in the pan on a wire rack. Cut into bars.

TERRELL GREEN
New Orleans, Louisiana
Nu Mu Citywide Chapter—Tulane—New Orleans

VANILLA-PECAN ICEBOX COOKIES

MAKES 4 DOZEN

❧

1 cup butter, softened

1 cup granulated sugar

¼ cup red decorator sugar crystals (optional)

1 large egg

1 teaspoon vanilla extract

2¾ cups all-purpose flour

1 teaspoon baking powder

½ teaspoon salt

1 cup finely chopped pecans

1 (16-ounce) jar maraschino cherries, drained and finely chopped

Beat the butter in a large bowl with an electric mixer at medium speed until creamy; gradually add the sugars, beating well. Add the egg and vanilla; beat well.

Combine the flour, baking powder, and salt in a medium bowl; add to the butter mixture, beating well at medium speed (dough will be stiff). Stir in the pecans and the cherries.

Cover and chill the dough at least 2 hours.

Shape the dough into two equal-size rolls. Wrap the rolls in wax paper, and chill or freeze until firm.

Preheat the oven to 350 degrees.

Cut the chilled dough into ¼-inch-thick slices; place on ungreased cookie sheets. Bake 10 to 12 minutes or until lightly browned. Remove the cookies to wire racks to cool.

MARY CHRISTMAS MARTIN
Rancho Palos Verdes, California
Rolling Hills–Palos Verdes Alumnae Chapter

BESSIE'S OLD-FASHIONED TEA CAKES

MAKES 4 DOZEN

½ cup butter, softened

1 cup sugar

2 large eggs, well beaten

1 teaspoon vanilla extract

3 cups all-purpose flour

2 teaspoons baking powder

2 tablespoons milk, as needed

Preheat the oven to 350 degrees. Lightly grease 2 cookie sheets.

Cream the butter and sugar in a large mixing bowl until the sugar almost dissolves. Add the eggs and stir until blended. Add the vanilla; stir until blended. Add the flour and baking powder; stir well. If the mixture is too thick, add up to 2 tablespoons of milk. Roll the dough to ¼-inch thickness, cut into squares, and place on prepared cookie sheets. Bake about 8 minutes or until lightly browned.

COOK'S TIP | *You can add a pecan to each square before baking.*

JOYCE WHITE
Jackson, Mississippi
Jackson Alumnae Chapter

OLD-FASHIONED TEA CAKES

MAKES 3½ DOZEN

MY MOTHER, Sarah, baked many cakes, including these, during the holidays when we were growing up in Florida. Some of my best memories are of coming home from school to find a plate of freshly baked tea cakes waiting for me.

½ cup butter, softened

1 cup sugar

2 large eggs

1 tablespoon sour milk

1 teaspoon vanilla extract

1 teaspoon baking powder

½ teaspoon baking soda

½ teaspoon salt

About 3½ cups all-purpose flour

Preheat the oven to 350 degrees.

Mix all the ingredients in a large bowl, adding just enough flour to make a stiff batter. Drop the batter by teaspoonfuls onto an ungreased baking sheet. Bake 10 to 12 minutes or until golden brown. Cool on wire racks.

COOK'S TIP | *Could add a pinch of cinnamon-sugar mixture to each cookie before baking.*

CURLEY SPIRES-POTTER
Bronx, New York
Bronx Alumnae Chapter

CHOCOLATE CHIP COOKIES

MAKES 6 DOZEN

½ pound butter

1 cup granulated sugar

½ cup packed light brown sugar

1 teaspoon vanilla extract

2 large eggs

3 cups all-purpose flour

1 teaspoon salt

1 teaspoon baking powder

1 teaspoon cinnamon

1 (12-ounce) package semisweet chocolate chips

1 (4-ounce) package walnut pieces

Preheat the oven to 350 degrees.

Cream the butter, sugars, and vanilla in a large bowl. Add the eggs, one at a time, beating well after each addition.

Combine the flour, salt, baking powder, and cinnamon in a medium bowl; mix well. Add gradually to the creamed batter. Add the chocolate chips and walnuts.

Drop the batter by teaspoonfuls onto an ungreased, nonstick cookie sheet. Bake 10 minutes or until light brown.

REGINA D. COOK
Columbia, Maryland
Columbia, Maryland, Alumnae Chapter

CHEWY CHOCOLATE COOKIES

MAKES 10 DOZEN

1¼ cups butter, softened

2 cups sugar

2 large eggs

2 tablespoons vanilla extract

2 cups plus 2 tablespoons all-purpose flour

¾ cup unsweetened cocoa powder

1 teaspoon baking soda

½ teaspoon salt

1 cup chopped nuts of your choice or raisins (optional)

2 cups semisweet chocolate chips

Preheat the oven to 350 degrees.

Cream the butter and sugar in a large bowl until light and fluffy. Add the eggs and vanilla; beat well.

Stir together 2 cups of the flour, the cocoa, baking soda, and salt in a medium bowl; blend into the butter mixture with an electric mixer at low speed.

Use the remaining 2 tablespoons of flour to coat the nuts or raisins, if using. Stir the chocolate chips and the nuts or raisins into the batter.

Drop teaspoonfuls of batter onto ungreased baking sheets. Bake 9 minutes—do not overbake. Cookies will be soft. They will puff while baking and flatten while cooling.

Let cookies cool a few minutes before removing them from the hot sheet, then transfer them to a wire rack to cool completely.

RHONDA WASHINGTON
Los Angeles, California
Rolling Hills–Palos Verdes Alumnae Chapter

SAND TARTS

MAKES 42 SMALL OR 25 LARGE TARTS

THIS RECIPE comes from my late mother's kitchen. They're great at Christmastime, and she always had them ready for us when we arrived home in North Carolina for the holidays.

3 heaping tablespoons plus 1 cup sifted powdered sugar
¾ cup butter
2 cups all-purpose flour
½ teaspoon salt
1 cup chopped nuts of your choice

Preheat the oven to 350 degrees.

Cream 3 tablespoons of the sifted powdered sugar and the butter in a large bowl. Add the flour and salt. Mix the ingredients with your hands. Add a little water to make the dough stick together. Form into small rolls with hands. Lay on cookie sheets. Sprinkle with the nuts. Bake 15 to 20 minutes or until they begin to brown. Roll the hot cookies in the remaining 1 cup sifted powdered sugar until

evenly coated. When cool, roll again in the sifted powdered sugar. Store in a tin.

DORIS LOWRY
Washington, D.C.
Washington, D.C., Alumnae Chapter

A Sand Tart and a cup of coffee

BUTTER NUT COOKIES

MAKES 3 DOZEN COOKIES

THESE COOKIES are a must for our study group before examinations and a picker-upper afterward. They melt in your mouth.

1 cup butter, softened
1 large egg
½ teaspoon grated lemon rind
½ teaspoon vanilla extract
1 cup ground hazelnuts, pecans, or walnuts
1¼ cups sifted all-purpose flour
Sweetening Mist (see following recipe)
Chocolate Cream Topping (see recipe opposite)

Preheat the oven to 375 degrees. Grease a cookie sheet.

Cream the softened butter with the egg in a large bowl; mix thoroughly. Add the grated lemon rind, vanilla, and ground nuts. Mix with an electric mixer at medium speed until the mixture has the consistency of whipped cream. Add the sifted flour gradually and mix thoroughly. Mixture should be stiff.

Drop by teaspoonfuls onto the prepared cookie sheet, or form small balls and flatten slightly with a fork for uniform size and shape. Bake for about 12 minutes or until the edges are slightly brown. Cool completely on a wire rack.

SWEETENING MIST

½ cup water
6 packets sugar substitute or 2 tablespoons sugar

Combine the water and sugar substitute or sugar until well dissolved. Pour into a pump-spray bottle. Mist cool cookies until wet. Repeat three or four times. Allow cookies to dry for about 2 hours before serving or adding topping or garnish.

CHOCOLATE CREAM TOPPING

2 (1-ounce) squares semisweet chocolate
4 tablespoons butter, softened
3 packets sugar substitute or 1 tablespoon sugar

Melt the chocolate and butter together over low heat. Remove from the heat and stir in the sugar substitute or sugar. Drizzle the hot chocolate cream over the dry Butter Nut Cookies. Allow the cream to harden before serving.

COOK'S TIP | *You can dust sifted powdered sugar over the cookies as a topping instead of the chocolate cream.*

JOHANNA WESTERFIELD
New Orleans, Louisiana
Nu Mu Citywide Chapter—Tulane—New Orleans

ALMOND KISSES

MAKES 3 DOZEN

3 large egg whites
1 cup sugar
⅛ teaspoon salt
1 tablespoon cornstarch
1 teaspoon vanilla extract
½ cup chopped almonds

Preheat the oven to 350 degrees.

Beat the egg whites in a large bowl until soft peaks form. Add the sugar, a little at a time, and continue beating until stiff peaks form. Stir in the salt and cornstarch. Stir in the vanilla. Add the almonds. Drop by tablespoonfuls on a parchment-lined baking sheet. Bake 20 to 30 minutes or until light brown. (Cookies are done when they don't break as you try to remove them from the sheet.)

WILINE JUSTILIEN
New Orleans, Louisiana
Nu Mu Citywide Chapter—Tulane—New Orleans

MOYÉ NOELS

MAKES ABOUT 30 COOKIES

THESE RICH, yummy cookies are worth the time it takes to make them, especially for holiday goodies.

1 (8-ounce) package pitted prunes
30 pecan halves
1¼ cups all-purpose flour
½ teaspoon baking soda
¼ teaspoon baking powder
⅓ cup butter, softened
¾ cup packed brown sugar
1 large egg
1 teaspoon vanilla extract
½ cup sour cream
Cream Cheese Icing (page 215)

Stuff the prunes with the pecan halves and set aside.

Preheat the oven to 400 degrees. Grease 2 cookie sheets.

Stir together the flour, baking soda, and baking powder in a medium bowl; set aside. In a large bowl, cream the butter and brown sugar until light and fluffy. Beat in the egg and vanilla until blended. Stir in the flour mixture alternately with the sour cream until blended.

Roll each stuffed prune in the cookie dough using two forks, until well covered. Drop 2 inches apart on greased cookie sheets. Bake about 10 minutes or until golden brown. Cookies will be soft to touch. Remove immediately to racks.

When cookies are cool, spread with icing. Store in an airtight container in the refrigerator.

LINDA EVERETT MOYÉ
San Antonio, Texas
San Antonio Alumnae Chapter

Happy Holidays Punch (page 19)

Devastating Delta Diva Dip (page 12)
with Chips

Pumpkin Dip (page 13) with Gingersnaps

Victory Garden Chicken-Vegetable Soup (page 53)

Sunday-Afternoon Roasted Chicken (page 74)

Nita's Southern-Style
Corn Bread Dressing (page 160)

Stacey's Sugary Sweet Candied Yams (page 154)

Skillet Greens with Balsamic Vinegar (page 144)

Foster's Cranberry Mold (page 45)

Uncle Roy's Light Pecan Pie (page 229)

Moyé Noels (page 265)

START YOUR HOLIDAY meal with a festive glass of punch, then sit down to a menu of traditional homemade dishes just like your mother and grandma used to cook. Getting everything done at the same time can be a challenge, but this schedule will keep you on track.

TO PREPARE:

❧ The day before, make the cranberry mold and store it in the refrigerator. Make the Moyé Noels and store them, covered airtight. Make the punch and store it in a covered container. (Mix with the ginger ale just before serving.)

❧ If you're making the soup from scratch, you'll need to cook the chicken a day in advance. If not, start it early in the day, then reheat and season it just before serving.

❦ On Christmas morning, prepare the chicken and bake the pie. Make the pumpkin dip and refrigerate it. If serving in a scooped-out pumpkin, don't put the dip in the pumpkin until just before serving.

❦ Bake the yams in the morning (or in the afternoon if this is an evening meal), then remove them from the oven and let them sit at room temperature, covered with foil, to reheat before serving.

❦ Prepare the corn-bread dressing so that it's ready to go into the oven 1 hour before the chicken is done. An hour before people are due to arrive, begin the Delta Diva Dip. Once the dressing is in the oven, begin to prepare the greens.

A DELTA CHRISTMAS

For Deltas, as for most African-Americans, Christmas is a time to gather with family and close friends, to decorate lavishly, and to indulge in a festive meal composed of traditional dishes that often have been passed down from one generation to the next.

The menu for this meal is composed of just the kinds of recipes that would have been lovingly copied, recopied, and saved over the years. Cover your table with an heirloom cloth that's been lovingly washed and stored but may well bear the stains of happy holidays past. Decorate it with a centerpiece of fresh holly and fragrant pine branches, perhaps some beautiful flowers, and a few of the family's ornaments.

Be sure your board is brimming with sparkling glassware, flatware, and china. As you sit down to eat, see the beauty of the setting and the occasion reflected in the faces of your family and loved ones.

GRAHAM CRACKER COOKIES

MAKES 2½–3 DOZEN

A GRANDMOTHER'S DELIGHT for high-noon tea or a holiday treat.

1½ cups finely crushed graham cracker crumbs (about 15 graham cracker squares)
½ cup all-purpose flour
2 teaspoons baking powder
1 (14-ounce) can sweetened condensed milk
½ cup butter or margarine, softened
¾ cup raisins or dried cherries or cranberries
¾ cup semisweet chocolate chips
1⅓ cups flaked coconut
1 cup chopped pecans or walnuts

Combine the first 4 ingredients and mix well. Stir in the remaining 5 ingredients. Chill the dough in the refrigerator for 30 minutes.

Preheat the oven to 350 degrees. Grease a baking sheet with butter.

Drop dough onto the prepared sheet in heaping tablespoons. Bake for 10 to 12 minutes or until golden.

SHIRLEY STAGG
Carson, California
Cerritos Area Alumnae Chapter

MICROWAVE PEANUT BRITTLE

MAKES 10–12 SERVINGS

½ cup light corn syrup
1 cup sugar
1 cup raw peanuts
1 tablespoon margarine
1 teaspoon vanilla extract
1 teaspoon baking soda

Cover a baking sheet with aluminum foil and spray lightly with nonstick cooking spray; set aside.

Pour the corn syrup into a 2-quart glass mixing bowl. Add the sugar and peanuts. Microwave on high for 4 minutes; stir. Microwave on high for 4 minutes longer. Stir in the margarine and the vanilla. Microwave on high for 1 minute; stir in the baking soda. Spread on the prepared baking sheet. Cool and break into pieces.

CORA LEE BOULDIN
Port Arthur, Texas
Port Arthur Alumnae Chapter

ALMOND BISCOTTI

MAKES 2 DOZEN

BISCOTTI ARE LONG, slivered, intensely crunchy Italian cookies, perfect for dunking in a cup of hot coffee.

½ cup butter, softened

1 cup sugar

1 tablespoon Kahlúa or other coffee-flavored liqueur

2 large eggs

2½ cups all-purpose flour

1½ teaspoons baking powder

¼ teaspoon salt

3 tablespoons Dutch cocoa or regular cocoa powder

1 (6-ounce) can whole unsalted almonds

Preheat the oven to 350 degrees. Lightly grease 1 baking sheet.

Beat the butter and sugar in a large bowl with an electric mixer at medium speed until light and fluffy. Add the Kahlúa and the eggs, mixing well.

Combine the flour, baking powder, salt, and cocoa; add to the butter mixture, beating at low speed until blended. Stir in the almonds.

Divide the dough in half. Using floured hands and a floured board, shape each portion into a 9-by-2-inch log and place on the prepared baking sheet.

Bake 28 to 30 minutes or until firm. Cool on the baking sheet 5 minutes. Remove to a wire rack to cool.

Cut each log diagonally into ¾-inch-thick slices with a serrated knife, using a gentle sawing motion. Place on ungreased baking sheets. Bake 5 minutes. Turn cookies over, and bake an additional 5 minutes. Remove to wire racks to cool.

M. SANDRA SEVERE
New Orleans, Louisiana
Nu Mu Citywide Chapter—Tulane—New Orleans

STRAWBERRY TOPPING

MAKES 1½ PINTS

THIS IS A very old, very good recipe.

1 quart strawberries

3 cups sugar

1 teaspoon butter

Wash the strawberries in a colander and remove the stems. Pour boiling water over the strawberries. Place the berries, enough water to cover, and 1 cup of the sugar in a large saucepan. Bring to a boil and cook 2 minutes. Stir in the remaining 2 cups sugar and boil 5 minutes longer, stirring constantly. Stir in the butter. Cool, stir, and store in the refrigerator.

Serve over ice cream or pound cake.

EDNA LEE LONG-GREEN
Washington, D.C.
Chair, National Commission on Arts and Letters
Washington, D.C., Alumnae Chapter

FOREST'S ALWAYS-CRUNCHY PECAN CANDY

MAKES 5 DOZEN

THIS IS MY grandmother's recipe from when I was a child (more than forty years ago). I give the candies for Christmas, Mother's Day, and birthday presents. I also give them to people who do special things for me. One batch is usually enough for three gifts.

2 (12-ounce) cans evaporated milk

4 cups sugar

½ cup butter or margarine

1 cup ice water, for testing hardness

1 teaspoon pure vanilla extract

2 cups lightly toasted whole pecans

Grease a cookie sheet with butter or margarine.

Combine the milk and sugar in a large pot over medium heat. Note the time because in 1 hour you will have crunchy pecan candy. Stir the mixture constantly for 45 minutes. As the mixture thickens, lower the heat, but maintain boiling consistency (do not scorch). After about 45 minutes the mixture will be golden brown, thick, and gooey. Whip in the butter or margarine. Cook for about 10 more minutes and test for hardness. Mixture should form a brittle ball when a small amount is dropped into ice water. Turn off the heat at the 1-hour mark and add the vanilla. Stir in the pecans. Pour onto the prepared cookie sheet and spread over the entire sheet with a spoon. Cool. Cut into ¾-inch squares.

FOREST DENT SMITH
Baker, Louisiana
Baker-Zachary Alumnae Chapter

1950s: Delta begins to study job opportunities for women through its Job Analysis Committee, helps to place more African-American women on public boards and commissions, and works to expand job opportunities for skilled and unskilled workers.

We launch a national voter registration drive and expand our National Library Project.

In 1953 Delta opens its first National Headquarters in Washington, D.C., with Patricia Roberts Harris serving as executive director.

The establishment of Delta's Five-Point Thrust Program in 1956 lays the foundation for our current areas of focus: Educational Development, Economic Development, Physical and Mental Health, Political Awareness and Involvement, and International Awareness and Involvement.

1960s: **In 1963** Delta marks its fiftieth anniversary of sisterhood service with a celebration attended by President John F. Kennedy and Vice President Lyndon B. Johnson.

1963 Establishment of the Teen-Lift program to build self-esteem in high school students.

1967 Establishment of the Delta Research and Educational Foundation to provide a vehicle for charitable giving and fund-raising.

In the wake of the assassinations of Dr. Martin Luther King, Jr., President John F. Kennedy, Robert Kennedy, and Malcolm X, Delta establishes the Social Action Commission, which becomes an influential voice in the passage of the Civil Rights Act. Today the commission continues to shape local and national policy.

1970s: **In 1971,** Delta receives a $500,000 grant from the U.S. Department of Justice to co-sponsor a program with OneAmerica, Inc., to rehabilitate women offenders.

Through DST Telecommunications, Inc., Delta creates, finances, and produces the major motion picture *Countdown at Kusini,* starring Ruby Dee, Greg Morris, and Ossie Davis. Released in 1975, *Countdown* was the first major motion picture produced by a Black women's organization.

1979 Delta commissions and erects the sculpture *Fortitude* on the campus of Howard University in honor of its twenty-two founders.

1980s: **The Distinguished** Professor Endowed Chair is established to provide a biennial award to a historically Black college or university for an outstanding professor who is noted in a particular field or to establish and/or enhance a course of study or research that is needed and not available to students at these institutions. Tuskegee Institute is the first recipient.

A "Call to Action" is issued in response to the social crises facing women in America. The program events, held throughout the 1980s as "Summit Meetings," focus on concerns paramount to Black women: supporting Black single mothers, and preparing boys for manhood.

1990s: In **1990,** Delta begins the renovation of a multimillion-dollar building in the historic Dupont Circle area of Washington, D.C., for its national headquarters.

In **1992,** Delta forms a partnership with Habitat for Humanity International and builds houses throughout America and conducts an international building of forty houses in Ghana, West Africa.

In **1996,** Delta launches Summit IV: Health and Healing, Let It Begin Within and receives funding from the Eli Lilly pharmaceutical company to conduct nationwide training on clinical depression screening and treatment. Concurrently Delta launches a second programmatic initiative, "The Dr. Betty Shabazz Delta Academy: Preparing Young Ladies for the 21st Century."

2000s: In **2000,** Delta launches Summit V: A Global Response to the Pandemic of AIDS and Other Health Issues.

In **2001,** chapters throughout the world implement our first International Day of Service to address a common issue—to heighten awareness of, encourage prevention of, and promote screening and testing for HIV/AIDS.

In **2001,** the first Technology Task Force is established. Delta's Internal Roster is placed on CD-ROM and on-line registration is implemented for 2001 regional conferences and the 2002 national convention.

From January 10 to 12, 2002, Delta dedicates its newly renovated and expanded national headquarters.

In **2002,** the first class of Leadership Delta is selected and begins their course of study in leadership training and professional development. Thirty-eight collegiate sorors with grade point averages of 3.5 and above are selected to participate in this historic program, which is funded by a generous grant from General Electric Company.

A **Delta** delegation travels to South Africa to conduct educational-training workshops for teachers and principals in Swaziland and Lesotho, and to establish a new connection with the ancestral homeland.

Delta receives a five-year grant from the National Science Foundation to implement the Science in Everyday Experiences Program (SEE) to promote interest in math, science, engineering, and technology, especially among young women.

In 2003, Delta celebrates her ninetieth birthday in Washington, D.C., and produces a thirty-minute video chronicling her history.

Delta is granted Non-Governmental Special Consultative Status with the Economic and Social Council of the United Nations. This entitles Delta to have NGO representation in New York and at the UN Offices in Geneva and Vienna.

Delta representatives travel to South Africa for the dedication of an orphanage funded by the sorority in Swaziland.

Delta creates a $1 million endowment scholarship at Howard University in honor of founders and past national presidents.

INDEX

A

African Chicken-Peanut Soup, 54
Alexander, Gloria H., 142, 143
Alexander-Calloway, Michelle, 150
Almond Biscotti, 270
Almond Kisses, 265
Ames-McConnell, LaShawn, 130, 245
Appetizers
    Cheese Ball, Delta, 14
    Cheese Ball, Sweet-and-Sour, 14
    Cheese Wafers, 15
    Chicken wings
        Robin's Buffalo Wings, 6
        Spicy Asian Wings, 9
        Tangy Baked Party Wings, 8
    Crabmeat Quiche, 133
    Dips
        Chicken Dip, 13
        Devastating Delta Diva Dip,
            12–13
        Mexican Dip, 15
        Pumpkin Dip, 13
        Spicy Spinach Dip, 12
        Taco Dip, 16
    Ham Biscuits with Poppy Seeds, 6
    Rumaki, 7
    Sandwiches, Fancy Party, 8
    Seafood Nachos, 7
    Shrimp, Italian, 12
    Shrimp Mold, 9
Apple
    Cake, Apple Caramel, 220
    Cake, Sister Vee's Apple, 216–17

Cheesecake, Apple, 224
Cheesecake, Taffy Apple, 224–25
Crumb Pie, Deep-Dish, Apple, 236
Dump Cake, 221
Pie, Crustless English Apple,
    236–37
Pudding, Apple, 253
Ashe, Jean McCray, 17, 227
Asian Wings, Spicy, 9
Asparagus, Marinated, 143
Atlanta Lemon Whip Lush, 254
Au Gratin Grits, 156–57

B

Banana
    Bread, Banana, 184
    Sassy Fruit 'n' Sauce, 251
    Tropical Fruit Dessert, 248
Beans. *See also* green beans
    Baked Beans, Faye's Meaty, 108
    Baked Beans, Lucy and Ethel's, 139
    Black-Eyed Peas with Attitude,
        Billy Bob's, 62
    Chili
        Heart-Smart Chili, 67
        Lavita's Slammin' Chili, 63
        Turkey Chili, 66
        Turkey Chili, Del Rio, 66–67
        White Chili, 67
        World's Best Chili (cook's tip),
            62–63

Dip, Mexican, 15
Dip, Taco, 16
One-Pot Dinner, 103
Red Beans and Rice, Mickey's, 111
Slumgully, 57
Turkey Dump Beans, 91
Beef
    Beef and Vegetable Soup, 52
    Devastating Delta Diva Dip, 12–13
    Everyday Meat Loaf, 102
    Fancy Meat Loaf, 102–3
    Lasagna Casserole, 108
    Meat Sauce, for Spaghetti Crust
        Pie, 105
    Meaty Baked Beans, Faye's, 108
    New Orleans Oyster Dressing,
        Peezie's, 160–61
    Old-Fashioned Vegetable Soup, 52
    One-Pot Dinner, 103
    Pot Roast, Beef, 100
    Pot Roast with Vegetables and
        Gravy, 101
    Red Beans and Rice, Mickey's, 111
    Slammin' Chili, Lavita's, 63
    Spaghetti Pizza, 107
    Stuffed Cheese, 104
    Taco Salad, Jett's, 26
    Tamale Pie, 106
    Tangy Beef-Spinach Lasagna, 92
    World's Best Chili, 62–63
Beets, pickled, 43
Belcher-Dixon, Peggy, 121, 139
Bell, Geneva C., 139, 170
Bellhouse Hot Rolls, 170
Benn, Rita, 82, 91

INDEX   277

Bennett, Gloria Freeman, 183
Berry. *See also* strawberry
    Blackberry Dumplings, 249
    Raspberry and Cream Blossoms,
        Crimson, 244–45
    Tartlets, Berry, 238–39
Bessie's Old-Fashioned Tea Cakes, 261
Beverages
    Baptist Punch, 17
    End-of-Day Punch, 19
    Happy Holidays Punch, 19
    Homemade Lemon-Raspberry
        Lemonade, Ida's, 17
    Hot Wine Cranberry Punch, 18
    Punch, Lenora's, 18
    Watermelon Lemonade, 16
Billy Bob's Black-Eyed Peas with
        Attitude, 62
Binns, Yvette, 152
Biscotti, Almond, 270
Biscuits, Ham, with Poppy Seeds, 6
Biscuits, Peaches Style Homemade,
        172–73
Blackberry Dumplings, 249
Black-Eyed Peas with Attitude, Billy
        Bob's, 62
Blueberry-Orange Bread, 185
Bouldin, Cora Lee, 269
Boyd, Alfredia, 17, 42, 56, 77, 93,
        109, 142, 144, 153, 157, 162,
        222
Boyd, Gwendolyn E., *xv*, 138, 210,
        214
Boyd's Clam Chowder, 56
Breads
    Biscuits, Ham, with Poppy
        Seeds, 6
    Biscuits, Peaches Style Homemade,
        172–73
    Cakes, Corny Cora Lee, 186
    Coffee Cake, 182–83
    Festivals, 177
    Fruit and vegetable breads
        Banana Bread, 184
        Blueberry-Orange Bread, 185
        Sweet Potato Bread, 183
        Zucchini Bread, 184–85

Monkey breads
    Mama's Monkey Bread, 175
    Potato Monkey Bread, 174
    Simple Monkey Bread,
        174–75
Rolls
    Bellhouse Hot Rolls, 170
    Cinnamon Rolls, 180
    Dinner Rolls, 171
    Dinner Rolls, Perfectly Easy,
        170–71
    Ice Box Rolls, 176–77
    Scones, Jean's, 182
    Sticky Buns, Christmas Morning,
        180–81
    Waffles, Sister Vee's Gingerbread,
        186
Breakfast foods
    Casserole, Breakfast, 190
    Corny Cora Lee Cakes, 186
    Country Pie, Breakfast, 190
    Garden Vegetable Quiche, 195
    Gingerbread Waffles, Sister Vee's,
        186
    Peach Crisp Pie, 237
    Quiche Lavita, 191
    Sausage
        Casserole, Breakfast Sausage, 187
        Sausage and Potatoes, 194
        Sausage Quiche, 194
Breese, Bertha "Bert" Hopkins, 19,
        246
Bristow, Hazel H., 118, 120
Broccoli
    Broccoli Casserole, 145
    Broccoli and Cheese Salad, 44
    Broccoli and Chicken Casserole, 88
    Broccoli Salad, 34
    Broccoli Salad with Sunflower
        Seeds, 38
Broome, Doris Flack, 89
Brown, Crystal R., 237, 256
Brown, Michelle Rhodes, 16
Brown, Mignon, 251
Brown, Rita L., 133
Brown, Stacey J., 83, 155
Brown, Tammara, 239

Brownies, Louise R. Wilson's
        Two-Way, 256
Brown-White, Carniece, 87, 235
Buckman, Renée McCarthy, 236
Buffalo Wings, Robin's, 6
Butter Bars, Delicious Gooey Delta,
        257
Butter Nut Cookies, 264

C

Cabbage, Pork Chops and, 109
Cabbage Pot, Virginia's Steamed, 144
Cabrera-White, Eloise J., 150
Cakes
    Apple Cake, Sister Vee's, 216–17
    Apple Caramel Cake, 220
    Carrot Cake, 214–15
    Carrot Nut Cake, with Pineapple,
        215
    Cheesecakes
        Apple Cheesecake, 224
        Charlotte's Cheesecake, 223
        Crimson Raspberry and Cream
            Blossoms, 244–45
        German Chocolate Cheesecake,
            225
        Ricotta, Lighter-Textured
            Cheesecake, 226
        Sweet Potato Cheesecake,
            226–27
        Taffy Apple Cheesecake, 224–25
    Chocolate
        Chocolate Cake à la Hicks, 211
        Chocolate Peppermint Cake, 212
        Chocolate Pound Cake, 204
        Chocolate–Sour Cream Pound
            Cake, 203
        Mocha Halo Cupcakes, 212–13
        Modern Marble Cake, 216
    Coca-Cola Cake, 209
    Coffee Cake, 182–83
    Dirt Cake, 243
    Dump Cake, 221

Gingerbread, Shoofly, 222–23
Holmes Cake, 220–21
Lemon-Filling Cake, Supreme, 217
Pineapple Poke Cake, 222
Pound cakes
    Chocolate Pound Cake, 204
    Chocolate–Sour Cream Pound
        Cake, 203
    Five-Flavor Pound Cake, 204–5
    Lemon-Thyme Pound Cake,
        206–7
    Miss Vernon Mundy's Pound
        Cake, 206
    Perfect Pound Cake, 202
    7-Up Pound Cake, 208
    Sour Cream Pound Cake, 202
Red Velvet Cake, 210
Rum Cake, 214
7-Up Cake, with Icing, 208–9
Sweet Potato (or Pumpkin) Nut
    Roll, 227
Canady, Hortense Golden, 76, 100
Candied Yams, Stacey's Sugary Sweet,
    154–55
Candied Yams with Brandy, 153
Candies
    Forest's Always-Crunchy Pecan
        Candy, 271
    Microwave Peanut Brittle, 269
Canty, Andrea, 246
Canty, Delores "Dee Dee," 105
Caramel Cake, Apple, 220
Caramel-Coated Yam Flan, 242–43
Carolyn's Cream Cheese Squares,
    258–59
Carr, Danette, 44, 190
Carrots
    Carrot Cake, 214–15
    Carrot Nut Cake with Pineapple,
        215
    Copper-Penny Carrots, 152
    Marinated Carrots, 38
Carter-Burnett, Charlotte, 43
Casseroles
    Breakfast Casserole, 190
    Breakfast Sausage Casserole, 187
    Broccoli Casserole, 145

Chicken
    Chicken All-in-One, 87
    Chicken and Broccoli Casserole,
        88
    Chicken and Rice Casserole,
        Gladys's, 89
    Chicken Macaroni or
        Spaghetti, 90
    Chicken Potpie, 83
Corn Casserole, 145
Crab Casserole, 132
Delta Executive Meeting
    Casserole, 81
Lasagna Casserole, 108
Lasagna, Tangy Turkey-Spinach, 92
Sausage and Rice Casserole, 110
Shrimp Casserole, 126–27
Spinach-Rice Casserole, 147
Squash Casserole, 151
Sweet Potato Casserole, 154
Tamale Pie, 106
Catfish, Fried, with Homemade Tartar
    Sauce, 121
Cato, Ciesta L., 244
Cheese
    Cheese Ball, Delta, 14
    Cheese Ball, Sweet-and-Sour, 14
    Cheese and Broccoli Salad, 44
    Mac and Cheese, Mom's, 163
    Macaroni and Cheese, 162–63
    Stuffed Cheese, 104
    Wafers, Cheese, 15
Cheesecakes. See under cakes
Cherries
    Fruit Pie, 235
    Fruit Salad, Cherry, 248
    Jubilee, Cherries, 246
    Pie, Cherry, 238
    Pizza, Cobb's Cherry, 245
Chewy Chocolate Cookies, 262–63
Chicken
    Breasts
        à l'orange, Chicken Breasts, 75
        Moroccan Chicken Breasts,
          77
        Scaloppine, Chicken Breast,
          76–77

        Supreme, Chicken Breast, 75
Chicken All-in-One, 87
Chicken and Broccoli
    Casserole, 88
Chicken and Rice Casserole,
    Gladys's, 89
Casserole, Delta Executive
    Meeting, 81
Chicken Chow Mein, 91
Chicken Croquettes, 86–87
Chicken Dip, 13
Chicken-Peanut Soup,
    African, 54
Chicken Salad, Mom's, 27
Chicken-Vegetable Soup, Victory
    Garden, 53
Chili, Lavita's Slammin', 63
Chili, White, 67
Curried Chicken, 82
Dirty Rice, 157
Drums, Jerk Chicken, 86
Fried Chicken, Stacey's Bodacious
    Buttermilk, 82–83
Gumbo, Flournoy's North
    Louisiana, 57
Gumbo, Rachel's To-Die-For
    Shrimp, 60–61
Jambalaya, Wilma's, 61
Macaroni or Spaghetti, Chicken, 90
Potpie, Chicken, 83
Pyramid Penne Rigate, 90
Roasted Chicken, Sunday-
    Afternoon, 74
Smothered Chicken, 76
Wings, chicken
    Robin's Buffalo Wings, 6
    Spicy Asian Wings, 9
    Tangy Baked Party Wings, 8
Chicken livers
    Dirty Rice, 157
    Dirty Rice Dressing, 157
    Rumaki, 7
Chiles, Sonya E., 243
Chili. See under soups and stews
Chocolate
    Chocolate Cake à la Hicks, 211
    Chocolate Chip Cookies, 262

Chocolate (cont.)
    Chocolate Cookies, Chewy,
        262–63
    Chocolate Peppermint Cake, 212
    Chocolate Pound Cake, 204
    Chocolate–Sour Cream Pound
        Cake, 203
    Mocha Halo Cupcakes, 212–13
    Modern Marble Cake, 216
    Two-Way Brownies, Louise R.
        Wilson's, 256
Chowder, Rozchel's Red-Hot Halibut,
    119
Chow Mein, Chicken, 91
Christmas Morning Sticky Buns,
    180–81
Cinnamon Rolls, 180
Clam Chowder, Boyd's, 56
Clark, Barbara Randall, 7, 229
Cobbler, peach
    Cobb's Peach Cobbler, 241
    with a Flair, Peach Cobbler, 240–41
    Quick Peach Cobbler, 242
Cobb's Cherry Pizza, 245
Cobb's Peach Cobbler, 241
Coca-Cola Cake, 209
Collard greens. See greens
Collins, Michele, 16
Connor, Delores L., 107, 146
Cook, Regina D., 195, 253, 262
Cookies and bars
    Biscotti, Almond, 270
    Brownies, Louise R. Wilson's
        Two-Way, 256
    Butter Bars, Delicious Gooey
        Delta, 257
    Butter Nut, 264
    Chocolate, Chewy, 262–63
    Chocolate Chip, 262
    Cream Cheese Squares, Carolyn's,
        258–59
    Gooey Squares, 257
    Graham Cracker Cookies, 269
    Ice Cream Crunch, 256
    Kisses, Almond, 265
    Lemon Bars, 254–55
    Noels, Moyé, 265

    Pecan Pie Bars, 260
    Sand Tarts, 263
    Tea Cakes, Bessie's Old-Fashioned,
        261
    Tea Cakes, Old-Fashioned, 261
    Vanilla-Pecan Icebox Cookies,
        260–61
Copper-Penny Carrots, 152
Corn
    Casserole, Corn, 145
    Easy Fried Corn, 149
    Pudding
        Elaine and Sheila's Corn
            Pudding, 151
        Eloise's Favorite Corn Pudding,
            150
        Mirian's Corn Pudding, 150
    Corn Bread Dressing,
        Mama's, 158
    Corn Bread Dressing, Nita's
        Southern-Style, 160
Corny Cora Lee Cakes, 186
Country Breakfast Pie, 190
Country Ham with Red-Eye Gravy,
    109
Crab. See under shellfish
Cranberry
    Mold, Cranberry, 153
    Mold, Foster's Cranberry, 45
    Punch, Hot Wine Cranberry, 18
    Relish, Cranberry, 44
Crawford, Robin Pennington, 6
Cream Cheese Squares, Carolyn's,
    258–59
Cream of Crab Soup, Mommadot's
    Easy, 56–57
Crème Anglaise, for Peach Cream
    Trifle, 250
Creole, Baked Fish, 118–19
Creole Pronto, Shrimp, 131
Crimson Raspberry and Cream
    Blossoms, 244–45
Croquettes, Chicken, 86–87
Crustless English Apple Pie, 236–37
Curried Shrimp, 125
Curry, in Shrimp Pilau (substitution),
    127

D

Dabney, Lorraine W., 75, 103
Davis, Barbara Moseley, 38
Davis, Era Jean, 252
Davis, Rachel R., 61
Day, Thelma James, 230
Delicious Gooey Delta Butter Bars,
    257
Del Rio Turkey Chili, 66–67
Delta Cheese Ball, 14
Delta Executive Meeting Casserole, 81
Delta Sigma Theta
    Deltas of Distinction
        Adams, Osceola McCarthy, 187
        Bethune, Mary McLeod, 203
        Blackwell, Harolyn, 24
        Burroughs, Nannie Helen, 207
        Catlett, Elizabeth, 43
        Cole, Johnetta B., 50
        Cosby, Camille O., xiii, 50, 51
        Dee, Ruby, 228
        Farmer, Sharon, 232
        Fobi, Helen J. Newton, 72
        Foster, Lesli, 239
        Hampshire-Cowan, Artis G., 73
        Harris, Patricia Roberts, 259
        Herman, Alexis, 89
        Jackson, Shirley Ann, 100
        Jamison, Judith, 107
        Jones, Ingrid Saunders, 103
        Jones, Stephanie Tubbs, 110
        Jordan, Barbara, 116
        Malveaux, Julianne, 117
        Seymour, Allison, 139
        Showell, Carolyn D., 156
        Stewart, Natasha J., 161
        Terrell, Mary Church, 173
        Wilder, Carolyn, 141
    Executive committee, ix
    Featured sorors
        Canady, Hortense Golden, 97
        Freeman, Frankie Muse, 3
        Harrison, Dorothy Penman, 137
        Height, Dorothy I., 199–201
        Jeffries, Essie M., 49–51

McKenzie, Floretta Dukes, 115–17
McKenzie, Vashti Murphy, 71–73
Mitchell, Keyana, 23–24
Smith, Stacy Nicole, 167
Founding sisters, *vi–vii*
History, 273–76
National presidents, *viii*
Occasions
    book club meeting meal, 40–41
    bridal or baby shower, 28–29
    chapter roundup barbecue, 122–23
    Christmas dinner for family and friends, 266–68
    Crimson and Cream Ball, 78–80
    Delteen tea, 178–79
    fiftieth (or fortieth or sixtieth) birthday party, 128–29
    graduation celebration, 98–99
    initiation year anniversary, 168–69
    installation dinner, 218–19
    Jabberwock dinner, 4–5
    Juneteenth backyard picnic, 84–85
    new members' celebration, 32–33
    prayer breakfast, 188–89
    reception to honor national officers, 10–11
    red-and-white midnight breakfast, 192–93
    step show afterparty, 64–65
    United Nations NGO luncheon, 36–37
    wedding reception buffet, 58–59
Desserts. *See* fruit desserts; *specific type of dessert*
Dessert toppings
    Frostings, 228
        Chocolate Frosting, 211
        Coca-Cola Frosting, 209
        Cream Cheese Frosting, 210
    Glazes, 205, 206, 207
        Peppermint Glaze, 212

Icings, 208–9, 220
    Chocolate Never-Fail Icing, 222
    Cream Cheese Icing, 215
    Dream Whip Icing, 204
    Fluffy White Icing, 213
Sauces
    Crème Anglaise, 250
    Fruit 'n' Sauce, Sassy, 251
    Strawberry Topping, 270
    Topping (pineapple), 221
Devastating Delta Diva Dip, 12–13
Dijon Green Bean Salad, 35
Dill Tuna Salad, 34
Dinner Rolls, 171
Dinner Rolls, Perfectly Easy, 170–71
Dips. *See under* appetizers
Dirt Cake, 243
Dirty Rice, 157
Dirty Rice Dressing, 157
Dixon, Phoebe Boykins, 160
Dobbins, Cheryl L., 30, 229
Douglas, Deborah Marina, 25
Dream Whip Icing for Chocolate Pound Cake, 204
Dressings
    Corn Bread Dressing, Mama's, 158
    Corn Bread Dressing, Nita's Southern-Style, 160
    Dirty Rice, 157
    Oyster Dressing, Peezie's New Orleans, 160–61
    Shrimp Dressing, 162
    Sylvia's Stuffing, 159
Drinks. *See* beverages
Dump Cake, 221
Dumplings, Blackberry, 249
Dyson, Ruth Berry, 131

Easterling, Victoria "Mickey," 111
Eggplant, Stuffed Baby, 148–49
Elaine and Sheila's Corn Pudding, 151
Eloise's Favorite Corn Pudding, 150

Emerson, Lavita Alston, 63, 191
End-of-Day Punch, 19
English Apple Pie, Crustless, 236–37
Evans, Felicia U., 237
Everyday Meat Loaf, 102

Fancy Meat Loaf, 102–3
Fancy Party Sandwiches, 8
Faulkner, Mary E., 60
Faye's Meaty Baked Beans, 108
Festivals, 177
Fish. *See also* shellfish
    Catfish, Fried, with Homemade Tartar Sauce, 121
    Creole, Baked Fish, 118–19
    Halibut, Rozchel's Red-Hot Chowder, 119
    Salmon, Sandra's Spicy, 120
    Salmon Steaks, Grilled, 120
    Savory Baked Fish, 118
    Seafood Velvet, 124
    Stuffed Cheese (cook's tip), 104
    Tuna Salad, Dill, 34
Five-Flavor Pound Cake, 204–5
Flan, Caramel-Coated Yam, 242–43
Fletcher, Flaxie, 77
Flournoy, Gloria Cobb, 57, 241, 245
Flournoy's North Louisiana Gumbo, 57
Floyd, Jean, 254
Fluffy Strawberry Pie, 238
Fobi, Helen J. Newton, 9, 147, 194, 209
Fobi, Ngelah Alyssa, 255
Forest's Always-Crunchy Pecan Candy, 271
Foster, Alyce F., 45
Foster, Jessie W., 9, 57, 253
Foster, Valerie A., 186, 217
Foster's Cranberry Mold, 45
Foster-Westerfield, Cherylann, 106
Franklin, Merle Allen, 14, 75, 93, 149, 153, 175, 206, 223

Frostings. *See* dessert toppings

Fruit desserts. *See also specific fruits; specific types of dessert*

Apple Pudding, 253
Blackberry Dumplings, 249
Cherry Fruit Salad, 248
Fruit Dessert, Tropical, 248
Fruit 'n' Sauce, Sassy, 251
Fruit Starter, Vintage, 251
Fruity Pound Cake Compote, 244
Lemon Breeze, 253
Lemon Pudding Soufflé, 252
Lemon Whip Lush, Atlanta, 254
Noels, Moyé, 265
Peach Cream Trifle, 250
Raspberry and Cream Blossoms, Crimson, 244–45
Strawberry Delight, 246
Strawberry Pretzel, 248–49

Fruits. *See also* fruit desserts

Banana Bread, 184
Blueberry-Orange Bread, 185
Cranberry Mold, 153
Cranberry Mold, Foster's, 45
Cranberry Relish, 44
Mandarin Orange and Romaine Salad, 39
Moroccan Chicken Breasts, 77
Pineapple, Baked, 152–53
Smoked Turkey Salad with Walnuts, 25
Waldorf Salad, 42
Watermelon Lemonade, 16

Fudge, Marcia L., 221

Game

Venison Roast, 93
Wild Rabbit, Fried, 92–93

Garden Vegetable Quiche, 195
Garner, Yvonne, 163
German Chocolate Cheesecake, 225
Gill, Chandra, 145

Gilmore, Denise E., 74
Gingerbread, Shoofly, 222–23
Gingerbread Waffles, Sister Vee's, 186
Gipson, Pamela C., 177, 180
Gladys's Chicken and Rice Casserole, 89
Glapion, Gussie J., 209
Glazes. *See* dessert toppings
Goings, Valerie Fleming, 182
Good, Teshine G., 154
Gooey Delta Butter Bars, Delicious, 257
Gooey Squares, 257
Graham Cracker Cookies, 269
Grandma's Southern Pecan Pie, 230
Grant, Angela, 149
Green, Terrell, 260

Green beans

Marinated (cook's tip), 143
Salad, Dijon Green Bean, 35
String Beans with Potatoes, 142

Greene, Bessie, 27

Greens

Collard Greens, Fried, 143
Kale Slaw, Spicy, 30
Old-Time Greens, with Smoked Ham Hocks, 146
Skillet Greens, with Balsamic Vinegar, 144
Steamed Cabbage Pot, Virginia's, 144

Grits, au Gratin, 156–57
Guillory, Rachelle Hollie, 119
Gumbo. *See under* soups and stews

Hairston, Dorothy L., 57
Halo Cupcakes, Mocha, 212–13

Ham

Ham Biscuits with Poppy Seeds, 6
Country Ham, with Red-Eye Gravy, 109
Country Breakfast Pie, 190

Crabmeat Quiche (cook's tip), 133
Ham Hocks, Smoked, Old-Time Greens with, 146
Sylvia's Stuffing, 159
Wilma's Jambalaya, 61

Hammond, Mary, 110, 222
Hampshire-Cowan, Artis G., 8
Happy Holidays Punch, 19
Hardaway, Eugenia B., 106, 226
Harrison, Dorothy Penman, 157, 217
Hash Browns, Sour Cream, 155
Heart-Smart Chili, 67
Height, Dorothy I., 233
Hicks, Chocolate Cake à la, 211
Hill, Ola, 131, 143
Hitchens, Linda Gipson, 177, 180, 231
Holmes, Anita, 221
Holmes Cake, 220–21
Hope, Marion Conover, 5
Hors d'oeuvres. *See* appetizers
Hot Wine Cranberry Punch, 18
House, Mildred, 109
Howard, Jacqueline Jackson, 243
Hudson, Cheryl Y., 249

Ice Box Rolls, 176–77
Ice Cream Crunch, 256
Icings. *See* dessert toppings
Ida's Homemade Lemon-Raspberry Lemonade, 17
Ingram, Iris, 7
Irvin, Nicol Davis, 19
Italian Shrimp Appetizer, 12

Jackson, Rosemary, 152, 159
Jambalaya, Wilma's, 61

Jazzy Piquant Shrimp
    with Angel Hair Pasta,
    124–25
Jean's Scones, 182
Jefferson, Vienna M., 90, 232
Jeffries, Essie M., 62, 240
Jerk Chicken Drums, 86
Jett, Debora L., 26
Johnson, Altheada L., 215
Johnson, Carolyn C., 13, 14, 202,
    204, 259
Johnson, Khaliah A., 127
Johnson, Renée, 108
Jones, Almetta J., 18, 242
Jones, Kimberly Perkins, 27
Jones, Willie Pearl, 52
Judge Trudy's Sensation
    Salad, 39
Justilien, Wiline, 265

Kale Slaw, Spicy, 30
Kenner, Sandi, 159
Keshi Yená, 104
Key Lime Pie, Yolanda's, 230
Kielbasa Soup, 54
King, Emma B., 202
Kisses, Almond, 265
Kugel, Peach, 152

Lasagna, Tangy Turkey-Spinach, 92
Lasagna Casserole, 108
Lavender, Blanche, 151, 157, 215,
    231, 235
Lavita, Quiche, 191
Lavita's Slammin' Chili, 63
Lawyer, Vivian Moore, 153
Lee, Gloria, 185

Lemon
    Lemon Bars, 254–55
    Lemon Breeze, 253
    Lemon-Filling Cake,
        Supreme, 217
    Lemon Meringue Pie, 231
    Lemon Pudding Soufflé, 252
    Lemon-Thyme Pound Cake,
        206–7
    Lemon Whip Lush, Atlanta, 254
Lemonade
    Lemon-Raspberry Lemonade, Ida's
        Homemade, 17
    Lemonade Pie, 232
    Watermelon Lemonade, 16
Lenora's Punch, 18
Liggins, Yolanda A., 230
Lillie, Charisse R., 125
Long-Green, Edna Lee, 53, 88, 102,
    103, 212, 213, 216, 270
Louise R. Wilson's Two-Way
    Brownies, 256
Lowry, Doris, 263
Lucy and Ethel's Baked
    Beans, 139

Macaroni. See pasta and noodles
Mama Ruth's Crab Cakes, 131
Mama's Corn Bread Dressing, 158
Mama's Monkey Bread, 175
Mandarin Orange and Romaine
    Salad, 39
Marble Cake, Modern, 216
Marinade for Grilled Steaks, Simple,
    106
Marinated Asparagus, 143
Marinated Carrots, 38
Marshall, Charlotte Y., 13, 83, 184
Martin, Christine, 66
Martin, Mary Christmas, 261
Mary McLeod Bethune's Sweet Potato
    Pie, 233

Meat Loaf, Everyday, 102
Meat Loaf, Fancy, 102–3
Menus
    after-theater buffet, 4
    anniversary celebration, 168
    barbecue bash, 122
    breakfast at midnight, 192
    bridal or baby shower, 28
    celebration breakfast, 188
    Christmas dinner for family and
        friends, 266
    cocktails and hors d'oeuvres, 10
    dancing and dining after-dark
        buffet, 64
    fiftieth (or fortieth or sixtieth)
        birthday party, 128
    food for thought: a book club
        meeting meal, 40
    formal luncheon, 140
    formal sit-down dinner, 78
    graduation celebration, 98
    Juneteenth backyard
        picnic, 84
    ladies' night out, 32
    luncheon for the ladies, 36
    summer sit-down dinner with
        friends, 218
    tea for more than two, 178
    wedding reception buffet, 58
Mexican Dip, 15
Mickey's Red Beans
    and Rice, 111
Microwave Peanut Brittle, 269
Miller, Tracy Stokes, 13, 257
Minted Onions, 146
Mirian's Corn Pudding, 150
Miss Vernon Mundy's Pound Cake,
    206
Mitchell, Keyana, 181
Mocha Halo Cupcakes, 212–13
Modern Marble Cake, 216
Molasses Pie, 235
Mommadot's Easy Cream of Crab
    Soup, 56–57
Mom's Chicken Salad, 27
Mom's Mac and Cheese, 163
Moncrief, Rosetta, 257

Monkey breads. *See under* breads
Moore, Jarita, 130, 183
Moore, Julia Bradford, 132
Morgan, Barbara D., 132
Morgan, Vicki L., 171
Moroccan Chicken Breasts, 77
Moyé, Linda Everett, 265
Moyé Noels, 265
Muhammad, Wanda N., 34
Mushrooms and Sausage, Vidalia
    Onion Pie with, 147
My Mom's Sweet Potato Pie, 234–35

New Orleans Oyster Dressing,
    Peezie's, 160–61
Newton, Mary Alice, 15
Nita's Southern-Style Corn Bread
    Dressing, 160
Noodles. *See* pasta and noodles
No-Sugar Pear Pie, 229
Nuts
    Almond Biscotti, 270
    Almond Kisses, 265
    Cake, Carrot Nut, with Pineapple,
        215
    Cookies, Butter, 264
    Peanut Brittle, Microwave, 269
    Peanut Soup, African Chicken-
        (peanut butter), 54
    Pecan
        Icebox Cookies, Vanilla-Pecan,
            260–61
        Pecan Candy, Forest's
            Always-Crunchy, 271
        Pie, Grandma's Southern Pecan,
            230
        Pie, Uncle Roy's Light Pecan, 229
        Pie Bars, Pecan, 260
    Roll, Sweet Potato (or Pumpkin)
        Nut, 227
    Walnuts, Smoked Turkey Salad
        with, 25

Okra, Old-Fashioned Fried, 142
Old-Fashioned Tea Cakes, 261
Old-Fashioned Vegetable Soup, 52
Old-Time Greens with Smoked Ham
    Hocks, 146
One-Pot Dinner, 103
Onion Pie, Vidalia, with Mushrooms
    and Sausage, 147
Onions, Minted, 146
Orange
    Chicken Breasts, Moroccan, 77
    Chicken Breasts à l'Orange, 220–21
    Orange-Blueberry Bread, 185
    Holmes Cake, 220–21
    Mandarin Orange and Romaine
        Salad, 39
Oyster Dressing, Peezie's New
    Orleans, 160–61

Parker, Sandra K., 87
Parrish, Lenora, 18, 63, 232, 238
Party foods. *See* appetizers
Pasta and noodles
    Angel Hair Pasta, Jazzy Piquant
        Shrimp with, 124–25
    Angel Hair Pasta, Shrimp with
        Vegetables on, 126
    Chicken Chow Mein, 91
    Delta Executive Meeting
        Casserole, 81
    Lasagna, Tangy Turkey-Spinach, 92
    Lasagna Casserole, 108
    Macaroni
        Mac and Cheese, Mom's, 163
        Macaroni and Cheese, 162–63
        Macaroni or Spaghetti,
            Chicken, 90
    Peach Kugel, 152
    Penne Rigate, Pyramid, 90

Shrimp Casserole, 126–27
Spaghetti
    Spaghetti Crust Pie, 105
    Spaghetti Pizza, 107
    Spaghetti Salad, Supreme, 27
Patterson, Ella, 228, 234
Peach
    Cobbler
        Cobb's Peach Cobbler, 241
        Peach Cobbler with a Flair,
            240–41
        Quick Peach Cobbler, 242
    Cream Trifle, Peach, 250
    Crisp Pie, Peach, 237
    Dump Cake, 221
    Fruity Pound Cake Compote,
        244
    Kugel, Peach, 152
    Sassy Fruit 'n' Sauce, 251
    Tropical Fruit Dessert, 248
    Vintage Fruit Starter, 251
Peaches Style Homemade Biscuits,
    172–73
Peanut Brittle, Microwave, 269
Peanut Soup, African Chicken-, 54
Pear Pie, No-Sugar, 229
Pecan. *See under* nuts
Peezie's New Orleans Oyster Dressing,
    160–61
Pembroke, June G., 38
Peppermint Chocolate Cake, 212
Perfectly Easy Dinner Rolls, 170–71
Perfect Pound Cake, 202
Phillips, Sandra, 120
Pickled Beets, 43
Piecrust, 228
Pies, dessert
    Apple Pie, Crustless English,
        236–37
    Apple Crumb Pie, Deep-Dish, 236
    Berry Tartlets, 238–39
    Cherry Pie, 238
    Fruit Pie, 235
    Key Lime Pie, Yolanda's, 230
    Lemonade Pie, 232
    Lemon Meringue Pie, 231
    Molasses Pie, 235

Peach Crisp Pie, 237
Pear Pie, No-Sugar, 229
Pecan Pie, Grandma's Southern,
    230
Pecan Pie, Uncle Roy's Light, 229
Strawberry Pie, Fluffy, 238
Sweet Potato Pie, 234
    Mary McLeod Bethune's Sweet
        Potato Pie, 233
    My Mom's Sweet Potato Pie,
        234–35
Pies, savory
    Chicken Potpie, 83
    Country Breakfast Pie, 190
    Onion Pie, Vidalia, with
        Mushrooms and Sausage, 147
    Quiche
        Crabmeat Quiche, 133
        Lavita, Quiche, 191
        Sausage Quiche, 194
    Spaghetti Crust Pie, 105
    Spaghetti Pizza, 107
    Tamale Pie, 106
Pineapple
    Baked Pineapple, 152–53
    Carrot Nut Cake with Pineapple,
        215
    Cherry Fruit Salad, 248
    Fruit Pie, 235
    Fruity Pound Cake Compote,
        244
    Poke Cake, Pineapple, 222
    Sassy Fruit 'n' Sauce, 251
    Strawberry Pretzel, 248–49
    Topping, for Holmes Cake, 221
    Tropical Fruit Dessert, 248
    Vintage Fruit Starter, 251
Pittman, Nancy, 203, 208
Polote, Sabrina, 34, 55
Pone, Southern Sweet Potato, 240
Pork. See also ham; sausage
    Fancy Meat Loaf, 102
    Pork Chops and Cabbage, 109
    World's Best Chili, 62–63
Potatoes
    Monkey Bread, Potato, 174
    Sausage and Potatoes, 194

Sour Cream Hash Browns, 155
    with String Beans, Potatoes, 142
Pot Roast, Beef, 100
Poultry. See chicken; turkey
Pound Cake Compote, Fruity, 244
Pound Cakes. See under cakes
Powell, Kimberly, 185
Pumpkin Dip, 13
Pumpkin (or Sweet Potato) Nut Roll,
    227
Punch. See beverages
Pyramid Penne Rigate, 90

Quiche
    Garden Vegetable Quiche, 195
    Quiche Lavita, 191
    Sausage Quiche, 194

Rabbit, Fried Wild, 92–93
Rachel's To-Die-For Shrimp Gumbo,
    60–61
Raspberry and Cream Blossoms,
    Crimson, 244–45
Red Beans and Rice, Mickey's, 111
Red Velvet Cake, 210
Reid, Carol Perkins, 27
Relish, Cranberry, 44
Rembert, Doris C. Rice, 35
Rice
    Baked Fish Creole, 118–19
    Casseroles
        Gladys's Chicken and Rice
            Casserole, 89
        Sausage and Rice Casserole, 110
        Spinach-Rice Casserole, 147
    Dirty Rice, 157
    Dirty Rice, Dressing, 157

Red Beans and Rice, Mickey's,
    111
Rice Salad, Crabmeat and
    Vegetable, 26
Shrimp
    Shrimp Casserole, 126–27
    Shrimp Dressing, 162
    Shrimp Pilau, 127
Rice, Louise, 147
Ricotta, Lighter-Textured Cheesecake,
    226
Roberson, Carolyn, 127
Robin's Buffalo Wings, 6
Robinson, Farella Esta', 108
Rodgers, Cynthia J., 6, 155, 251
Rolls. See under breads
Romaine Salad, Mandarin Orange
    and, 39
Rose, Mary Duncan, 26
Rozchel's Red-Hot Chowder Halibut,
    119
Rumaki, 7
Rum Cake, 214

Salads
    Beets, Pickled, 43
    Broccoli, 34
        Broccoli and Cheese, 44
        Broccoli with Sunflower
            Seeds, 38
    Carrots, Marinated, 38
    Cherry Fruit Salad, 248
    Chicken, Mom's, 27
    Crabmeat and Vegetable Rice, 26
    Cranberry Mold, Foster's, 45
    Cranberry Relish, 44
    Dill Tuna, 34
    Green Bean Salad, Dijon, 35
    Kale Slaw, Spicy, 30
    Mandarin Orange and Romaine
        Salad, 39
    Sensation Salad, Judge Trudy's, 39

Salads (*cont.*)
    Spaghetti Salad, Supreme, 27
    Taco Salad, Jett's, 26
    Turkey Salad, Smoked, with
        Walnuts, 25
    Vegetable Salad, Stacy's
        Marinated, 31
    Waldorf Salad, 42
Salmon. *See* fish
Sand Tarts, 263
Sandwiches, Fancy Party, 8
Sassy Fruit 'n' Sauce, 251
Sauces, dessert. *See* dessert toppings
Sauces and marinades
    Marinade for Grilled Steaks,
        Simple, 106
    Meat Sauce, 105
    Piquant Sauce, 102
    Tartar Sauce, 121
Sausage
    Black-Eyed Peas with Attitude,
        Billy Bob's, 62
    Breakfast Sausage Casserole, 187,
        190
    Devastating Delta Diva Dip, 12–13
    Dirty Rice Dressing, 157
    Jambalaya, Wilma's, 61
    Kielbasa Soup, 54
    Meat Sauce, for Spaghetti Crust
        Pie, 105
    and Potatoes, Sausage,194
    Quiche, Sausage,194
    Red Beans and Rice, Mickey's, 111
    and Rice Casserole, Sausage, 110
    Shrimp Gumbo, Rachel's To-Die-
        For, 60–61
    Slammin' Chili, Lavita's, 63
    Slumgully, 57
    Stuffing, Sylvia's, 159
    Turkey Chili, Del Rio, 66–67
    Turkey Dump Beans, 91
    Venison Roast, 93
    Vidalia Onion Pie with
        Mushrooms and Sausage, 147
Scones, Jean's, 182
Scott, Hurlene, 125
Seafood. *See* shellfish

Sellers, Vasa "Peaches," 173
Sensation Salad, Judge Trudy's, 39
7-Up Cake with Icing, 208–9
7-Up Pound Cake, 208
Severe, M. Sandra, 270
Sexton, Dyani, 8, 92, 225
Shears, Sheila Dean, 44, 151
Shellfish. *See also* fish
    Clam Chowder, Boyd's, 56
    Crab
        Crab Bisque, 55
        Crab Cakes, Mama Ruth's, 131
        Crab Casserole, 132
        Crab Fingers, Fried, 132
        Crabmeat and Vegetable Rice
            Salad, 26
        Crabmeat Quiche, 133
        Seafood Gumbo, South Carolina
            Style, 60
        Seafood Nachos, 7
        Shrimp Casserole, 126–27
        Soup, Mommadot's Easy Cream
            of Crab, 56–57
    Gumbo, Flournoy's North
        Louisiana, 57
    Oyster Dressing, Peezie's New
        Orleans, 160–161
    Seafood Gumbo, South Carolina
        Style, 60
    Seafood Nachos, 7
    Seafood Velvet, 124
    Shrimp
        with Angel Hair Pasta, Jazzy
            Piquant, 124–25
        Appetizer, Italian Shrimp, 12
        Black-Eyed Peas with Attitude,
            Billy Bob's, 62
        Casserole, Shrimp, 126–27
        Crabmeat Quiche (cook's tip),
            133
        Creole Pronto, Shrimp, 131
        Curried, Shrimp, 125
        Dressing, Shrimp, 162
        Gumbo, Flournoy's North
            Louisiana, 57
        Gumbo, Rachel's To-Die-For,
            60–61

        Gumbo, South Carolina Style
            Seafood, 60
        Jambalaya, Wilma's, 61
        Mold, Shrimp, 9
        Pilau, Shrimp, 127
        Scampi, Shrimp, 130
        Scampi, West Indian Shrimp,
            130
        Seafood Nachos, 7
        Seafood Velvet, 124
        Slumgully, 57
        Stuffing, Sylvia's, 159
        with Vegetables on Angel Hair
            Pasta, Shrimp, 126
Shoofly Gingerbread, 222–23
Shrimp. *See under* shellfish
Silas, Robin, 119
Simpkins-Smith, Rita L., 205
Sister Vee's Apple Cake, 216–17
Sister Vee's Gingerbread Waffles, 186
Skillet Greens with Balsamic Vinegar,
    144
Slaw, Spicy Kale, 30
Slow cooker recipes
    Jerk Chicken Drums, 86
    One-Pot Dinner, 103
    Turkey Dump Beans, 91
Slumgully, 57
Smith, Beverly Evans, 31, 124, 175
Smith, Corey Minor, 15
Smith, Danyell P., 186
Smith, Elease M., 139
Smith, Forest Dent, 271
Smith, Jennifer R., 223
Smith, Pamela, 91
Smith, Peola, 161
Smith, Rosanne Anderson, 52, 171
Smith, Sondra L., 225, 248, 256
Smoked Turkey Salad with
    Walnuts, 25
Smothered Chicken, 76
Snacks. *See* appetizers
Soufflé, Lemon Pudding, 252
Soups and stews
    Beef and Vegetable Soup, 52
    Black-Eyed Peas with Attitude,
        Billy Bob's, 62

Chicken-Peanut Soup, African, 54
Chicken-Vegetable Soup, Victory
    Garden, 53
Chili
    Heart-Smart Chili, 67
    Lavita's Slammin' Chili, 63
    Turkey Chili, 66
    Turkey Chili, Del Rio, 66–67
    White Chili, 67
    World's Best Chili, 62–63
Clam Chowder, Boyd's, 56
Crab Soup, Mommadot's Easy
    Cream of, 56–57
Crab Bisque, 55
Gumbo
    North Louisiana Gumbo,
        Flournoy's, 57
    Seafood Gumbo, South Carolina
        Style, 60
    Shrimp Gumbo, Rachel's
        To-Die-For, 60–61
Jambalaya, Wilma's, 61
Kielbasa Soup, 54
Slumgully, 57
Vegetable Soup, Old-Fashioned, 52
Sour cream
    Chocolate–Sour Cream Pound
        Cake, 203
    Hash Browns, Sour Cream, 155
    Pound Cake, Sour Cream, 202
South Carolina Style Seafood
    Gumbo, 60
Southern Pecan Pie, Grandma's, 230
Southern-Style Corn Bread Dressing,
    Nita's, 160
Southern Sweet Potato Pone, 240
Spaghetti. See pasta and noodles
Spencer-Dupree, Treva J., 224
Spicy Asian Wings, 9
Spinach
    Dip, Spicy Spinach, 12
    Quiche, Garden Vegetable, 195
    Quiche Lavita, 191
    Spinach-Rice Casserole, 147
    Spinach-Turkey Lasagna,
        Tangy, 92
    Stuffed Baby Eggplant, 148–49

Spires-Potter, Curley, 12, 261
Squash Casserole, 151
Stacey's Bodacious Buttermilk Fried
    Chicken, 82–83
Stacey's Sugary Sweet Candied Yams,
    154–55
Stacy's Marinated Vegetable
    Salad, 31
Stagg, Shirley, 269
Stamps, Beulah R., 174
Starters. See appetizers
Stews. See soups and stews
Sticky Buns, Christmas Morning,
    180–81
Stockton, Margaret C., 54
Strawberry
    Delight, Strawberry, 246
    Pie, Fluffy, Strawberry, 238
    Pretzel, Strawberry, 248–49
    Sassy Fruit 'n' Sauce, 251
    Topping, Strawberry, 270
String beans. See green beans
Stuffed Baby Eggplant,
    148–49
Stuffed Cheese, 104
Stuffings. See dressings
Sunday-Afternoon Roasted
    Chicken, 74
Sunflower Seeds, Broccoli Salad
    with, 38
Supreme Lemon-Filling
    Cake, 217
Supreme Spaghetti Salad, 27
Swanson, Mayme, 241
Sweet-and-Sour Cheese Ball, 14
Sweet potatoes and yams
    Bread, Sweet Potato, 183
    Candied Yams, Stacey's Sugary
        Sweet, 154–55
    Candied Yams, with Brandy, 153
    Casserole, Sweet Potato, 154
    Cheesecake, Sweet Potato,
        226–27
    Flan, Caramel-Coated Yam,
        242–43
    Nut Roll, Sweet Potato (or
        Pumpkin), 227

Pie, 234
    Mary McLeod Bethune's Sweet
        Potato Pie, 233
    My Mom's Sweet Potato Pie,
        234–35
    Pone, Southern Sweet Potato, 240
Sylvia's Stuffing, 159

Taco Dip, 16
Taco Salad, Jett's, 26
Taffy Apple Cheesecake, 224–25
Tamale Pie, 106
Tangy Baked Party Wings, 8
Tangy Turkey-Spinach Lasagna, 92
Tanner, Kathy E., 211
Tartar Sauce, Homemade, Fried
    Catfish with, 121
Tea Cakes, Bessie's Old-Fashioned,
    261
Tea Cakes, Old-Fashioned, 261
Thomas, Joy M., 81
Thompson, Kimberley Reed, 67
Tijani, Debbie W., 190, 238
Toomer, Virginia R., 101, 249
Toppings, dessert. See dessert toppings
Trice, Mary, 208
Trifle, Peach Cream, 250
Tucker, Renée, 220
Tuna Salad, Dill, 34
Turkey
    Chili, Turkey, 66
    Chili, Del Rio Turkey, 66–67
    Country Breakfast Pie, 190
    Dump Beans, Turkey, 91
    Fancy Meat Loaf, 102–3
    Lasagna Casserole, 108
    Lavita's Slammin' Chili, 63
    Smoked Turkey Salad with
        Walnuts, 25
    Spaghetti Pizza, 107
    -Spinach Lasagna, Tangy
        Turkey, 92

Uncle Roy's Light Pecan Pie, 229

Vanilla-Pecan Icebox Cookies, 260–61
Veal, in Fancy Meat Loaf, 102–3
Veeris, Cessna, 104
Vegetables. *See also* greens; *specific vegetables*
  -Chicken Soup, Victory Garden, 53
  and Gravy, Pot Roast with, 101
  Quiche, Garden, 195
  Rice Salad, Crabmeat and, 26
  Salad, Stacy's Marinated, 31
  Sautéed, Vegetables, 138
  Soup, Beef and Vegetable, 52
  Soup, Old-Fashioned Vegetable, 52
  Winter Vegetables, Roasted, 138–139
Venison Roast, 93
Victory Garden Chicken-Vegetable Soup, 53
Vidalia Onion Pie with Mushrooms and Sausage, 147

Vintage Fruit Starter, 251
Virginia's Steamed Cabbage Pot, 144

Waffles, Sister Vee's Gingerbread, 186
Waldorf Salad, 42
Walker, Doris McEwen, 67
Walker, Ngwebifor Fobi, 250
Walker, Paulette C., 194
Walnuts, Smoked Turkey Salad with, 25
Wamble, Wilma, 61
Ward, Antoinette M., 12
Ward, Jodie R., 146
Ward, Tracie J., 177
Ware, Carol E., 126, 163
Washington, Rhonda, 263
Washnitzer, Margaret J., 39
Watermelon Lemonade, 16
Watson, Tanya W., 187, 227
Wellington, Irene Lee, 145
Westerfield, Johanna, 264
West Indian Shrimp Scampi, 130

White, Joyce, 90, 261
White, Judge Trudy M., 39
White, Marion T., 207
White Chili, 67
Wilder, Carolyn, 141, 248
Wilkerson, Donna Maria, 86
Williams, Jeanette Perkins, 27
Williamson, Judith, 54, 67
Wilma's Jambalaya, 61
Wilson, Yvonne S., 144
Wine Cranberry Punch, Hot, 18
Wings. *See under* chicken
World's Best Chili, 62–63

Yams. *See* sweet potatoes and yams
Yolanda's Key Lime Pie, 230
Young, Arlene Hanton, 235

Zucchini Bread, 184–85